POTLUCK, POSTSCRIPTS & POTPOURRI

POTLUCK,
POSTSCRIPTS
&
POTPOURRI

Jean Gay Mussleman

MINDBRIDGE PRESS
Florence • Alabama

Through the years, an amazing number of people,
all kinds of people from all walks of life,
have "put their feet under our table."
There is always room for one more . . .

Library of Congress Control Number 2008941284

ISBN 978-0-9822151-0-4

Printed in the United States of America

Published in Florence, Alabama, by MINDBRIDGE PRESS

First Edition

ACKNOWLEDGEMENTS

MY HUSBAND DAVID PROVIDED ME the constant loving encouragement that enabled me to write this book. Believing like Eudora Welty that stories should be read aloud, I read them over and over to David, and he listened loyally as I revised and rewrote them. He laughed and cried with me, he picked me up and cheered me on, and his enthusiastic encouragement led me to follow my dream.

My son, Dee, was on call 24/7 for any and all computer crises, and there were many. With great effort and patience, he miraculously managed to keep my computer and me on the same page . . . no small task. Other family members and friends generously shared stories, recipes, and photos while offering loving support.

Pam Kingsbury, my friend who is a University of North Alabama English professor, edited my manuscript and provided the direction, aid, and support that made this book possible. She has been my mentor and encourager; she has provided exceptional professional guidance as we worked together to get my manuscript ready to print.

Pam introduced me to Ed Garner of MINDBRIDGE PRESS who has become my publisher, skillfully shepherding me and my book through all the difficult steps and the necessary hoops through which one must jump. I can never thank him enough for the fantastic job he has done to produce this book.

The talented artist, Mark Sandlin, from his Atlanta studio, provided the terrific artwork and design for my book. Mark played on the Bradshaw High School tennis team with my sons, Dee and Matt. David and I were High School friends with Mark's parents, Jesse and Kathryn. My parents and Jesse's parents were lifelong friends. What a history!

Thanks to Felicia Kahn Michelson of Atlanta for her exceptional production design.

At ElderCare Services, Care Coordinator Tracie Reid graciously covered for me in the office, and Sammi Jo McConnell was an invaluable computer whiz.

William Lindsey McDonald—beloved cousin, Methodist minister, retired U. S. Army Colonel, author, and historian—has shared a wealth of family history with me. His many books, especially *The Legacy of Our Lindseys*, have enriched my knowledge of my family's heritage.

Willie Ruff, himself such great copy, graciously gave his blessing to quote and to share material from his fascinating autobiography, *A Call To Assembly*.

Executive Editor, Wayne Mitchell, granted permission to reprint items from our local newspaper, the *Times Daily*, including a story about my Daddy and an early map of Florence.

The Birmingham News, "At Wit's End," Erma Bombeck, 2/28/1986.
Readers Digest, "Life in These United States," October, 1991 issue.
A Brief Look At The University of North Alabama History, 2005.
Al Hausmann created the W.C. Handy sculpture for Wilson Park.
Greg Crenshaw for his portraits of family and grandchildren.
Harold Parker for his photograph of Cypress Creek Bridge.
THE CLUB of Birmingham, Alabama, for their Poppy Seed Dressing recipe.

CONTENTS

RECIPES BY CATEGORY

GRAVY

VEGETABLES

SALADS

SAUCES & SALAD DRESSINGS

FRUITS

DESSERTS

CAKES & ICINGS

PIES

COOKIES & SUCH

INTRODUCTION

DEAR FRIENDS,

THROUGH THESE PAGES, YOU ARE INVITED to be the guests of our lively family of five now grownup children, reigned over by a veterinarian father turned entrepreneur (who re-turned to veterinary practice) and a social worker mother turned politician and business founder.

You will meet my one-of-a-kind husband David (Dad) and (from the oldest to the youngest) daughter Lindsey, sons Dee and Matt, and Janna and Laura (the "Little Girls"): all very special indeed. Since I am the "I" in this book, you don't exactly meet me, but the children call me Mom, and Dad sometimes calls me Mother Superior.

You will also meet neighbors, friends, and more than one generation of unique but still beloved kinfolk from both sides of the family.

You may be confused as you meet family animals because they have people names like Rachel, Maggie, and Walter, and not pet names like Spot, Rover, or Fluffy … except for that incorrigible English Bull Dog who was already named Spike when we adopted him.

You will view us through the kaleidoscope of strengths, successes, frailties, and failures of people bound together in that marvelous, indestructible unit known as The Family.

So Dear Friends, in celebration of our family life, please share with us the stories that entertain us, the foods and recipes that maintain us, and the traditions, love, and fellowship that sustains us.

Regards,

Jean Gay Mussleman   December 1986

WHY & WHEN
I WROTE THIS BOOK

PERHAPS IT WOULD HELP TO KNOW know why and when I wrote this book. The why has to do with my ninety two year old father who was living independently until he fell, broke his hip, suffered a massive stroke, and spent the final months of his life in a nursing home. I was devastated. This was not what I had planned, nor what I had promised. At the proper time, Daddy was supposed to come live with our family, and we would lovingly care for him the rest of his life. But sometimes the best laid plans fail, and loving promises are broken.

When I could not find the necessary home care for Daddy, I sat down in frustration and wrote a business plan for a company that could. I pondered all of this in my heart, and then eventually decided to retire from a twenty year career in school social work to pursue my dream. I dusted off my business plan and founded ElderCare Services. I was, after all, a helping professional who knew first-hand what it was like to seek and not find home care resources. Today, I am comforted by the fact that, with a full staff of care givers, I can now provide the kind of home care for others that I was not able to find for my own father. I am gratified that, as a Geriatric Care Manager, I can offer counsel and direction to families struggling with the complicated issues of aging. I am blessed that my eldest son Dee joined the staff early on, committed himself to ElderCare Services, and will someday take over the management from me.

Back in 1986, grieving my father's death, I realized that as family matriarch I was also the keeper of family stories. I reminisced, recalled, and wrote down some of these stories. Daddy would have been proud, hearing the stories of his family he so loved. I discovered that writing was therapy and that it gave me peace.

As a Christmas gift that year, I presented each of my children a copy of this "first edition," inspired by Daddy and dedicated to them. My first book effort circulated among extended family and friends, and many made suggestions on what absolutely must be enhanced, changed or added, and, yes, subtracted. I got a lot of, "Did you remember to tell about the time ... " or "Where is that story about ... ?" or "Gee, I never heard that before!" One time, my brother Rivers approached me at a church gathering and demanded to know,

"Did you remember to tell what a great storyteller Mother was?" I soon discovered it was much easier to start the book than it was to stop the book!

Now about the when: these writings have been a work in progress off and on for more than twenty years, during which time, as it is with families, much has happened, and many changes have taken place.

Today, all five of our children are married, blessed with their own children, homes, careers, and active lives. I am sometimes reluctant to admit to friends whose children and grandchildren live in far away places that three of our children—Lindsey, Dee, Janna—and their families all live close by and in the same subdivision where we live; that Laura and her family live across town, only fifteen minutes away; and that Matt and his family live just across the Tennessee line, all of forty five minutes away. But best of all, we are now grandparents to eleven delightful, beautiful, and (of course) above average grandchildren!

Throughout the book, I have used abbreviations for the measurements in the recipes. This is the way I and generations of my family have always written them, so it didn't feel right representing them any other way. Refer to the following legend for equivalents.

c	=	cup	pkg	=	package
gal	=	gallon	pt	=	pint
in	=	inch	qt	=	quart
lb	=	pound	t	=	teaspoon
oz	=	ounce	T	=	tablespoon

Fall, 2008

Jean Gay Mussleman   Florence, Alabama

DEDICATION

*Dedicated to my beloved children and to all
others in my family, past and present.*

This quick and dirty guide can help you identify the main characters in this book.

GRANDCHILDREN

Rebecca	Lauren	Alex	Sydney	James, Liles,
Forrest	Anna Beth	Macie		Laura Alice
				& Mary

OUR CHILDREN

Lindsey	Dee	Matt	Janna	Laura
& Butch	& Amy	& Deanna	& Blaine	& Jim
Davis	Mussleman	Mussleman	Childers	Hillhouse

MOM & DAD

Jean Gay **(Mom/Memaw)**		David **(Dad/G-Doc)**
Rivers Jr. (brother)		Mary Ellen (sister)

OUR PARENTS

Pauline & Rivers Lindsey, Sr.		**Ruby & Carl Mussleman, Sr.**	
Lenice	Clyde	Allen	Augazelle
		Grace	Ellen
		Virginia	Paul

GRANDPARENTS

Will & Missie Cauhorn	**Dee & Blanche Mussleman**
Barbee & Lizzie Lindsey	**Ross & Mattie Gaines Pierce**

Generations of kin preceded us, dear souls with names like Chisholm, Kennedy, Walston, Barbee, Malone, Noel, Price, and Crowe. From the Mitchell side of my family, Mother's cousins Elba and Iola were able to prove enough Indian blood to claim their birthright and settle land in Oklahoma.

Dear children,

FAMILY RECIPES AND STORIES ARE TREASURES to be shared and passed down from generation to generation as a valuable part of our heritage. Recipes recall family and friends, past and present, and grant them life for the future. But the stories and the fond memories I most wish to share are my love gift to you.

Food and fellowship have always been the trademarks of our family life. While I am confident that our good eating habits have enhanced our good health, we are blessed to have come from inherently sound stock!

One family tradition, an abiding enthusiasm for eating and cooking—compliments of Dad—has engendered other traditions, such as our collective commitment to sit down together at mealtime even when the hour was late and you little ones were so sleepy, and also the ritual of giving a mealtime demonstration (a rousing round of applause) to congratulate, compliment, or encourage.

It is my hope that you will continue the tradition in your homes that has prevailed in ours: that Mom, Dad, sons, daughters, all learn to cook and learn to love cooking. Learn to cook "by ear," knowing that some recipes require careful measurement while other recipes beg creativity. Master the art of gracious entertaining, even for a crowd. Learn that quantity cookery is not a task to be feared but a talent admired by others and enjoyed by all.

Remember how you each could pick one food you never had to eat? Until this day, Lindsey does not eat sweet potatoes. Never have I found a food that Dee and Matt would not eat heartily (except sometimes raisins). Even as a toddler, Janna avoided spinach by stuffing it in the hole in her warmer plate. As a child, Laura would not eat tomatoes.

We are blessed with an abundance of rich, growing-up memories: summertime picnics under the apple tree or on the deck, hot dog suppers at Little League Park, tailgating with Pearl-Fried Chicken and Dad-made Potato Salad, Easter Sunrise Services and neighborhood get-togethers, Barn Parties and Hunt Breakfasts, everyday meals that began with a child's simple blessing, and birthdays that you children somehow managed to stretch into birthweeks! Speaking of birthdays, have you ever wondered or computed how many birthday cakes a five-childrened mom has baked? Remember the cakes decorated with footballs and tennis racquets, airplanes, and horses … Raggedy Ann and Raggedy Andy cakes … white cakes with chocolate icing … chocolate cakes with white icing … pink cakes and blue cakes … all baked by Mom.

Through the years, an amazing number of people—all kinds of people from all walks of life—have "put their feet under our table." There was always room for one more, as there was for Stacy, our "Boy's Ranch son," whom you graciously and lovingly accepted as brother.

Then there was our memorable 25th wedding anniversary. I am still amazed that five youngsters (ages nine to nineteen) could have managed the unbelievable gift of a grandfather clock. Surely, there was no way to top the spectacular children-cooked meal (and Dee's flaming Cherries Jubilee finale), but you did, Dear Children, with the surprise party that followed. I won't even try to describe the elegant 50th Anniversary Brunch you children hosted at Turtle Point. It was fantastic!

And who will ever forget the first W. C. Handy Music Festival and the party at our house afterward when the famed Dizzie Gillespie, Willie and Dwike (the Mitchell Ruff Duo), and the rest of the great performers—along with a few hundred other guests, some invited and some not—"put their feet under our table" that night, while I, the helpless and increasingly anxious hostess, sat enthroned in an easy chair with my broken ankle propped on a foot stool (autographed cast and all)?

I remember Dwike's fingers caressing the piano keys, calling forth pianissimo and forte, passionato and dolce, until night faded into dawn and the artist's restless spirit found peace.

Lest I make us sound like a jolly band of merrymakers who never got mad, disagreed, or argued (we all know better), I confess there were times we parents took advantage of your mealtime presence to lecture or scold; or at times we tried to settle the affairs of state, school, and family at the expense of dinner time peace and digestive tranquility. Surely, valuable lessons can be learned from both the negative and the affirmative experiences of family life.

However, the good times must have outweighed the bad, because one young visiting friend—perhaps coveting the yard full of pets, the barn full of horses, and the creek full of splashing fun—expressed her wish to come back reincarnated as a Mussleman child.

Who will ever forget when Mom closed down her kitchen to enter politics and all of you, Dear Children, not only campaigned but cooked? After Mom was elected as our city's first female City Council member, we not only found that kitchens as well as lives can be reopened, but that one's true worth is measured in terms greater than elections lost or won.

I agree with Erma Bombeck who in her infinite wisdom said, "It takes a lot of courage to show your dream to someone else." But those who do are "rewarded with a legacy for others to follow."

In our living, sometimes there are dreams we must follow. Even though we risk failure, we also risk success. But not to dream … not to risk … that would be the ultimate failure.

Just as you have been open to new foods and flavors, may you be open to new experiences, ideas, and dreams. Always remember to give back something of value to a world that has given so much to you. Always remember what the Scriptures teach us: "To whom much is given, much is expected."

I hope we will all continue to know the pleasure of gathering together, including those you have chosen to love and cherish into our expanded family circle that, with the added joy of grandchildren, now has truly come full circle.

I pray that we have nourished you both spiritually and physically and that, as parents, we have passed on to each of you, our cherished children, the valued gift of both roots and wings.

Giving life to these pages, Dear Ones, has been much like giving life to you, with the joy of conception, the labor of birth, and the wonder of life itself. As surely as I have nurtured each of you, then let you go to become your own best selves, I must now do the same for my literary creation. It is bittersweet, this letting go of what I have for so long worked on and held so close.

But is it not through the holding close and letting go that we are liberated to seek the fullness of life and to claim its promises?

Accept this gift, My Dear Children,

of *Potluck, Postscripts & Potpourri*,

written especially to you,

for you,

and because I love you,

Mom

Christmas 1986

ANY OF ITS SEASONS

THE MOST PRECIOUS MEMORIES OF MY CHILDHOOD were spent mainly in Oakland, a neighborly crossroads community seven miles west of Florence, tucked into the northwest corner of Alabama, not far from the Tennessee line to the north and the Mississippi line to the west. Back then, Oakland had two bustling general stores, a part time cafe, two cotton gins, and a blacksmith shop that could shoe your horse or grind your ears of corn into meal while you waited. We were close enough to the Tennessee River to hear sounds of river traffic on a foggy night, the mournful blast of a horn, barge groaning against barge.

It seems to be a universal truth that none of us can truly value the heritage that is our own until we view ourselves and our past from the perspective of time, and age, and fond memory.

Growing up in the rural South of the '30s, I basked in those day-to-day experiences that may have been common to all but which I believed were uniquely mine. As a child, I loved the smell of rain approaching, of fresh turned earth, of honeysuckle in the evening, and of tar when our county road was first paved. Encountered today, these same scents call me back to days long past.

Never will I forget the delight, after a summer rain, of loblollies and the warm red mud oozing up between my toes. Never will I forget the rattle of raindrops on the tall tin roof of the barn, the hours spent building hideouts in the hayloft, the breeze that whispered through the broad shady hall of the barn, and the peaceful crunch, crunch, crunch of horses leisurely munching grain.

Memories of my playhouse in the plum thicket are as sweet as the fruit that pinkened and ripened around me. I recall the shiny, savory blackberries that grew in wild abundance on the fence rows near the barn. And the first tentative taste of Autumn's frosted persimmon, which, if prematurely judged ripe, would positively and absolutely turn your mouth wrong-side out.

I will remember always how big I felt the first time I was allowed to walk up the road to the store by myself, a coin proudly clutched in my hand, and how agonizing the decision of which penny's worth of candy to buy. Displayed in the shiny glass candy case was a virtual wonderland of bright colors and luscious flavors—candy canes striped peppermint and lemon, silver wrapped chocolate drops, golden squares of banana kisses, all-day suckers, BB-Bats that melted to your teeth, and jawbreakers so big that just looking at them set your jaws to aching—all for my delight.

I experienced the same sense of importance when I managed to gather eggs from the henhouse without cracking any, and when I was finally able to shell corn with a cob fast enough to keep ahead of the hungry clucking chickens as I proudly called over and over again: "Chick-chick … chick-chick … chick … EEE!"

I will love forever the beauty of a cotton field in any of its seasons, when furry little leaves push up through the soil and long straight rows stretch into the distance where earth meets sky. Next, the pink blossoms are transformed into hard round bolls, choice ammunition for childhood battles. But best of all, I love the glorious finale when snow-white bouquets of cotton spill out of the sharp, delicate fingers of the bursting bolls when God and weather-willing green fields explode into whiteness and proudly proclaim the good news: "COTTON PICKIN' TIME IS HERE!"

I was at my happiest when I was allowed to go to the cotton fields with my daddy. During cotton pickin', poor children stayed out of school, and entire families turned out into the fields to pick. Blacks and whites worked companionably side-by-side. Canvas pick-sacks were made in various sizes and lengths so that children, I suppose, could begin to economically justify their existence. Everybody wore straw hats against the sun and denim before it was fashionable. Babies sometimes rode on the pillowy pick-sacks of their mothers, who would pause long enough to nurse their babies or to holler at the older ones to pick more, play less, and quit throwing cotton bolls.

Hour after hour, in the still hot sun of Alabama's late summer, some "hands" (as farm workers were then commonly called) stooped down low over the cotton stalks, and others picked from their knees. Up and down the long rows, the hands deftly plucked the soft cotton and poked it into the long pick sacks that hung from their shoulders and trailed along behind them. When full, the sacks were weighed on the old balance scales hanging from a nearby tree or from the side-boards of Daddy's red (the only color he ever owned) pick-up truck. As soon as the truck was heaping full of cotton, Daddy and I would head for the gin.

Once at the gin, we could count on a long line: trucks of assorted vintages and models, makeshift trailers and mule-drawn wagons, all overflowing with cotton. Weary, dusty workers in search of such refreshment as ice cold RC Colas and Moon Pies milled in and out of the two general stores: Mr. Arthur Smith's on one side of the road and Mr. Hugh L. Rice's on the other. Worn and hungry workers lined up for a juicy ten-cent hamburger loaded with onions and dill pickles at Mr. Jolly's Cafe, which was sometimes open around the clock at that time of the year. The proprietor, despite his promising name and prosperous business, rarely smiled and seemed to me the grumpiest man around.

When it was finally our turn at the gin, Daddy drove up onto the platform, and we climbed up into the bed of the truck. Daddy guided the giant overhead vacuum until all of the cotton was sucked up into the … boom … boom … booming machinery that separated seed from cotton and ultimately turned out, at the other end of the cavernous gin, a huge burlapped bale.

In the meantime, I had been bouncing around in the diminishing mound of cotton. Giggling in anticipation of what always happened next, I would squeeze my eyes shut and cover my ears with my hands. Daddy would then playfully hold the roaring tube just above my head, and with my hair literally standing on end, we together laughed at the funny sight I must have been.

Back in the fields, amidst the revelry and rivalry at day's end, weights were carefully tallied and totaled in Daddy's dog-eared ledger, and accounts were settled on account or in cash. Prosperity, however relative and short-lived, was a welcome relief from the prevailing poverty, which I later learned were the Depression Years.

During the height of the season, the steady, comforting, around-the-clock throb of the cotton gin could be felt for miles around. This spoke to a good harvest and underscored how bound our lives were to the cotton, which in those days was still very much King.

Even from the perspective of a safe, secure childhood was an emerging awareness of the prejudice and inequalities that existed in my otherwise perfect world. But I was blessed. By precept and example, I learned from my parents about tolerance and fairness. I was helped to define what it was I believed in, and to identify what was valuable enough to stand up and fight for … and against.

I understood early on that because my Daddy owned the fields my world was somehow different from the world of those who worked the fields. Yet, at every point where my world encountered theirs, I felt privileged by that connection.

I have a wonderfully clear memory of the rich voice of old Ruth and of her dilapidated cabin in the field across the road from our house. With floors scrubbed clean and walls papered with newspaper to ward off the cold, Ruth's house stood primitive but proud. In winter, smoke curled through the chimney from the fireplace that heated her house, and year round smoke rose from the fire under the big black wash pot out in the yard where she washed clothes. I would watch Ruth walking up and down the road on her way to deliver white folks' laundry—which she tied up neatly in a clean sheet and balanced gracefully on top of her head—or she'd go up the dusty path to draw a bucket of water from the well up on the hill. Whatever her destination, the soulful sounds of Ruth's singing would drift across the road to my little girl self who sat on the front steps of one world while quietly observing and listening to another.

By the time I was eight, we had built nearby a handsome new one-and-a-half-story sandstone home in a beautiful wooded setting. Benches, hand-hewn by our stone mason, graced the yard, and cheerful buttercups, many from the Walston family home place that were lovingly planted by my mother, soon lined the circular driveway.

The only thing that separated our new home from Eleven Grove Missionary Baptist Church was a dense stand of trees, mainly oak, pine, sassafras, and sweet gum. In those days, country churches, especially black churches, were social as well as religious gathering places. At Leben Grove, preachin' went on all Sunday afternoon and by coal oil lamplight into the night. Drawn again to my front steps, I waved and watched the lively comings and goings of the church-goers, all dressed up in their "Sunday-go-to-meetin" clothes. Sometimes I crept closer through the woods where I listened enthralled as the congregation's spirited singing grew more fervent and, like the preacher's, their shouting more frenzied.

In the workday cotton fields, the song might begin with a mother's gentle singing or the humming of a familiar refrain:

O, I know the Law-aw-d, I know the Law-aw-d
I know the Lawd's laid His hands on me …

As others joined in, the song would pick up momentum …

Did ev-ah you see the likes befo-uh   *King Jesus preachin' to the po-uh …*
Some seek the Lawd and don't seek Him ri-ight   *Dey fool all day and pray all ni-ight …*

Then after each verse, the voices would crescendo into a chorus of unparalleled pathos and beauty …

O, I KNOW THE LAW-AW-UD
I KNOW THE LAWD'S LAID HIS HANDS ON MEEE …

Sometimes victorious or jubilant, melancholy or slow, the beloved songs and spirituals that I grew up hearing from the fields and front steps of my childhood became a part of my tap-roots, too.

I am thankful that babies are no longer nursed in cotton fields and that today's children are found in places of learning rather than places of laboring. Yet, when I see one of those mammoth mechanical cotton pickers at work, I can still hear in my heart of yesterday music far more beautiful than any today's farmer will ever hear in his air-conditioned, stereo-filled cab.

The scenes and sounds of the cotton pickin' times of my childhood are gone now and exist only in my memories. Artists have captured the scenes on canvas, but modern technology has stilled forever the sounds I so well knew and loved, sounds of laughter … and singing … and camaraderie.

STEWS & SUCH

The Aroma of Chicken Stew

DURING THE HOT ALABAMA SUMMERS of the 1930s, I traveled down dusty country roads with my mother in her automobile. A trail of dust curled lazily behind us, then settled back in on us through the rolled-down windows. I well remember driving from one farm house to the next, collecting donations for the Annual Chicken Stew, then as now a favorite fund-raiser of local country churches.

Though richer in spirit than anything else, farm folk of the Depression Years shared generously from the bounty of their gardens. Before long, we were loaded down with butter beans, potatoes, fresh-picked roast'n'ears, red-ripe tomatoes, onions, and live, wild-eyed hens, their feet tied together with string. When the car would hold no more, we would turn back to the shady park next to the weathered frame schoolhouse where my father was principal. There, we unloaded the vegetables into piles and the squawking hens into coops. Firewood, sawhorses, and lumber for tables were brought in and set up in preparation for the big event.

At daybreak on the big day, workers descended on the park, slaughtered and plucked the chickens, then cooked them tender in big black iron pots over an open fire. The vegetables, to be added later, were shucked, shelled, and peeled. By mid-morning, the men were stirring with long wooden boat-like paddles the pots full of simmering stew. The blended aroma of wood smoke and stew drifted over the entire community, heralding the event and broadcasting the standard invitation: "Y'all ALL come!"

Soon, clean white cloths covered the rough tables. Homemade cakes and pies appeared by the dozens. Bottled cold drinks—Co'colas, RCs, orange and grape Nehis—were iced down in fat wooden tubs. With tree branch fans, women shooed the flies away from the food and shooed the children away from the tempting, tantalizing chipped ice.

Before they chose up sides for the big afternoon ball game, the men-folks pitched horseshoes and speculated about the chance of rain or the price of cotton. Children of all ages, carefree and barefoot, ran and romped and played simple games like Tree Tag, Red Rover, or Hop Scotch scratched out in the dirt. Throughout the day, the older ones fought for space on the ever-popular, ever-whirling Flying Jenny.

Often scheduled after the crops were laid by, this was a time of community-wide fellowship and celebration. Even today, the delicious aroma of chicken stew momentarily takes me back to a time and a place where life was not necessarily better but at least seemed simpler.

Since I grew up assuming chicken stew was a universal food, I was astonished to discover that the rest of the world did not share my heritage and that it was, in fact, a local rather than a global tradition. Thus it was that through the years chicken stew became the specialty I served to many a gathering of friend and family.

Our eldest daughter Lindsey loves to tell about the time she was copying my trademark chicken stew recipe for her files. She was beginning to wonder where she was going to get a big enough pot before she noticed she had mistakenly pulled the recipe that feeds 100 (the recipe for church suppers or fund-raisers).

Now the making and serving of my chicken stew should not be a terribly stressful event, but crises will happen. The most memorable stew crisis of all was the time we fed the Mooreland Hunt. Family horseback riders, stock ties in place and boots polished, had already loaded tack and horses, tails and manes proudly braided, into the trailer and had embarked before dawn to Huntsville, more than an hour's distance away.

It was our turn to host the hunt breakfast, and we had worked out a careful strategy to assure delivery of enough stew to feed the field of hungry hunters on their return from the hunt. Friends Joyce and Wayne helped load all the food into the station wagon: two brand-new thirty gallon plastic garbage cans filled with chicken stew, the piece-de-resistance of my plan. We were not even out of the city limits when Wayne, in a calm, controlled voice, ordered: "Jean Gay. Don't look back. Just turn around and head straight back home. FAST."

But like Lot's wife, I did look back, and what I saw almost made me wish I could turn into a pillar of salt! To my horror, what I saw was Wayne, hanging over the back seat, bear-hugging both garbage cans. He was valiantly trying to prevent any more stew from spilling through large gaping splits in the sides of the cans … cans obviously not sturdy enough to contain all those pounds and gallons of hot chicken stew!

I can hardly remember, or perhaps I choose to forget, how we ever managed to get all that stew into sturdier containers with a minimum amount of loss and spillage … but somehow we did.

It was, to say the least, an unforgettable Saturday. The mounted hunters, gentlemen in red coats and ladies in black, pursuing the wily fox through field and forest to a chorus of baying hounds, "Tally-Hos," and the huntsman's horn would never know how much more exciting my ride to Huntsville had been. And they would never know how dangerously close they had come to having no stew a'tall.

I do remember this. Until the day we traded that station wagon, everyone who got into it, including me, vowed that it still possessed the unmistakable, aroma of chicken stew.

Oakland Chicken Stew

SERVES 12	SERVES 60	INGREDIENTS

1. In a large pot, half full of water, cook until tender:

1	5	3 lb chicken(s)

2. Cool, bone, and return to broth.

3. Add and simmer for 2 or more hours:

1	5	1 can (28 oz) tomatoes
2-3	10-12	med onions, chopped
5-6	10-12 lb	potatoes, diced
1 pkg	5 pkg	1 pkg (16 oz) frozen limas

4. Add and stir until the bread is well blended:

1	5	1 can (16 oz) kernel corn
1 (1 lb) loaf	5 loaves	white bread

5. Add salt, pepper, Tabasco to taste. Add more water if needed to keep it soupy. Stir frequently to keep stew from sticking. Simmer until ready to serve, the longer the better.

3

The Tale of DaDa's Famous Escape

AFTER MY MOTHER'S DEATH at the fairly young age of sixty two, my father was a lonely, disconsolate man. Two or three brief and unsuccessful marriages later (depending on how you count his marriage to the same woman twice), Daddy made a great discovery: if you cooked and invited folks in to eat, you were not so lonely, which is a far less complicated solution to loneliness than marriage.

Well into his seventies at the time, Daddy started his culinary career with what he knew best: Chicken Stew. Like all great Southern cooks, he improvised and created his own recipe, omitting lima beans because he didn't especially like lima beans and omitting corn because it was bad to stick to the bottom of the pan. It was not uncommon to encounter in his stew an unexpected ingredient or two, such as spaghetti or green beans, but you could always count on a big favorite of his, lots of carrots. As age made chopping more difficult for him, Daddy (Dada to grandchildren) grated all the vegetables, creating a different textured (but still delicious) version of what we call DaDa's Chicken Stew.

Chicken Stew was his offering, a ritual to celebrate family homecomings. No matter where they traveled from—Paige from as far away as Israel or England; Meredith, Courtney, Stacie, and Barbara from as near as Birmingham and Nashville—his granddaughters/my nieces could always count on a simmering pot of Chicken Stew; there was also homemade coleslaw on the side when they came home to visit DaDa.

But Daddy didn't limit his guest-list to family. He believed that being around young people kept him young, and it certainly seemed to work for him. Daddy was always befriending and inviting to lunch nice young ladies wherever he met them: at church, the bank, the doctor's office, or at the hospital (as was the case with his favorite group, the entire Eliza Coffee Hospital physical therapy staff). He laid out his best china and silver and hosted whatever number appeared at his famous luncheons. He cared, counseled, and comforted them through their assorted crises. He rejoiced at their weddings (often pictured in the wedding party as grandfather of the bride) and celebrated job promotions and new babies. All were "his girls." They became an important part of his life, and he of theirs.

With equal generosity, he would give one of his girls a semester's tuition or one of their children a trip to summer camp. He treated them with little gifts and sent them home with leftover stew for their suppers. They loved him, hugged and kissed him, and the notes and cards they sent him were cherished treasures. He built shelves to display their many photographs, and no guest ever escaped a tour of his prized picture gallery.

Daddy's luncheons remind me of what we call the Tale of Dada's Famous Escape. One time after Daddy had been hospitalized, I insisted he recuperate at our house until he was strong enough to manage at home. This was, of course, most unsatisfactory with him. Home was where he wanted to be, and he was growing more restless by the hour.

Realizing I had confined him about as long as I was going to get by with, I quietly slipped out of the house early one morning, with Daddy still asleep, to finalize arrangements with a temporary helper for him. When I got back to the house, Daddy's bed was empty. Just-awake Janna and Laura had not seen their grandfather (Dada, to them) and had no idea where he was. Since his hearing aid was still on his bedside table, we assumed he'd not gone far, and we continued the search.

Suddenly, our housekeeper, Pearl Barnett, frowning and fussing, came bursting through the door. Her words tumbled ahead of her, "You not gonna like what I done, but I couldn't hep it. When I drove up t'th' house he was awready waitin' on the curb, an' 'fore I knew what was happenin' he hopped right in th' front seat beside me an' said he'd invited some o' his girls fo' lunch and tole me I better take him home RIGHT THAT MINUTE and.... "

When Pearl finally stopped for breath, I assured her it was OK. She was not to worry, and surely Daddy could manage by himself for a few hours. By midmorning, Daddy had meekly called to explain how (but not why) he really needed to 'get on home.' I coolly reminded him I would still be there, as scheduled, that afternoon with the hired help.

Cruel though it may seem, as I packed his belongings, I figured it was poetic justice he'd had to entertain his girls without his very essential hearing aid. Daddy had lost hearing in one ear during World War I, and his good ear was not as good as it used to be. However, a bigger portion of poetic justice than deserved was served later in the day. When I arrived at his house with Daddy's hearing aid, his suitcase, and the hired help in tow, Daddy (then in his 90s) snatched the bag from my hand and to my utter amazement shouted, "DID YOU BRING MY TEETH?" Only then did I realize that he who had pulled off such a daring escape was not daring enough to call his daughter (before he entertained guests for lunch) and request the two essentials that he, in his haste, had left behind: his hearing aid and his teeth! Later, in a condolence note, a favorite neighbor well described Daddy as "One who found each day a gift from God … a day to serve Him and to reach out to others."

Daddy's determination to live a full, busy, productive life and his resourcefulness in accomplishing this left his children and grandchildren a rich legacy. And part of that legacy is Dada's Chicken Stew.

Dada's Chicken Stew

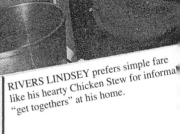

RIVERS LINDSEY prefers simple fare like his hearty Chicken Stew for informal "get togethers" at his home.

Retired Man Finds Cooking A Catalyst For Fellowship

By CINDY GREENE
Times-Daily Writer

"I was raised on a farm without any girls," says Rivers Lindsey of Florence, "so I had to learn to do a little of everything — including help with the cooking."

The art has only become a major interest for Lindsey in the last few years, however. Living alone at 83, he finds cooking to be a great way to bring people together and he frequently entertains friends and family at his home on Riverview Drive.

"Now that I'm retired," Lindsey explains, "I don't have anything I have to do and these get togethers help me keep in contact with young people."

Gatherings at the Lindsey home usually take on a casual atmosphere with simple fare such as his favorite — chicken stew with slaw and hot bread. It's the kind of meal guests can relax over and enjoy a visit and that, after all, is the whole idea.

CHICKEN STEW

1 whole fryer
3 to 4 Irish potatoes, diced
2 to 3 onions, diced
4 to 5 carrots, diced
1 medium can tomatoes or 1 small can tomato sauce
1 cup celery
Salt and pepper to taste
Bread crumbs, if desired

Pressure cook or boil fryer until tender. Cool and remove from pan, reserving stock. Debone and cut up fine. Cook potatoes, onions and carrots in stock until tender. Add chicken and tomatoes and cook slowly until very well done. Bread crumbs may be added if mixture is too "loose."

Lindsey suggests varying the recipe by adding other vegetables such as corn, lima beans or English peas, if desired.

6

She'll Be Comin' Round the Mountain

IT WAS A LONG TIME AGO, but I still remember the loving touch of my mother's arms wrapped around me, as together we rocked in the big wicker rocking chair, and she sang verse after verse one of my favorite melodies:

She'll be comin' round the mountain when she comes,
when she comes …

She'll be ridin' six white horses when she comes, gee haw …

She'll be wearin' red pajamas when she comes, ooh wee …

We will all go out to meet her when she comes, hey, babe …

We will kill the ole red rooster, when she comes, chop, chop …

We will have chicken'n dumplin's when she comes, yum, yum …

We will have chicken'n dumplin's …

We will have chicken'n dumplin's …

We will have chicken'n dumplin's when she co-omes …

In the old days, it was a hen past her prime and productivity, or even a cranky old rooster, whose lot it was to be featured as Chicken 'n Dumplin's. Today I prefer the tenderer and less personal store-bought, shrink-wrapped chicken.

Miss Kathy

THIS RECIPE COMES NOT FROM the past but instead from someone very beloved by our present family. Miss Kathy became a member of our family when Lindsey and Butch's Rebecca, our first grandchild, was born. Miss Kathy came to take care of the new baby, never dreaming that she would end up helping to raise, one way or another, every last one of our grandchildren. She graciously fills in whenever, wherever, and however any of us need her. Her role has evolved from changing diapers and rocking babies to such duties as picking up children after school and delivering them to wherever growing-up children need to go next. She cried when she realized that she had picked up for the final time an almost sixteen-year-old Rebecca (who would now drive herself to school). Miss Kathy has accepted her role in our family with patience, love, and good cheer.

Miss Kathy's Chicken 'n Dumplin's

Her Chicken 'n Dumplin's is the most favorite dish of all that Rebecca and her brother Forrest most often request that their favorite Miss Kathy cook for them.

1. In **6 c water**, cook 45 minutes (or until tender in a big pot) **1 chicken (2-3 lb)** (or an equal weight of breasts).

2. Add **1 T salt** and **½ t pepper**

3. Cool, bone chicken, and discard skin. Cut up chicken. Set aside. Add to broth after dumplin's are cooked.

4. Sift **2 c self-rising flour** into a bowl.

5. Cut in **⅓ c shortening**, using a pastry blender (or 2 knives), until shortening resembles coarse meal.

6. Add **½ c water**; then stir with a fork until mixture is sticky.

7. Place on well floured wax paper and work out by hand. Roll or pat out to ⅛ inch thick, and cut into strips about 1x4 inch. Drop dumplin's one at a time into slow boiling broth. Stir gently to keep from sticking. Add cut-up chicken to broth. Cook uncovered for 10 minutes. Cover and simmer 5-10 more minutes before serving. Yum … Yum!

Flookie

DURING MY HUSBAND DAVID'S CHILDHOOD, families in his neighborhood got together near the Price Spring for a big summer picnic. Early in the day, everybody took their hens down to Uncle Jim Price who lived down the road a piece. He set up a big black pot over an open fire and by evening had cooked the hens into his own brand of delicious chicken stew.

Back then times were hard, and recreation usually centered around wholesome family fun. The women enjoyed a respite from the heat of their kitchens, while the men swapped stories and took turns cranking the ice cream freezers before icing them down 'til supper time. Meanwhile, the children splashed and played in the nearby swimming hole. Surely those slow, hot summer days and happy times still echo in the hearts of those who were there: mostly Prices and Harrisons and Musslemans. They were all kin, one way or another, and every last one of them seemed to have a nickname. Even today, few people could tell you that Hap Harrison's real name was Cecil, or that Uncle Jim's son Chicken was really named James Edward (which had nothing to do with Uncle Jim's chicken stew but instead with his son's down-like hair when he was little). And for reasons nobody remembers, my David's nickname was Flookie. These friends and kin—Hap and Chicken and Flookie— were known by no other names throughout their growing-up years.

However, you cannot imagine my relief when, at a much later time, my beloved fiancé and I went to the Courthouse to get our marriage license, and I discovered I was, in fact, to become Mrs. David and not, thank goodness, Mrs. Flookie Mussleman.

Jim Price Chicken Stew

1. Cook **1 chicken (2-3 lb)** in **5-6 c water** until tender.

2. Remove bones and skin and return meat to broth.

3. Add to broth, and cook until done:

   3-4 med potatoes, peeled and diced

   1 large onion, chopped

   Salt

   Lots of pepper to taste

4. Add ½ **loaf white bread** torn into pieces, and stir until it thickens.

5. Simmer until ready to serve.

   Note: Unlike Uncle Jim's original, this is a 1-chicken recipe.

The Manly Sport of Anvil Shooting

THERE WAS A LONG TIME TRADITION of anvil shooting where Dad grew up in the Bailey Springs Community. Anvil shooting is a sport that requires two anvils, though today few families own even one anvil. Fewer still own two, but our family does. One of our anvils, once used in the neighborhood blacksmith shop, began as community property.

Now it came to pass that a few years ago Dad answered a veterinary call to treat a sick cow at Cousin Hobson Price's barn. He spotted the rusting anvil, dusty and abandoned, where the old shop had been. Dad asked his elderly cousin if he could buy the old anvil. Perhaps considering the legal complexities regarding community property, Hobson hesitated briefly; then he graciously bestowed it on Dad with the blessing: "I want you to have it, Flookie. I reckon it's as much your anvil as it is mine."

Understand that at this time we had a barn full of horses that required endless grooming, training, feeding, stall mucking, and shoeing. And there were still fences to repair and broken water lines to contend with. When I, too frequently pregnant to enjoy the horseback riding I also loved, caustically complained that our horse-shoeing budget exceeded our children-shoeing budget, Dad added to his chores as in-house veterinarian the backbreaking task of shoeing our horses (donning leather apron and all). Please note that our original lust for an anvil was for utilitarian rather than recreational purposes.

It was through another's misfortune that we had the good fortune to acquire a second anvil and thereby resurrect the almost lost art of anvil-shooting, an art I understand came down to us through the Appalachians. Dad's recently divorced receptionist Karen, moving to smaller quarters, needed a good home for her gold-painted anvil she used as a door stop. There is, I am pleased to report, a happy ending to what sounds like a sad story. Karen later remarried Spooner Oldham, a world-renowned piano player who shares labels with the likes of such recording artists as Linda Ronstadt and Kris Kristofferson. The couple—and now their daughter—are too busy living happily ever after to need an anvil for a door stop.

Anvil shooting will probably never replace the Super Bowl or the America's Cup Race, but it has certainly provided our family with much world class entertainment. One time our friend Eleanor in Louisville met some Florence acquaintances of ours, who, when pressed, confessed they had never even heard of an anvil shoot. Snapped Eleanor, "You damn well must not be very good friends if you've never attended a Mussleman Anvil Shoot!"

By now, you are probably as confused as was Eleanor's husband Fred, who had first heard wild talk of anvils from Dad's sister Mary Ellen and her husband Bill. Before he himself became a firsthand fan of anvil shooting, Fred's question was: "What in the hell do you do with the anvil after you shoot it?"

I can't exactly answer Fred's question, but since this is a cookery book, I can share with you our very own recipe for anvil shooting:

Recipe for Anvil Shooting

1. Take 2 anvils (100 lb each). Stir in 1 determined Dad and 2 compatriotic sons. Mix with cheering, curious friends/family/fans.

2. Place first anvil on the ground with hole in the base facing up.

3. Fill hole heaping full of dry gunpowder.

4. Add 1 fuse (6-8 inch) made of twisted paper sprinkled with gunpowder. (We admit, a commercial fuse can be used and is more efficient.)

5. Place flat surface of second anvil on top of first anvil at right angles, making sure powder-filled hole of first anvil is firmly covered by flat surface of second anvil.

6. Light the fuse, using a sturdy match and a steady hand.

7. For the first-timer's sake, show no fear, but run like the devil. Cover both ears with hands.

8. Wait 15-20 seconds for earth shaking explosion.

9. Watch for falling anvils (even if they do jump only a few feet).

Anvil Innovations

Two DEAR FRIENDS—big anvil shooting fans—must be recognized for their contributions. Jack Pounders, a certified diver with a knowledge of blasting, is fascinated with anvil shooting. With his ingenuity, Jack wanted to bring 21st century technology to the ancient art of anvil shooting. The gift was presented with much pomp and circumstance. It was a metal box with the letters Pyronator 2000 printed on the outside. Within were a mega amp battery, connecting cables, a brick-mounted double-throw switch, and seventy-five-feet of paired twenty-two gauge copper ignition wire. The final item was a step-by-step instructional video (narrated tongue in cheek) by Jack himself. The Pryonator was technologically correct and fun, but our cranky old anvils never adapted well to today's technology.

Steve Davis, another long time anvil-shooting fan, used his sophisticated machine shop staff and equipment (whose paying clients were mainly Taiwanese industries) to enlarge the powder hole, cut a groove for the fuse, and mill the anvil's flat surfaces to mirror-like perfection. We thanked Steve for his generosity, but sadly an automobile accident took Steve's life before he had a chance to hear for himself how much bigger the **BOOM** was after he overhauled our anvils.

And traditions can be improved upon or even changed. Recently, Dad and I were listening to classical music on public radio when we heard the distinctive notes of a familiar song. In the manner of couples long married, we suddenly looked at each other and smiled. We were of one mind. Yes siree, next time we shoot the anvils, it will be to the background music of the "Anvil Chorus!"

Twelve Squirrels and Six Rabbits

SINCE HORSES IN GENERAL AND HUNTER-JUMPERS in particular had become such an important part of our family's life, we were delighted when Dad's sister Mary Ellen and her family moved to Louisville, Kentucky, in the very heart of real horse country. We soon made a practice of paying them at least one visit during the fall racing season. Mary Ellen's deep love for us as family and her unconquerable love for anything fun made for a delightful time and a memorable visit. She always had elegant, delicious food ready to serve, as if she had magically pulled it out of a gourmet chef's hat. One time, Mary Ellen invited us to invite several Florence couples to accompany us; the food was just as special and the hospitality as gracious as ever.

Although Mary Ellen lived in the city that was home to the Kentucky Derby and Churchill Downs, it was Keeneland Racetrack in nearby Lexington that we most enjoyed. Approaching by the sweeping roadway and welcomed by the rich colors of autumn, our hearts quickened at our first glimpse of the classic grey, vine-covered stone and the grandness that was Keeneland.

Dressed in their casual tweeds and polished leather, owners and trainers brushed shoulders with the likes of us whose attire patterned theirs. Grooms were ever-present, washing, brushing, and walking their nervous equine charges. Bandy-legged jockeys strutted about, sporting the distinctive silks of their owners, listening for the huntsman's horn calling the next race as they waited to mount the magnificent, fine-boned thoroughbreds under the huge sheltering trees. This unique tradition of mounting the horses with anybody and everybody milling around and underfoot—rather than in the traditional, restricted-area paddock of most tracks—adds greatly to Keeneland's charm.

When we first ate this superb stew at Keeneland Racetrack, I did not even know how to spell it, much less make it. It was no easy task, but I collected all available Burgoo recipes from far and near. I could find no one who had ever cooked it and only a few who had eaten it, but one friend unearthed a recipe from one of her historical cookbooks that called for "twelve squirrels and six rabbits … " Given our friendship with such neighborly animals, I rejected that one and continued my quest. Eventually locating several more contemporary versions of that recipe, I mixed and matched, combined and copied until I arrived at this one. It takes a long time to cut up all the vegetables and to cook three meats, but the flavor is unsurpassed in mouth-watering pleasure. Making Burgoo is well worth the required effort, but let there be no doubt about it: either it feeds lots and lots of folks or the leftovers last a long, long time.

Kentucky Burgoo

1. Cook **3 lb *each*** of **pork, beef, and chicken** until fork tender in **6 qts of water.**

2. Remove from stock and cool. Bone, pull apart chicken, cut up beef and pork, and return to stock.

3. Chop and add to stock:

   2 c cabbage   **2 lb potatoes**

   2 lb onions   **1 lb carrots**

   2 green peppers   **1 c celery**

4. Also add:

   ½ bottle Worcestershire sauce **2 cans (16 oz each) whole kernel corn**

   1 pkg (16 oz) lima beans **1 can (16 oz) green beans, chopped**

   2 c okra, sliced   **Salt**

   Tabasco to taste   **Cayenne pepper**

5. Simmer several hours, stirring occasionally, until thick but still "soupy."

6. Before serving, add **2 T fresh chopped parsley.**

Barn Party

DURING THE YEARS when our family had a barn full of horses, we would invite in a bunch of friends for a pot of chicken stew or burgoo, push back the bales of hay in the loft, and have ourselves a party. Guests came casually attired in plaid shirts and blue jeans, and somebody in the crowd was sure to bring along a banjo or a guitar. But one time, a couple (who had attended dress-up parties at our home but who had never attended what we called a Barn Party) arrived dressed just a little less than black tie. The somewhat embarrassed lady (she will remain nameless) in her long gown required a bit of help getting up the ladder to the loft, but once accomplished she was a good sport, and a jolly good time was had by all.

MEATS

Two Heads Are Better Than One

NO RECIPE IN EXISTENCE HAS PROVIDED more repeated funny stories in our family or provoked more smoldering hostility in me than has Scrapple, a recipe passed down through the Musslemans from the dim mists of time. In the first place, no one, unless actually born a Mussleman, should be expected to follow a recipe that reads: "Cook one hog's head and four feet …." In the second place, in my early scrapple-making days, David insisted that two hog's heads were better than one. So we doubled the recipe, a perennial source of conflict. This meant I had to double the necessary scrubbing, shaving, and teeth brushing (let me explain that the hog is deceased at this point) to prepare the creatures for the long hours of slow cooking. It was a family tradition to shock any new girl or boy friends who had not been around the previous Christmas (traditional scrapple-making season) by suddenly exhibiting the hog's head leering in a box or cooking in a pot. The faint of heart never did too well around our house, especially during Scrapple Season.

It was at the final stage of preparation that Dad and his mother would take over center stage and together make their cameo appearance. Dad "worked the bones" out of the meat, and she appeared, bearing her pot full of cornmeal mush, the final important scrapple ingredient. While I collapsed exhausted on the couch, the two of them mixed the mush with the meat, seasoned it, and poured it into pans to cool. Insult was added to injury as they heartily congratulated themselves and took a bow, once again, for having done a masterful job of making scrapple.

Since Dad's sister Mary Ellen always came home at Thanksgiving rather than Christmas, delivering Scrapple to her in Louisville in time for her Christmas morning breakfast required considerable coordination and resourcefulness. I assure you, it did not go unnoticed, that she who was born a Mussleman did not have the same enthusiasm for making that she had for eating Scrapple.

Travelers headed her way were subject to being called into service—into delivery service, that is. One year, when all else failed, the Scrapple was dispatched to Louisville on a Greyhound bus. We alerted Mary Ellen, and there she was, waiting at the bus station alongside those meeting loved ones home for the holidays, greeting with equal joy her package of home-made Scrapple, hailing all the way from Alabama.

The one other and essential task was ordering the hogs' heads and feet, which became increasingly difficult when health regulations eventually prohibited the sale of hogs' heads altogether. Back when our county was dry, I knew folks who had bootleggers for booze, but ours was the only family I ever heard of who had a bootlegger for pig parts.

For the boys, going down in the country to pick up the contraband hogs' heads was considered a high point of the season. Obviously, such a mission lent itself to unforgettable pranks and jokes. Once, on the way home from a rural slaughterhouse, mischievous son Matt decided to tuck the hogs' feet inside the cuffs of his jacket sleeves, and the effect was not lost on startled fellow motorists. Driving down the road in his dad's beloved 1955 Army jeep, (top off, of course) Matt, clutching the steering wheel with cloven hooves, looked like some misplaced mythical creature. Sitting beside him like Pan, the god of mirth, his brother Dee roared approvingly with laughter.

At long last, we discovered that a Boston Butt and four pig's feet—available at local grocers (at least here in Alabama)—provide all the quantity and quality of Scrapple we can ever eat for our traditional Christmas morning breakfast. What a wonderful relief it was to finally get out of the pig parts bootlegging business and rejoin the ranks of respectable, law-abiding citizens!

Old Fashioned Scrapple

1. Cook slowly in large pot half full of water for 6-8 hours (or until meat falls from bone):

   1 hog's head, scrubbed and thoroughly cleaned

   4 hog's feet, scrubbed and shaved

2. Drain off and discard liquid.

3. When cool, "work bones" out of meat.

4. Discard bones and fat. Place meat back in pot.

5. Mix **hot mush** thoroughly with meat. See directions for corn meal mush.

6. Season with **salt** and plenty of **pepper**.

7. Pour into pans and refrigerate.

Corn Meal Mush

1. In a large pot, bring **4 c of water** to boil.

2. Measure **2 c cold water** in a bowl, and blend in **2 c corn meal**. Mix until smooth; then pour slowly into boiling water.

3. Bring to a boil, stirring constantly until mush is thick and smooth.

To Cook and Serve Scrapple

1. Cut **Scrapple** into thick slices, and roll in **flour**. Fry in skillet over medium heat in a small amount of **oil**.

2. Turn when upper surface bubbles and lower surface is crisp and brown. Cook until both sides are brown. Drain on paper towels.

3. Serve Scrapple hot with home-made biscuits, sorghum molasses, cheese grits, and eggs any way you like them.

New Fashioned Scrapple

1. Cook until tender and meat falls from bone:

   6 lb Boston Butt (instead of hog's head)

   4 hog's feet, scrubbed and shaved

2. Follow directions for Old Fashioned Scrapple.

Surprise Meatloaf

Potato-stuffed meatloaf, a family favorite recipe, is a surprise nice enough to serve company.

1. Mix together:

1 ½ lb lean ground beef	**½ c chopped onion**
¼ c dry breadcrumbs	**1 egg**
¼ c catsup	**1 t salt**
¼ t pepper	**¼ t crushed basil leaves**

2. Press half of mixture into 9x5 loaf pan.

3. To make potato filling, heat **¾ c water** to boiling and add:

   2 T margarine

   ½ t salt

4. Remove from heat and add:

   ⅓ c milk

   1 ½ c potato flakes

5. Stir in:

   1 egg

   ¼ c shredded cheese

6. Spread potato mixture over meat in loaf pan. Top with remaining meat. Bake for about 35 minutes at 350 degrees. Let cool 5 minutes. Drain off fat and liquids. Invert onto serving plate. Garnish with **catsup** or **chili sauce** and a **few sprigs of parsley**.

Eastside . . . Westside . . .

My good and dear friend Martha Daniel and I have been together in this business of school social work for a long time. While we have never (in the manner suggested in song) done New York together, we have (in the manner suggested by our chosen profession) covered Eastside, Westside, all around our hometown here in Florence, Alabama, where the opposite ends of town are sometime referred to as "the Eastside" and "the Westside." We social workers are bound by the same "neither snow nor rain nor heat nor gloom of night" code as mailmen, but if they had to deal with the mess of problems we did, the U.S. Postal Service probably would have shut down a long time ago.

One time Martha and I together made a home visit to one of our toughest homes on one of the roughest sides of town. Martha, first to sit down on the dilapidated old sofa, sort of squirmed and then scooted over a space. Assuming she was graciously making room for me, I sat down on the spot she vacated, a spot so lumpy I decided she must have been seeking a softer seat. Whatever lumps I was sitting on were hard, but I shifted to as comfortable a position as possible and did my best to keep our home visit as brief as possible.

We were back in the car before I noticed Martha was shaking, now more from laughter than from fright. She soon stopped shaking enough to tell me that the reason she had moved so quickly was to avoid sitting on a mean looking pistol half hidden (and probably hastily hidden) between the sofa cushions, where first she and then I had been sitting during our visit. Then it was my turn to shake!

Martha Daniel's Jambalaya

1. Cook together in **3 c water** until tender.

   1 lb smoked link sausage, cut in large chunks

   9 chicken thighs

   1 bay leaf

2. Bone chicken, cut up, and return to broth (discard bay leaf).

3. Chop and sauté in small amount of **olive oil:**

   3 onions

   5 ribs celery

   1 bell pepper

4. Add to broth:

   Sautéed vegetables

   2 cans (16 oz each) stewed tomatoes

   1 small can of tomato paste

5. Season to taste with:

   Tabasco

   Creole seasoning

   Worcestershire sauce

   Chili powder

   Salt and pepper

6. Cook **2 ½ c rice** in broth.

7. Simmer 30 more minutes before serving.

   Optional: Add **1 lb shelled shrimp** 5 minutes before serving.

Mom's Chili

My original chili recipe came from the Auburn Alpha Psi Veterinary Fraternity House. In those days, I too made it in frat house quantities on football weekends. Little did I know then that frat house numbers of young folks would be sitting down at our family table many times over the years. However, through those years, I have created my own simpler recipe with a special tasty ingredient added to the pot.

1. **Brown 3 lb ground beef** in large pot, stirring often.
2. Add **3-4 chopped onions**, and stir until transparent.
3. Drain off fat.
4. Add:

   4 cans (16 oz each) chili beans

   2-3 c vegetable cocktail juice (the tasty ingredient)

   2 T chili powder

   1 can (15 oz) diced tomatoes
5. Bring to a boil, and simmer for at least a half hour, preferably longer. Serve steaming hot, with coleslaw on the side.

Jean Lynch's Chili

OUR FRIENDSHIP WITH JEAN AND AARON LYNCH dates back to the same busy years when they were raising their four children, and we were raising our five. Through the years, we have enjoyed updating our friendship by enjoying food and fellowship together. Jean Lynch serves her chili over tortilla chips and tamales, sprinkles it with chopped onion and cheese, and melts in the microwave just before serving. She makes it more appetizing by garnishing the dish with lettuce, tomatoes, and jalapeno peppers.

James's Pepper Steak

Alva Fields was the ultimate, liberated professional woman. She was far more experienced than I, but we both were hired as school social workers at the same time by the Florence City School System. The recipes she talked about and shared, in the sort of recipe-swapping that prevails in offices were, often as not, her husband's.

The two of them moved back to Chattanooga before I got a chance to know James very well. However, gastronomically speaking (because of his Pepper Steak recipe), I'll never forget him.

1. Cut **2 ½ lb round steak** in ½ inch strips.
2. Coat with:

   ½ t salt

   ⅛ t pepper

   Garlic salt

   ¼ c flour
3. Brown steak in **¼ c vegetable oil**.
4. Add and simmer for 1 hour 15 minutes.

   Juice from 1 can (16 oz) tomatoes

   1 ¾ c water

   ½ c sliced onions

   2 t Worcestershire sauce
5. Add **2 bell peppers** cut into strips, and simmer for 5 minutes.
6. Add reserved **canned tomatoes**.
7. Simmer for 5 more minutes.
8. Serve over a bed of **hot cooked rice**.

A Shared Past

THE SMITHS HAD MOVED FROM ENGLAND TO AMERICA as newlyweds and from another Alabama town to ours when their Ethel was a little girl. Having never before heard English spoken by the English, I was captivated by its clarity and its cadenced beauty.

Mrs. Smith, who did not drive, and my mother, who did, were close church friends and traveling companions to meetings as nearby as area churches or as far away as the Methodist Retreat at Lake Junaluska in the North Carolina Smoky Mountains. Ethel and I were schoolmates and, daughters like mothers, lifelong friends.

Our high school years were those strange post-World War II years when there was a joyful frenzy to make up for what had been lost and to catch up on what had been missed. Raymond Graham and his twin Ralph were among those who had as boys dropped out of high school to serve their country and returned as men to continue their high school education. Teachers, some little older than these students, puzzled over how to manage war heroes in the classroom. Zealous football coaches and starry-eyed school girls alike were dazzled by the mature, muscled young veterans. It was a time when both superior ball teams and stellar romances flourished.

Raymond and Ethel's romance flourished into marriage during the summer David and I were living in England. We delighted in visiting their Coventry kin who talked about, asked about, and loved hearing about A-thel, Rye-mund, Uncle Rye-lif, and dear Aunt-ee Mice-ee (Mrs. Smith, known as Eleanor in America, was Maizie to her British family).

By the time we made our way back home to live, Raymond had reentered the U.S. Army to become a helicopter pilot, and by the time he retired, he was a Lieutenant Colonel. Whenever Raymond's assignments carried him to such places as Korea or Vietnam, Ethel returned home with the children, and yet another generation became friends. Our generation, as old friends do, simply picked up and began our friendship where it had been before.

When David and I made the decision to settle in our hometown, we considered the risk that we might forget and that our children might never discover life beyond the city limits of Florence, Alabama. Through the years, the Graham's visits and their greetings postmarked from faraway places served to remind us of the world beyond our doorstep. The sharing of themselves and their experiences helped expand our horizons and keep our windows open to the rest of the world. In return, I suppose we provided them a view of hometown life, the who-what-when-where and even why of small town news and the sometimes provincial views of hometowns everywhere.

Looking back, wondering where the years have gone, I am sobered by how swiftly our todays become tomorrows. More than ever before, I find myself savoring time and valuing friendships. Now that they too have come back home to live, we continue to build on our shared past and to enjoy the present pleasure of Raymond and Ethel's company.

Today, it is as it has always been. We are there for each other, in the joyful times and the sad … in the good times and the bad … when friends can count on friends.

Note: During our growing up years, Ethel was known only as Ethel, but during her years as a military wife, she was called Nicki (as she is today), short for her middle name, her mother's maiden name, Nicholson.

Corn Pone Pie

This recipe Nicki gave me years ago may seem a strange one to credit to such a well-traveled gourmet cook, but Nicki tells me that folks all over the world have enjoyed the regional taste of her Corn Pone Pie.

1. Brown **1 lb ground beef** in skillet.

2. Drain off fat.

3. Add and simmer 10-15 minutes:

   1 can (16 oz) of tomatoes

   1 can (16 oz) of kidney beans, drained

   2 t chili powder

   ½ t salt

   1 t Worcestershire sauce

4. Pour into bottom of buttered casserole.

5. Mix corn bread (pone) batter:

   1 c self-rising corn meal

   2 T self-rising flour

   ¾ c buttermilk (or enough to make batter pourable)

   1 egg

   1 T vegetable oil

6. Pour batter over meat mixture.

7. Bake at 425 degrees for 20 minutes.

FISH & SEAFOODS

29 Cents a Pound

WE ACQUIRED AN INSATIABLE TASTE for shrimp while we were college students at Auburn University. This may seem strange, since the little town of Auburn, located halfway between Atlanta and Montgomery on the eastern plains of Alabama, was never, even in ancient times, anywhere near the Gulf Coast or its bountiful shrimp beds. However, a local grocery store did, in ancient times when we lived there, frequently run a weekend special: a 5-pound box of shrimp at 29 cents a pound. That was extremely good, cheap eating (important to struggling students) that could with sufficient quantities of baked potatoes and hot buttered French bread be extended to feed a goodly number of other struggling student-guests. It is still a favorite food, and I'd sure like to get my hands on a few boxes of those shrimp at that price.

Boiled Shrimp

1. Pour **2 cans beer** in large pot (or enough beer to cover shrimp), and bring to a rolling boil.

2. Add **1 pkg shrimp boil**.

3. Add **shrimp in the shell (½ lb per person)**.

4. Bring to boil again. Cook 3-5 minutes 'til shrimp turns pink.

5. Drain and chill before serving.

Seafood Pasta

This is a delicious way to enjoy the variety of seafoods available at the beach, or even from a well stocked local market. The recipe, if you can call it one, is left over from the times our family vacationed with the families of cousin John Paul, Margaret, and their friends on the Gulf Coast. Believe me, there's room a-plenty for originality on the part of the cook!

1. Bring **2 jars (1 lb 10 oz each) of spaghetti sauce** to a boil.
2. Add:

   Rinse jars with 1 c water

   2 bell peppers, chopped

   1 large onion, chopped

   1 lb pkg fresh sliced mushrooms or 1 can (4 oz)

   3 t Tabasco
3. Simmer 15 minutes, then add:

   ½ lb scallops

   ¼ lb crab meat

   2 lb catch-of-the-day, filleted and cubed

   (White Fish, like Orange Roughy, is good.)
4. Cook slowly about 20 more minutes, then add:

   2 lb or more peeled shrimp

   1 c red wine
5. Cook for 5 more minutes, or until shrimp are pink.
6. Serve generously over hot **spaghetti or pasta** of your choice.

   Of course, you may mix and match any way you chose, adding your favorite sea foods and subtracting those which are not.

A Stew By Any Other Name

FOR YEARS I HAD HEARD HOW GREAT this dish was, especially at the beach for a crowd. Gulf Coast folk call it Cajun Feast, but for reasons I do not know and dare not ask, Carolina folk call it Frogmore Stew. By whatever name, whenever our family goes to the beach, serving it has become a family tradition. Back before all our daughters were married, they agreed … no matter how delicious or how much fun it is to eat, this is not what you serve the first time you invite a new guy home for dinner. Gentility, one of our cherished Southern traditions, takes its leave when a pot of Frogmore Stew is placed in the middle of a newspaper-covered table.

By the time everyone is full and finished with the feast, the table resembles some porcine paradise. But never mind, rolling up all the corn cobs, potato skins, and shrimp shells in the newspaper tablecloth is quick and easy, and no evidence remains to indicate what pigs everybody just made of themselves.

Frogmore Stew/Cajun Feast

1. Fill a large pot half full of **water** and bring to a boil.

2. Add and cook for 5 minutes:

   Polish sausage cut in chunks   ⅛ **lb per person**

3. Next, add and cook for 10 minutes:

   New potatoes scrubbed and in the jacket   **2-3 per person**

4. Add and cook for 10 more minutes:

   Ears of fresh corn broken in half   **1-2 per person**

5. Add and cook for 3-5 minutes or until pink:

   Shrimp in the shell   ½ **lb per person**

6. Drain water from the pot. Place the steaming, hot feast in pot or bowl in the middle of that newspaper-covered table we keep talking about. Serve on paper plates. Clean-up is as easy as rolling up the paper, debris and all, and throwing it away.

Newbern's Catfish and Hush Puppies

MOST SOUTHERN COOKS CAN TELL YOU how to fry Catfish to just the right shade of brown and degree of crispness, and how to chop the exact amount of onions for perfect hush puppies. But since I've never fried Catfish in my kitchen anywhere near as good as local fish restaurants fry catfish in their kitchens, I offer no such recipe. Anyway, this was all my mother-in-law's fault.

Greatmommy Mussleman's most memorable quote was: "Why on earth would anybody ever eat Catfish anywhere else but at Newbern's?" Her next memorable quote was: "Their fish are so brown, so crisp, and so piping hot …." We agreed. Therefore, we never ate Catfish and hush puppies anywhere else either. Or if we ever did dare to eat fish elsewhere, we certainly did not tell our grandmother.

As long as Greatmommy was physically able to make the trip, "going to Newbern's" was an established tradition. And today, for us, it still is. It usually takes no more than five phone calls and five minutes to round up enough family members for what we call a "fish night out." We have a theory that the fish is at its crispest and brownest when the parking lot is full, the restaurant is crowded, and the cooking oil is probably hottest.

It is amazing how graciously and efficiently tables are pulled together to serve the full complement of Musslemans (up to a party of twenty three). However, you do not want to get to Newbern's too late. This is a family restaurant (shoes and shirts required), and no alcohol is served. So as soon as the supper rush is past and the crowd thins out, the wait staff (still topping off our glasses with sweet tea) begins to refill the salt and pepper shakers and the catsup bottles … finally sweeping under the tables before closing time at 9 p.m.

But we never go to Newbern's Restaurant without missing Greatmommy, and we smile with the memory of how she loved coming here. We know exactly what her words would be, and we discover for ourselves that, sure enough, those little fishes are always just right … so brown and crisp … and ever so piping hot.

Note: In earlier times, before our waterways were so polluted, local fish eateries used to proudly proclaim: "Our Catfish slept in the Tennessee River last night."

Today, their fish may be just as fresh and tasty, but there is simply no poetry to "Our Catfish slept in a pond last night."

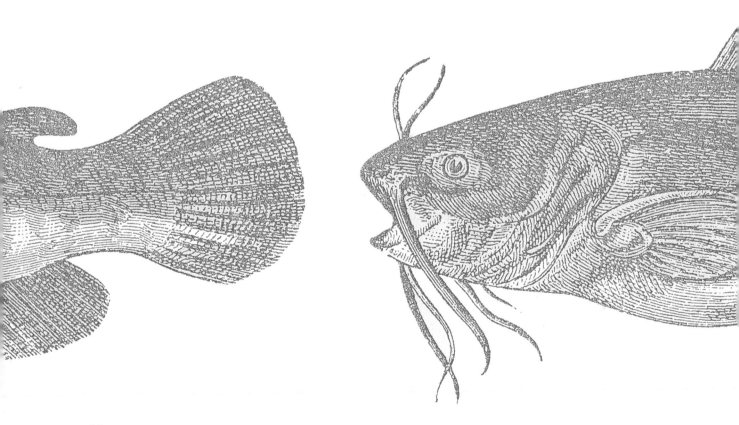

POULTRY & FIXINS

Remember Me?

WHEN OUR YOUNGEST TWO CHILDREN, Janna and Laura began nursery school—we lovingly referred to them as the Little Girls—I decided that full-time motherhood could spare me long enough to earn my master's degree, to seek my fortune, and, if not fame, at least to enhance my identity. Pursuing this goal was dependent upon securing reliable and responsible household help. I had already experienced too many rejections when potential ladies-who-help interviewed me by phone and inevitably asked that critical question: "Now, how many kids ya' got?" When I reluctantly admitted and muttered, "Five," it was not uncommon for the interview to end abruptly with a quick click, a slam-bang, or an unprintable expletive before the line went dead in my hand. Pearl Barnett, bless her heart, did not hang up on me, and after a quarter of a century she was still holding the line. Today, Pearl cares for her invalid husband, but she will always be a beloved part of our family. Having only one son of her own, Pearl also proudly claims (as her own) our three daughters and two sons.

However, if Pearl could have foreseen the multitudinous tasks that would grow and become hers, she, too, might have hung up that phone. Pearl, much like Mary Poppins, could by her mere presence whisk a house into cleanliness and orderliness. Even way back then, she stayed caught up with the washing and ironing, a heretofore unheard of accomplishment at our house. She even got the right socks and underwear in the right drawers, also unheard of B.P. (Before Pearl).

Pearl even included in her love and responsibilities the care of the assortment of eccentric and sometimes unlovable animals that were ours. Understand that a veterinarian's family is often approached to adopt animals that another family, for various reasons, may be unable to keep. Lucy, momentarily expecting her first litter, became our boxer when neither party, during divorce proceedings, would consent to the other owning the dog. So far as I know, the only point they agreed upon was that Dad was legally decreed her new owner.

Whatever needed doing, Pearl willingly did. She helped round up horses when they would jump the fence and gallop through the neighborhood on their way to frolic in the creek. She watched over whichever pet goat was currently in residence. She lovingly warmed milk in the microwave for Bud, Janna's aging cat.

Pearl was one of the few souls ever brave enough to manage our notorious English Bulldog Spike. Once she bodily rescued him by his choke chain out of the jaws of a dog-eating garbage truck where he had leaped in pursuit of the garbage men who themselves were barely one leap ahead of man-eating Spike. Surely they were awestruck as they clung precariously to the sides of the truck, as Pearl, holding Spike by the scruff of his neck, proceeded to give the bad dog a noisy verbal and physical scolding. I'm sure if Spike had possessed one, Pearl, as the saying goes, would have justifiably "jerked a knot in his tail."

When Pearl accepted the job (actually a career) with our family, she did so with only one major condition: No cooking. That agreement was essentially honored, but as she grumbled through the years about how much she hated to fry the chicken that husband Troy and son Bill so loved to eat, we eventually talked her into frying some for us. The rest of the story is history. For special occasions and tailgating events, nothing would do but Pearl-Fried Chicken. Even though she grumbled about frying chicken for us, I am convinced that the praise and appreciation (plus the extra incentive the grateful Dad slipped in her pocket) made it worthwhile for all.

Pearl Fried Chicken

Cut up many Chickens as you want
Wash Chicken in Warm Water
lay the Chicken on a plate
drain off the water add salt & pepper
and self rising flour all over the Chicken
put Crisco or Crisco oil in a
skillet or pan until hot
add Chicken never let your Chicken
touch each other before it browns
turn often as it browns do not
Cook Chicken to high or to low
when it done place on a plate
on paper towels.

Remember me?

As school and work increasingly kept us all away from home during Pearl's workday, she took to writing us notes: a reminder, a telephone message, a grocery list. Notes congratulated, scolded, or praised. But with the children grown and gone, Pearl's notes addressed such serious family matters as my cat Sam and his behavior:

Mrs Mussleman
You Cat Sam have been so bad
today I could have spank him
good he pull my iron off the
ironing board and tore it
up so bad I dont think it
can be fix and I am mad
with him to. I ask hem to leave it alone
but Sam dont mine at all remember me?
Pearl

Whatever the message, the note, like Pearl's recipe, always concluded with her trademark query, "Remember me?" In gratitude and love, our response is, "How could we NOT remember Pearl?"

The Pully Bone

WHILE DAVID AND I WERE STUDENTS at Alabama Polytechnic Institute (now Auburn University), we bought a lot of groceries (including chicken) at Southside Grocery, a small market down on Gay Street between our home and the campus. The butcher was outfitted in a white cap and a once white apron well stained with his trade. He was usually about a day behind a shave, a cigarette drooping permanently from the corner of his mouth, one eye squinting against the smoke. He was a bit crotchety, but if he wasn't too busy, he would cut up your chicken at no extra charge. I preferred to buy chicken on the days he wasn't too busy, but David, for reasons never clear to me, preferred I buy it whole and cut it up myself. The Wife resisted, the Man of the House insisted, and I usually lost. Now I am glad I had to learn how to cut up a chicken the old fashioned way. I can practice the almost lost art of cutting up a chicken that creates that very special piece we Southerners love and know as the pully bone. I don't know of any place you can buy a pully bone any more (either cooked or uncooked): not at any grocery store I know, nor even from that paragon of Southern fried chicken, the Colonel himself.

To Discover and Recover the Pully Bone
(also called wishbone):

1. Place a whole chicken, back down, breast up, on a flat surface.
2. Insert a sharp knife under the triangular bone in top center of the breast, and carefully carve out this choice piece with the bone intact.
3. Cut the remaining breast piece down the middle and into two pieces.

Historically, in most families, the issue of who got the pully bone was such a standing source of sibling rivalry that some system of turn-taking was required. The pully bone was the most sought after and fought over piece of chicken of all. After you had eaten the crisp-browned outside, the juicy white meat inside, and had nothing left but the bone, you chose someone to "pull" the bone with you. It was a ceremony. You both made a wish, and whoever held the piece that broke long had the absolute guarantee that their wish would come true.

How sad it would be if today's or tomorrow's children never knew the pleasure of a pully bone or the hope of a wish-come-true.

The Family Fire Buff

W<small>E COUSINS GREW UP TOGETHER</small> with many a leisurely Sunday afternoon spent at the farm home of Tommy's grandparents, my Great Aunt Jo (Grandfather Cauhorn's sister) and Uncle Archie Ray out in the country near Greenhill. One such time is forever etched in my memory. It was a typical warmish Alabama winter afternoon when the gathered family sat around talking and visiting as families back then did. The repeated slap-slap of the screened door marked how frequently the young cousins were back and forth, inside and outside to the porch, the yard, and the barn where the pony was stabled.

Then suddenly, all of us, all the children and all the grownups, were urgently called inside. We crowded ourselves into the small front room and joined those listening intently to the radio. All of us stared at it in disbelief, as if that could somehow change its message. A frantic voice broke through the spasms of static enough to repeat the news. Japan had bombed Pearl Harbor in Hawaii. We were shocked. Stunned. Silent. With tears in her eyes, my mother held me close and hugged me to her. We clung tightly to each other as Daddy's arms encircled us both. I was eleven years old, old enough to understand that my seventeen-year-old brother Rivers, away in college, was old enough to go to war.

It was an unforgettable day, a day frozen in time, a day that President Franklin Roosevelt would describe as "a date that will live in infamy." It was December 7, 1941.

By the time World War II was over, Tommy's family had moved to Florence, and even though my precocious cousin was a year younger, we were graduated in the same high school class. By the time we both ended up at Auburn University, Tommy, an Navy ROTC scholar, was dating Janet, and David and I were married. Sometimes we were a foursome and sometimes even a twosome. One winter quarter, David and Janet went to the basketball games together, and Tommy and I joined them after our night classes. Tommy married Janet, completed a tour of duty as a Naval officer, earned a PhD in nuclear engineering, and eventually settled in the nucleus of nuclear research at Oak Ridge, near Knoxville, Tennessee.

As far back as I can remember, Tommy has had an absolute passion for fire engines and anything associated with them. Perhaps it all began in nearby Tuscumbia where he lived as a child. There, the number of blasts on the fire siren—heard all over the small town— signaled a fire's location. Townspeople considered this an invitation (which they accepted) to attend the fire. His sister Katherine tells about the time young Tommy, in his haste to get to a fire, was seen hunched over his handlebars, speeding down the middle of the street on his tricycle. Intent on his mission, he was almost run over when he failed to yield to a car.

And matters haven't changed a great deal since. During college, Tommy hung around the fire station so much he was finally invited to move in, bag and baggage. Later, whenever he and Janet relocated, their first stop, almost before finding a place to live or checking in at the new job, was to check out the fire station. Always available as a volunteer fire fighter, Tommy often arranged home hookups for fire calls and has been known to beat the firemen to the fire. He has also been known to abandon family wherever they are, whenever he hears a siren. They have an understanding. Janet simply finds a way home, knowing that her spouse in due time will do the same.

It is not surprising that Tommy and Janet's new home is designed with room enough for Tommy's impressive collection of fire memorabilia and garages enough for his three antique fire trucks. Nor is it surprising that in good spirit Janet accompanies Tommy to Fire Musters all over the country.

I can assure you, if the opportunity ever presents itself, I certainly intend to nominate the patient, long-suffering Janet for Sainthood.

Many summers ago, while vacationing at the Smoky Mountain resort of Cobbly Knob near Gatlinburg, Tennessee, we were frightened awake during the middle of the night by a crackling flickering brightness, running footsteps, banging doors, and loud shouts of "FIRE! FIRE!! FIRE!!!"

Shaken but safe, our young family huddled in blankets on the hillside and watched volunteer fire fighters battle the blaze. None of us will ever forget the experience of that roaring, raging inferno. We were mesmerized as the furious flames fueled by the cedar shake construction engulfed the clubhouse. Spellbound, we watched the grand piano that had provided our dinner music the evening before crash through the fiery floor of the restaurant into the Pro Shop below.

Someone observed it was a shame Cousin Tommy was missing such a spectacular fire. Every volunteer fire department in East Tennessee seemed to be headed our way, and every time another fire truck with sirens screaming arrived on the scene, we half expected Tommy to come leaping from it. The next time we saw Tommy, we told him all about what was certainly the biggest fire we'd ever witnessed up close, and he apologized for missing our fire. Because of the more than fifty mountainous miles of winding road between Cobbly Knob and Oak Ridge, he'd consoled himself by monitoring it on his fire radio. But, he assured us, had he known we were there, he surely would have somehow come.

Then there was Tommy's older brother Zeke. Years ago, while having dinner with him and his wife Minnie, we were chuckling and swapping stories about our family fire buff when we heard the unmistakable sound of a distant siren. Zeke's ears pricked up like an old fire horse. By the time the siren was closer and louder, Zeke was out of his chair, through the door, and gone. That was the first I knew that Zeke suffered from the same affliction as his brother, and that our family actually had more than one fire buff, all of which would cause anyone, especially an old sociologist like me, to ponder and to raise the age-old question of heredity versus environment.

Cousin Ruby May assured me that she was never, while pregnant with Zeke or Tommy, frightened by a fire engine, so could the answer simply be their Tuscumbia upbringing? Or did the coincidence that Tommy was born on October 8—the date that Mrs. O'Leary's cow kicked over the lantern that started the great 1871 Chicago fire—somehow mark him for life? Since I have carefully searched and researched the family tree and can find no branch of it that explains how my cousins came to be how my cousins are, this causes me to wonder about all the skeletons families reportedly hide in closets … and to wonder if perhaps there was a pyromaniac or a mad arsonist hidden in ours!

Janet's Oven-Fried Pecan Chicken

We Southerners love our chicken fried all kinds of ways, and to prove it we have many recipes, like this wonderful fried-in-the-oven recipe of Janet Scott's!

1. Mix together:

   1 c biscuit mix or flour   **1 ½ t salt**

   2 t paprika   **2 T sesame seed**

   ½ t poultry seasoning (optional)

   ¼ to ½ c finely chopped pecans

2. Dip serving pieces of **1 cut-up fryer** (or an equal amount of your favorite pieces) in **½ c evaporated milk.**

3. Coat with dry mixture.

4. Place chicken in 9x13 inch baking dish.

5. Drizzle **¼ to ½ c melted margarine** over chicken.

6. Bake at 375 degrees for 1 hour, or until brown.

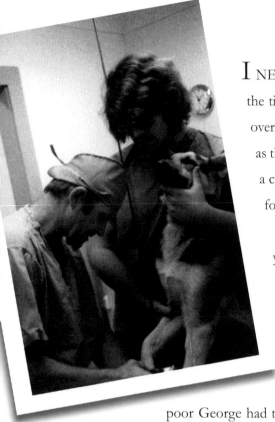

Great Eaters Make Great Cooks

I NEVER UNDERSTOOD HOW David's veterinary hospital staff found the time, much less the stomach, to discuss food as passionately as they did over the years, but some awfully good recipes came home via this route. Even as they treated the ill, sutured the wounded, struggled to save a victim hit by a car, or wrought other major and minor Veterinary Medical Miracles, they found time to ruminate about food and to swap recipes.

An array of interesting folks worked at David's office through the years. Some, students and veterinary interns, were not there for long, but for years big George Asher was a permanent fixture at Ellis and Mussleman Animal Hospital. George—way over six feet tall and three hundred pounds big—was a gentle black man who had a kind way with the patients and a warm smile for their owners. Fortunately, the triple-X coveralls provided by the hospital were large enough to fit him, but poor George had to pay out hard earned cash to have his Sunday suits tailor made. Now George liked to eat as much as the rest of them and could out-eat most of them, but his best offerings were the entertaining stories he loved to spin about the times he used to help his brother run his moonshine whisky operation and their ongoing backwoods battles with the revenuers. But, of course, his brother paid his debt to society by serving time, and those days were long past, over and done with.

Then there was Alan Machtoff, who worked as a Veterinary Assistant before he settled on his own career. Alan was not only a great eater, but he was an even greater cook. We all laughed because his favorite lunch was a combination of McDonald's hamburgers with Hardee's French fries (or was it Hardee's hamburgers with McDonald's French fries?). Much of his lunch hour was spent in his car, shuttling back and forth between the two fast food eateries, while at least half of his lunch got cold.

This recipe, shared by Alan, was originally credited to the Olympic gold-medal swimmer and titled Chicken Mark Spitz. We long ago renamed it Chicken David. Anyway, I'd be willing to bet that David has made a lot more of it than have Alan Machtoff and Mark Spitz combined!

Chicken David

1. Place **2 cut-up chickens** or an equal amount of pieces (we prefer breasts and thighs) in a large Dutch oven.

2. Add:

   2 cans cream of chicken soup   **2 cans cream of mushroom soup**

   2 cans cream of celery soup   **½ c red wine**

   Salt and pepper to taste

3. Cover and cook at 325 degrees, at least 2 to 3 hours.

4. Serve chicken and the good rich gravy over a **bed of rice**.

A Christening Chronicle

WHILE WE LIVED IN AUBURN when Dad was a senior Veterinary student, our first child Lindsey was born at Lee County Hospital in nearby Opelika, Alabama. Lindsey was christened by the greatly revered and beloved Joel McDavid only a few years before he was elected a Methodist Bishop. Of course, there is no proof, but I am confident that his role in our first-born's christening must have greatly enhanced his chances for Bishop-hood.

Another life-long family friend, Dr. Lambuth Archibald, christened our eldest son Dee, born soon after we moved back to Florence. "Dr. Archie" also christened our home with the Methodist New Home Blessing. Alice, his saint of a wife and my mother's dearest friend, further blessed this occasion by giving us a copy of her poem titled "Prayer For A New Home."

"Dear Lord,
On wings of prayer
We lift to thee
This precious home
That it may be

A household of
Charming grace,
And grant that tender love
And holy virtues
May abide within this place.
Amen."

Dr. Tillman Sprouse who next served Florence First Methodist Church was the only minister to christen two of our children. He and his dear wife Anne laughed about young Matt's ability after church to bounce off all four walls of the sanctuary and mount the pulpit before we could capture him. Tillman vowed that I suggested he consider re-christening Matt since it was obvious that the first time did not "take."

Janna was also his to christen, but every time we scheduled it, one of our children got sick, somebody's animal got sick, or something interfered. The Sprouses were appointed to another church with Janna still un-christened, so one Sunday afternoon we all traveled over to Huntsville's Trinity Methodist Church for her private christening by Dr. Sprouse.

While a student at Birmingham Southern College, Laura expressed a great truth about the nature of friendship in general as well as a great truth about our friends in particular. After the Sprouses had invited her out for lunch, Laura wrote us, "I think it's neat. I wasn't even born when they lived in Florence, but I feel like I've known them forever."

Laura, the baby of the family, was christened by our minister Duncan Hunter, who shared many late night Sunday suppers in our home debating the social issues of the 60s. All the children, as was our custom, stood beside us in proud stair step order at Laura's christening at the Florence First Methodist Church.

Of course, after christening all five children, the task of raising five children and raising them right began. Every Sunday morning, we claimed our front row pew where we had discovered that the children's behavior was much improved when the entire congregation could help keep an eye on them. It was amazing how this "Front Row Magic" worked throughout their growing up years.

In fact, the only time I ever lost control of the whole lot of them was when they were all home for the holidays from college and beyond. I lovingly watched them fill our pew—with a good bit of excitement and hilarity—for the Christmas Eve Service. No one ever confessed how the mischief got started, but I suspected it was Matt who was in the middle of it. For whatever reason, somebody got tickled, and it spread like wildfire down the pew. By then, all five were silently laughing so hard they cried, and the pew literally rocked. I poked whoever was sitting next to me, and I looked sternly at anybody's eye I could catch. But the pew rocked on. I was mortified. To their credit, my children did manage to settle down before it was time for Communion. But then I knew: the "Front Row Magic" did not work for grown-up Mussleman children.

Anne Sprouse's Chicken In Wine Sauce

When the Sprouses were appointed to another church, Anne gave me a copy of her special recipe as a farewell gift.

1. Dredge **8 fryer breasts** in **salt, pepper, and flour.**

2. Melt **⅛ lb butter and 2 T olive oil** in large skillet.

3. Brown chicken breasts.

4. Arrange chicken pieces in Dutch oven.

5. Bring to a boil in skillet and pour over chicken:

   1 can (4 oz) sliced mushrooms   **¼ c tomato juice**

   ¼ c sherry (Methodists can forgive a modest amount)

   ¼ t Basil   **1 small clove garlic or garlic salt**

6. "Rinse" skillet with **¼ c water**, and pour over chicken.

7. Cover and bake in oven at 350 degrees for 1 ½ hours.

8. Cook **2 boxes (6 oz) mixed long grain and wild rice** as directed.

9. Serve chicken over rice.

The Brethericks

THE BRETHERICKS WERE KIN through my mother's side of the family. According to my mother, her grandma Mahannah Bretherick Cauhorn had come to America from England when she was three years old, yet she always spoke with a hint of her native tongue. Grandpa, a warm fun-loving man, adored his diminutive wife, but she was far too reserved to overtly display her affection for him. She did have the habit of quietly pulling her rocking chair up close to his, and before long their hands would touch. Both of these dear souls died long before I was born, and I never saw nor met one of the Brethericks, but Mother told me lots of entertaining stories about these strange, even by the family's admission, kinfolks.

In my memory, the Brethericks owned a large farm out near Cloverdale, reportedly didn't trust banks, and had a good amount of money, but were never known to spend much of it. They lived reclusive, isolated lives, somewhat untouched by modern times. While living in England, niece Paige delved into family history and confirmed that this branch of the family's roots, as we'd been told, could indeed be traced back to British aristocracy. Perhaps the Brethericks retained some vestige of this heritage, for as an old country neighbor said of them, "They'd as soon read a book as talk to ya'. They ain't crazy. They's just quare."

My cousin, Catherine Scott, did know them and on occasion visited them. She told a story she vowed was true, and I believed her. While there, Catherine and Cousin Sarah Bretherick decided to walk down to Clear Creek, which ran in back of the house. As they walked through the primitive kitchen, she noticed an ancient six shooter lying on the table. That didn't make her too nervous, but when a bold Dominecker rooster wandered in through the open door, leaped onto the table, and began to flex his claws close to the trigger, that did. Catherine's moment of fear was tempered by her usual, unusual sense of humor, because (as she told it) it was not her life story that flashed before her eyes, but instead the headline: "LOCAL CITIZEN GUNNED DOWN BY DOMINECKER CHICKEN."

After the death of the last member of that branch of the family, my mother and several relatives (a host of antique- hunters and curiosity seekers) went to the auction that settled the estate. Mother returned with a treasure for me, my only link to the cousins Bretherick: a small tattered round top trunk.

Mom's Chicken Paprika

This recipe has no-kinship-to-nor-origin-with the Brethericks. It instead originated with me, just one of the ways I like to cook chicken. But I think you will agree with me that this Bretherick chicken story clearly belongs in the poultry section.

1. Remove and discard skin of **6 chicken pieces**.

2. Marinate chicken pieces (I prefer breasts) 15 minutes in:

   ¼ c soy sauce

   1 T lemon juice

   Dash of Tabasco

3. Place chicken in baking pan, pour marinade over it.

4. Place a **small pat of butter on each piece.**

5. Sprinkle with **salt and plenty of paprika.**

6. Bake until brown, about 45 minutes at 350 degrees.

7. Baste 2 or 3 times during cooking.

8. Cover and cook until tender and moist, about 15 more minutes.

Casseroles and Churches

Back in the days when mother was active in the leadership of the North Alabama Methodist Women, she returned from a Birmingham meeting raving about a chicken dish served by a friend who was a member of McCoy Methodist Church, which was located across the street from Birmingham Southern College campus. Mother—always generous with her recipes but amused when this friend declined to share hers—was telling the story to our new neighbor, Virginia Ray, who had recently moved to Florence from Birmingham and who had been a member at the same church. Virginia, also amused, laughed heartily. As it turned out, she had a copy of that very same recipe and (unlike their mutual friend) gladly shared it with us. Since then, Divan recipes and variations of them are common, but at the time we enjoyed the culinary conspiracy that led to the acquisition of this recipe.

To put the matter into proper perspective, understand that any Southern cook worth her salt can always pull a delicious casserole out of her oven for a Covered Dish Supper, today's version of yesterday's Dinner-On-The-Ground. Good cooks are constantly on the prowl for new recipes, and there is no better source than a local church cookbook. Rare is the church that has not published its own, and every single one of these cookbooks is a virtual treasury of the region's best-ever recipes.

I have warm childhood memories of those long ago church suppers when there was such an abundance of good home-cooked food that you could scarcely tell any had been eaten ... when the ladies gathered in the kitchen to wash up and perhaps even to gossip a little ... while the men carried on church business (and who knows, perhaps they gossiped some, too?) ... while the children ran outside, laughing and giggling and shouting, chasing each other in all directions around the church yard. When it was time to go home, we were called away from the fun and (along with the leftover food and dishes) were loaded into the family car. Hanging out the rolled down car windows and waving our goodbyes, we children could hardly wait for the fun, food, and fellowship of the next Church Supper.

Chicken Divan

1. **2 pkg (10 oz) frozen broccoli**, slightly cooked and drained.

2. **4-5 chicken breasts**, cooked, boned, and pulled apart.

3. Blend together:

   2 cans cream of celery soup

   ½ can water or broth

   1 c mayonnaise

   2 T lemon juice

4. Arrange broccoli in large buttered casserole.

5. Add boned chicken, and then cover with sauce.

6. Top with:

   ½ c buttered bread crumbs

   ½ c grated cheese

7. Bake at 375 degrees until brown, about 20-30 minutes.

A Blessing

WE DO NOT ALWAYS DISCOVER from our adult children that as parents we might have done some things right. However, in a recent letter Matt sent to his Dad during an Emmaus Walk, he recalled a transforming incident from childhood. Matt wrote: "I think we may have forgotten how much time we spent together as a family when we were young. Think of all the times at the hog farm, bailing hay, building fences, tennis, litter patrol police, fish night at Howard Johnson's, prayer time around the stool in the den at night, and any and everything related to horses (too numerous to list). These were some really wonderful times, and you never seemed to miss an opportunity to teach us something about others and ourselves. I specifically remember one time like it was yesterday. I remember we were eating out, and the waitress was being pretty rude, and how smart I was at the time and said if she did not like her job she should just quit. You said, how do you know her husband doesn't abuse her or is an addict or she is a single mom who has to work two jobs to feed her family? I will never forget that and will carry that lesson with me the rest of my life. I am also teaching what I learned from you to my children, Alex and Macie as well, and it is amazing the difference in them and so many of their friends.

Thank you for giving me a lifetime's worth of life lessons on just being a better person."

As Mom, I'll add, "What a blessing!"

New Vistas, New Fools

As I GATHER THESE RECIPES TOGETHER, I am amazed at how many come from the days when David, Lindsey, and Dee rode to the hounds as members of the Mooreland Hunt in Huntsville, Alabama. Horse people not only ride hard and drink long, they also eat well and gladly share recipes. While I can't remember my years of tennis netting me one single recipe, I've often wondered if we took up a sport like ultra-lighting that Dee once wanted to do, or skiing like Matt once and only once painfully did, or even writing like I like to do, would we discover with new vistas new recipes?

Included in my first ever "acceptance letter" was a bumper sticker proclaiming: "I EARNED MONEY, FAME AND GLORY. READER'S DIGEST BOUGHT MY STORY!" While these claims may be considerably overstated (and certainly produced me no new recipes), I did enjoy hearing from friends around the country when they read my story in the October 1991 issue of Reader's Digest.

A little background on this story: My dear friend and co-worker Rena Roy and I were in San Francisco attending a Social Work Conference, but the town was crowded with World Series fans. We were to fly home later in the day (just hours before that big earthquake hit), but that's another story. Rena and I were taking one last walk around this charming city. I was wishing for some special baseball souvenir for my sons Dee and Matt (obviously, better baseball fans than was I), when (out of nowhere) this rare opportunity for a famous autograph was mine. But read on.

IT WAS THE DAY of the second game of the 1989 World Series and I, not much of a baseball fan, was attending a conference in San Francisco. As I walked past one of the city's most elegant hotels, I noticed a tanned, muscled ballplayer standing at the curb resplendently decked out in his Giants uniform.

Not about to pass up a rare opportunity, I rushed up to him, pressed a pen and paper into his hand and asked for his autograph. He graciously wrote a message. I didn't want the player to guess that I didn't know who he was, so I waited until I was out of sight to read: "Best wishes from Charlton McKay—Doorman, St. Francis Hotel."

—JEAN GAY MUSSLEMAN *(Florence, Ala.)*

Believe me, it is indeed a humbling experience to admit making a fool of myself in a story printed in seventeen different languages and read by twenty eight million readers, so one more time surely can't matter!

Chicken and Wild Rice Casserole

This casserole was a mainstay of many a delightful and delicious hunt breakfast held after the return of horses, hounds, and riders of the Mooreland Hunt in Huntsville.

1. Cook **chicken breasts (3-4 lbs)** in **2 c water**.

2. Bone and pull meat apart.

3. Cook as directed:

   1 box (6 oz) wild, long grain rice

   1 additional c rice

4. In a heavy skillet, sauté **3-4 chopped onions in 2 sticks of melted butter.**

5. Blend in:

   3 T flour

   2 cans mushroom soup

   1 c milk

   1 can (4 oz) sliced, drained mushrooms

   Salt and pepper to taste

6. Grate **1 ½ c cheese.**

7. In large 9x12 casserole, alternate layers of sauce, rice, chicken, and cheese last.

8. Bake at 350 degrees about 20 minutes until bubbly.

Mystery of the Missing Turkey

EVERY FAMILY MUST HAVE ITS OWN favorite turkey story. Greatmommy Mussleman will never forget the time her turkey, all picture-perfect and garnished with fresh parsley and pickled peaches, slid right off the platter as she was carrying it from the oven to the table. I figured the culprit was those slippery peaches. The bird hit the floor, skidded the length of the kitchen, and hit the far wall before Greatmommy could capture it.

But let me tell you our story. Back then, it was my habit to place the turkey in the sink for its final thawing the night before, then arise in the wee hours to start the big 20-25 lb bird cooking in the oven. One such night, young son Dee, taking his turn at kitchen duty, did an especially thorough job. It was not until I was bumbling around the kitchen half asleep in the half light of morning that I realized just how thorough. I woke up in a hurry when the turkey was not in the sink where I had left it. But I finally I found it.

At this point, I rushed to Dee's room, woke him up (gently, of course), and demanded to know (sweetly, of course): "Why, Dee? Why did you put the turkey back in the freezer?"

His sleepy but perfectly logical explanation (at least to him) was, "But Mom, when we clean up the kitchen, we are never supposed to leave anything in the sink."

What could I say to such an obedient child? I hastily rearranged the dinner menu, and we all had a good laugh about the turkey who did not come to dinner!

Roast Turkey

1. **One turkey**, large enough to provide ½ lb per guest (plus enough for leftovers). I purchase at least a 20 lb bird.

2. Rinse turkey with cold water and pat dry with a paper towel.

3. Rub skin lightly with **margarine** or **butter**.

4. Sprinkle **1 T salt** in cavity of bird.

5. Rinse **turkey giblets and ¼ lb each of chicken livers and gizzards,** purchased when you buy turkey. Cook for 45 minute in pan of water ahead of time, and refrigerate for use in dressing and gravy, or cook them in the pan with the turkey.

6. Bake: Follow cooking time on label or cook for 20 minutes per lb at 350 degrees in covered roasting pan.

7. Turkey is done when drumsticks can be moved freely. To be sure it is tender, cook a bit longer.

8. Baste several times during cooking.

9. Brown by cooking uncovered during final 30 minutes of cooking.

10. Baste as needed until skin is a golden brown.

11. Remove turkey to a platter or another pan.

12. Reserve 2 c of broth for gravy.

13. Use rest of the broth for dressing.

Note: When you buy turkey, if you like giblets in your dressing, also buy **¼ lb each of chicken livers and gizzards** for the dressing.

Down South Down Home Cooking

EVERY SOUTHERN COOK'S CORNBREAD DRESSING is distinctive and different. Greatmommy Mussleman's was a light color, made with biscuits and cornbread with the crust removed. Mine, like my mother's, is made with "light bread" and cornbread, and is golden brown with crisp dark edges.

Early on, a very young Matt crawled up on a stool and got seriously into the act and art of dressing-making. He delighted in "meeping" (his word for mixing) the dressing with his hands, and I have to tell you, there is no other way to mix it. I always felt that the fascination in meeping dressing was that dressing is to hands what *loblollies are to feet.

Liz Brennan, Lindsey's law school classmate, far away from her own large Catholic family, spent enough time with us to become one of ours. She watched with fascination, learned to meep, and carried detailed instructions and recipe back "Up North." For years, we kept in touch with our New Jersey child by phone on Thanksgivings and Easters to thank her for the beautiful flowers sent in honor of those holidays spent with us. However, last time we asked, she still had not been brave enough to prepare this Southern dish for her Northern family.

*Today's children are deprived of one of the simple pleasures of my country childhood: loblollies. The way to make a loblolly is to find, after a warm summer rain, a mud hole filled with water. Next you pump up and down, up and down with your bare feet until you are ankle deep in mud. I can only vouch for the efficiency of Alabama red clay. Now for the ultimate ecstasy: having created a vacuum, you cannot extract a foot without the mightiest of efforts and the noisiest of slooops. Loblollies are traditionally served with generous helpings of happy squeals.

Southern Cornbread Dressing

1. Crumble (meep with hands) **cornbread** into small pieces in large mixing bowl.

2. Prepare according to directions:

   1 ½ cornbread recipe, (page 227)

   White bread, 1 lb loaf, torn into pieces

   Broth and water, enough to make mixture smooth and soupy

3. Add and meep:

   3-4 onions, chopped

   6 ribs of celery, diced

   4 eggs

   2 T sage

   Salt and pepper to taste

4. Add last (stirring gently so they won't get all mashed up): **turkey giblets**, cooked and chopped.

5. Optional: Reserve several slices of turkey liver and gizzard for gravy: ¼ lb each of chicken livers and gizzards, cooked and chopped. If you do not like giblets, make dressing with fewer or none.

6. Pour dressing into large baking pan. Then cover and cook at 350 degrees for about 1 ½ hours, until dressing is "set" or looks firm.

7. Remove cover and continue baking about 20 minutes until edges and top are brown.

   Note: Remove turkey to a platter, cover with foil, and then cook dressing in the same pan the turkey was cooked in.

GRAVY

The Truth About Gravy

EVERYTHING I KNOW ABOUT GRAVY … the rich, brown, creamy kind that hot biscuits were made for … I learned from my mother. I watched her stir in handfuls of flour to make a smooth paste in the smoking grease left in the iron skillet from whatever meat she had just fried. The one basic rule is that you must use equal amounts of grease and flour. Don't ask me how she measured it by handfuls, but my mother did. Today, you might simply say, "Make a roux." But we did not know words like that back then. I also learned that gravy bears the delicate flavor of the meat (like pork chops) that it was made from to whatever it was poured over (like mashed potatoes). Of course, if like some Southerners, you pour it over everything on your plate, then it's not so delicate.

Sawmill Gravy

1. After **bacon, sausage,** or **other meat** is fried in a skillet, stir in an amount of **flour** equal to the amount of remaining fat (add fat if needed) to make a smooth paste.
2. Stir constantly until the flour is lightly browned.
3. Slowly stir in **water (1 or 2 c)**. Continue stirring until gravy is thick and creamy.
4. Add **salt** and **pepper** to taste.

Giblet Gravy

1. Bring to a boil in a saucepan:

   Reserved turkey or chicken broth plus **water** to make 2 c
2. Mix and add to broth, stirring constantly until broth is clear:

   4 T corn starch dissolved in 1 c cold water
3. Stir constantly until broth is clear.
4. Add and stir gently:

   Sliced turkey giblets

   2 Sliced hard boiled eggs

   Salt and pepper to taste

Red Eye Gravy

Absolutely nothing but sho'nuff **Country Ham** will make Red Eye Gravy. In case you are not familiar with this kind of ham, it's the kind you may have seen looking all dried up and even a bit molded, hanging in Southern groceries or roadside markets.

1. Fry slices of **ham** to crisp brown, and heat skillet smoking hot to brown residue of meat.
2. Add **2 c of water** (or coffee) and reduce heat; then stir and cook down (to about 1 c) until gravy is rich and dark in color.

   Note: DO NOT add salt. Believe me, Country Ham is salty enough!
3. Serve over split biscuits, or sop (dip) biscuits in gravy.

Anita's Tomato Gravy

1. Place seasoned iron skillet over medium high heat, and when skillet is hot, add ⅓ **c fat** (bacon grease, lard, peanut oil, or mixture).
2. When fat is hot, stir in ⅓ **c flour**, stirring with wire whisk. Continue constant stirring until mixture brown to the color of an old copper penny, careful not to allow burning.
3. Add **2 medium tomatoes**, peeled and chopped, along with **1 c water.**
4. Allow mixture to return to a full simmer before removing from heat.
5. Add **salt and pepper** to taste.
6. Serve on split biscuits or rice.

VEGETABLES

Willie, Dad, and Mr. Handy

It ALL STARTED BACK IN THE LATE '70S when weather delayed David's flight out of our local airport. He was on his way to meet Lindsey in Atlanta. Together they would proceed to Louisville to visit his sister Mary Ellen and attend Bill Stansbury's inauguration as Louisville's new mayor.

Among the waiting passengers was an interesting looking black man with a red beard. The man carried a strange looking canvas case. Intrigued both by the man and the case, David eventually made contact, introduced himself, and discovered that inside the case was a French horn. During that initial meeting, Willie didn't mention that he sometimes traveled with his big string bass, affectionately called Mr. B. Fiddle, which was the way the name appeared on the passenger list, reserving the seat that the big bass fiddle occupied.

According to David, the conversation went something like:

Dad: "Where are you headed?"

Willie: "New York."

Dad: "Business or pleasure?"

Willie: "I work up there."

Dad: "And what do you do there?"

Willie: "Teach school."

Dad: "What do you teach?"

Willie: "Music."

Dad: "Where do you teach?"

Willie: "Yale."

In his fascinating autobiography, *A Call To Assembly*, Willie Ruff describes the same incident: "Then one day as I waited in the Muscle Shoals airport for a flight back to Yale, a congenial local veterinarian, Dr. David Mussleman, showed unusual curiosity about the horn I always carry with me aboard airplanes. I introduced myself, and a warm friendship developed. Two years later, David and I founded the W.C. Handy Music Festival."

David is deeply honored to have been included in Willie's fascinating and remarkable life story. Finding his name indexed in our autographed copy of *Call To Assembly*, the delighted David marveled that he was "Right in there on the same page as Mozart!" By whichever version, their first meeting did indeed mark the beginning of a warm and lasting friendships between Willie, our family, and our town.

Willie grew up in nearby Sheffield, in a poor part of town known as "Baptist Bottom," but, he didn't exactly finish growing up there. He consumed enough water and bananas to meet the minimum weight requirements, lied about his age, and as a skinny fourteen year old joined the United States Army a year after World War II ended.

During these World War II years, segregation was still very much enforced, even in the military. It was, however, Willie's good fortune to be assigned to an all black post, for there he was encamped with many of our country's finest black musicians. There he was introduced to, and began his romance with, the French horn. A long way from "Baptist Bottom," he is today a faculty member at Yale University, where he earned a degree in music. He is the Ruff of the internationally acclaimed Mitchell- Ruff Jazz Duo, with Dwike on piano and Willie on bass and horn.

During that initial meeting at the airport, after exchanging information with each other about each other, Willie and David were soon deep in conversation. Willie shared his dream to pay musical homage to his idol, Florence born W. C. Handy, known as Father of the Blues for his signature work, "Saint Louis Blues." Mr. Handy loved his roots, and, in Willie's young years, Handy visited local black schools to perform and inspire black children. David shared his dream to do something positive for our community, which was suffering deeply from the recession. David and Willie spoke of a common dream, one of greater racial understanding, and each man saw in the other's dream an opportunity to make that dream come true. David's enthusiasm was readily ignited, and by the time the Atlanta flight was finally called, the two had made plans to keep in touch and to get together the next time Willie was in town.

These were the first seeds planted from which would grow and blossom the W. C. Handy Music Festival, today an established and nationally recognized event held every year, around the first of August, here in Florence, Alabama.

The rest is a matter of record. The unlikely team of a Yale music professor and an Auburn veterinarian charged forward. Bolstered by an inflamed and hard working "kitchen cabinet" of friends, family, music lovers, tireless volunteers, and gracious local sponsors, the Music Preservation Society was incorporated to produce the festival. My brother, Dr. Rivers Lindsey, was actively involved from the beginning, following David as president; our daughter Lindsey followed him. Janna was the next Mussleman family member to serve on the Board of Directors.

During that first summer, David, with his boundless enthusiasm, and Peggy Clay, with her quick wit, presented their bi-racial—or "living color" as the two of them described it— dog and pony show to every community civic club and group that would listen. With their hopes high and their dreams contagious, they gathered up great support and growing excitement along the way.

Willie was the pro who led the way, himself directing the Mass Choir (singers from local black church choirs) in a hand clappin', foot stompin' performance at historic Greater Saint Paul A.M.E. (African Methodist Episcopal) Church, where Mr. Handy's father, like his father before him, served as pastor.

Willie organized the concert and engaged the performers. What a stellar group it was! The Mitchell-Ruff Duo hosted on-stage ... from San Francisco, Willie's talented scat-singing brother, Nate ... and from Hollywood, the renowned Harlem Copasetics, led by that old-time tap-dancing team, Honi Coles and Chuck Green ... and for the headliner, Willie's good and loyal friend, none other than the inimitable and amazing Dizzy Gillespie.

Dizzy was finishing a show in London and had a tight schedule from there to our local airport. Few knew just how tight and even fewer (mainly David and Willie) were privy to the knowledge that no contracts had been signed with any of the musicians. I confess that those of us who knew breathed a mighty sigh of relief when the smiling Dizzy and his crazy mixed-up horn bounced off that plane just hours before curtain call. All that talent was here for their friend Willie, because that's what friends do, and that's what Willie's friends did for the maiden performance of a fledgling festival in a little Alabama town with precious more to count on than a promise of pay.

The Handy Festival has now celebrated many wonderful successful years, but that special first year in 1982 set an unforgettable and unbeatable standard of excellence. Willie fulfilled his dream to honor Mr. Handy, and David fulfilled his dream to contribute something good and positive, something of lasting value to our fair town.

Every year on the first Sunday evening of Handy Week, on the lawn of the restored log Handy Home, a chosen local musician keeps tradition, raises his horn to his lips, and plays the first notes that open the W.C. Handy Music Festival. The huge crowd in lawn chairs and quilts on the ground is hushed, listening to the soulful solo notes of Mr. Handy's "Saint Louis Blues." We are reminded that this special week is not over until (in the words of this great song)"the evenin' sun goes down" on the final concert performance held the following Saturday evening.

During the Handy Festival,
blacks and whites, rich and poor, young and old,
together work and play,
hold hands, pat feet, sway to the same beat,
and through the universal bond of music
break down barriers and build bridges,
share in the joy of our common heritage
and fulfill the dream common to us all …
to achieve greater understanding one with another.

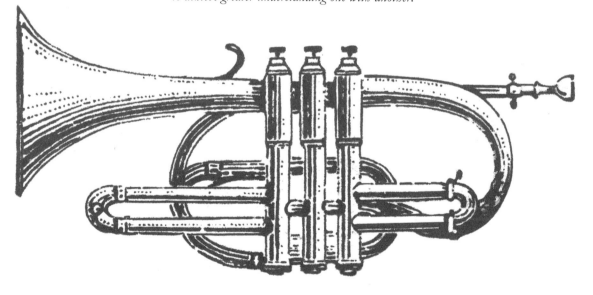

Jean Gay and Mr. Handy

I TOO HAVE A STORY ABOUT MR. HANDY. It dates back to when I was in Junior High School and a member of the Florence Junior Music Club. Each month, we studied a different famous musician, and this time our program was about W. C. Handy, Father of the Blues. The year was 1944, and even today it sounds unusual that at that time a group of white kids was honoring a black musician, even if he was born a native son in Florence. As was customary back then, the meeting was written up, listing all who attended in the social section of the Florence Times. (Does that tell you how little news happened in our small southern town?)

Within weeks, each member listed in the paper, including me, received a warm and gracious personal letter, a glossy picture, and a piece of his sheet music autographed by Mr. Handy. My sheet music is titled "Rough Rocky Road."

"Rough Rocky Road"
(I'm Most Done Traveling)
Negro Spiritual
arranged by W.C. Handy

On the front cover, he wrote:

"To Miss Jean Gay Lindsey
With all good wishes,
W. C. HANDY
4-20-1944"

Today, this framed sheet music hangs proudly over the piano in our home.

While best known for composing Blues and Jazz, W.C. Handy was deeply committed to preserving the Spirituals, and he compiled, arranged, and published many in music books or as sheet music.

His love of his hometown is well known and well documented. I was told he subscribed to the Florence Times and maintained local contacts as long as he lived. Back then, even with failing eyesight, Mr. Handy regularly visited area black schools, playing his horn, encouraging the students, and serving as their beloved role model. Certainly, I have never forgotten Mr. Handy's kindness, nor have I forgotten his encouragement to a group of white students to continue our love of music. I consider myself blessed indeed to have been touched by Mr. Handy in this very special way.

Collards and Other Greens

GREENS OF ALL KINDS (collards, turnip greens, mustard, and kale) are traditional fare for Southerners. We all know how to cook 'em, and most of us know how to eat 'em, too.

Back in the days when David's generous veterinary client Mr. Brown inundated us with bushels of the many kinds of greens he raised in his garden, there was always, in season, a potful simmering on the stove in our kitchen. It was the family joke that our children's favorite after-school snack was greens, (please forgive us, Miss Manners) eaten by fingers or forks-full straight from the pot. It sure must have been good for them, too, because today all five of them are hale, hardy, healthy grownups.

It fell the lot of our housekeeper, Pearl, to "wash and pick" the sacks of greens when they appeared unannounced and, according to her, unwelcome on our doorstep. Usually the paragon of patience, Pearl regularly threatened acts of violence … if she ever "got a holt" of him … against poor, dear Mr. Brown.

On one occasion, Willie Ruff somehow heard that I had put on a pot of greens, and he just happened to drop by when we happened not to be at home. Willie, always welcome, made himself at home, helped himself to a he'pin' of greens, and, gentleman that he is, left me a thank you note.

Greens

Wash and pick greens. Pick over greens, carefully removing heavy stems and bad leaves as you wash them thoroughly in sink. Repeat 2 or 3 times. My friend Joyce claims she washes her greens in the washing machine (gentle cycle?), but I've never had the nerve to try it.

1. Place **greens** in big pot with **2 c water**, bring to boil, and then simmer several hours.
   Note: Pile greens high. They cook down.
2. Add **1 ham hock**, or what we call fatback or streak o' lean.
3. Add **salt and pepper** to taste.
4. Serve in bowls with plenty of pot likker, the savory juice from the greens: If you want to sho'nuff "get down," serve the greens "on the side" in a bowl. Sop up the pot likker with cornbread and enjoy.
   Note: Some like to add pepper sauce or vinegar at the table.

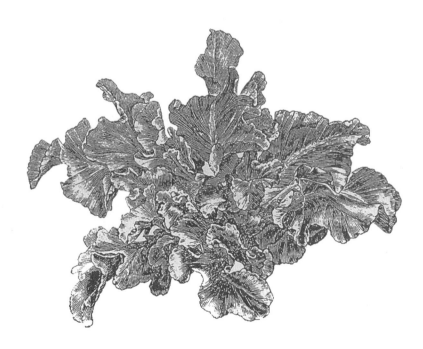

Final Tribute

DOWN HERE, POKE SALLET GROWS WILD near barns and fence rows and is an early Spring delicacy for those of us who consider ourselves connoisseurs of Soul Food. Sallet, I'm told, is an old English word meaning "cooked greens." At maturity, Poke Sallet grows four or five feet tall and is loaded with poisonous purple berries. I'm also told that Civil War soldiers used poke berry juice to write letters home. But for cooking, only the most tender, youngest sprouts are picked. As a child, I always knew where to find a good patch, but today I'd have to hunt hard to find me a mess of Poke Sallet. In case you wonder, a mess is what we call food enough to cook for one meal, with leftovers for the next meal. Remember that fresh greens wilt as they cook down, so it takes a bunch of greens to make a mess.

To illustrate just how special Poke Sallet is to some of us, I'm going to tell you a story that, I promise, is a true one. Some time ago, we went to pay our last respects to a childhood neighbor, lifelong friend, and kin of David's. Hap was special. It was Hap who taught David how to hitch a mule to a plow, how to chop cotton, how to spit and cuss and bird hunt. Always a character, Hap lived out his life in his own unique way.

Befitting his World War II POW status, his casket, between two overflowing urns of flowers, was draped with an American flag. With tears in her eyes and a smile on her face, his daughter Elizabeth took my hand, led me closer, and pointed to some unusual foliage in the arrangements. I nodded approvingly, gave her a hug, and smiled back at her. Hap would have been proud. In a final tribute from his children, discreetly peeping through the masses of daisies, roses, and lilies, were a few delicate green shoots, fresh from their father's farm, of Poke Sallet.

Poke Sallet

1. Wash **poke sallet** thoroughly.
2. Cover with **water**, and add **salt**.
3. Bring to a boil, and drain off water.
4. Repeat 3 times: this kills the strong flavor and also, I'm told, the toxins. Add small amount of water before cooking them for final time.

   Note: Like spinach, poke sallet can be served with an egg scrambled in.

Collardsickles

JOHN PAUL, OUR CITY COUSIN who lives in Birmingham's prestigious Mountain Brook, was so amused by our country habits regarding greens that he wrote a recipe in rhyme describing a new way to prepare a delicacy he describes as Collardsicles. I had intended to preserve this clever recipe for posterity by framing it for our kitchen. Too bad it was lost in the move to our new house.

Of course, if John Paul were not such close kin, he would never have gotten away with this. Down South, we don't take kindly to folks joking about such sacred subjects as our collard greens. While I don't remember the recipe exactly, I do remember that you fill Auburn cups (the kind you buy cokes in at the stadium and bring home after the game) with collards and pot likker, insert popsicle sticks (Come to think about it, I wonder if tongue depressors might bear the load better?), freeze, and VOILA: Collardsicles! The perfect (at least according to John Paul) Mussleman after-school snack!

Eggplant Casserole

I have always thought this delicious recipe tastes just like oysters, but David disagrees: he likes this recipe but dislikes oysters. This is one of the first dishes I remember eating at the Mussleman's before we were married. My mother-in-law, Ruby Mae Pierce Mussleman, says that this eggplant casserole, like many of her recipes, originally came to her from the kitchen of her mother-in-law, Fannie Blanche Crowe Mussleman. Now it's Jean Gay Lindsey Mussleman's time to pass on the recipe to yet another generation.

1. Peel and slice **1 medium eggplant.**
2. Cook tender in **salt water.** Then drain.
3. Add and Mix well:

   1 egg

   1 c milk

   1 T margarine

   8-10 crumbled crackers

   Salt and pepper to taste
4. Pour into buttered casserole.
5. Garnish with cracker crumbs.
6. Bake at 375 degrees for 20 minutes.

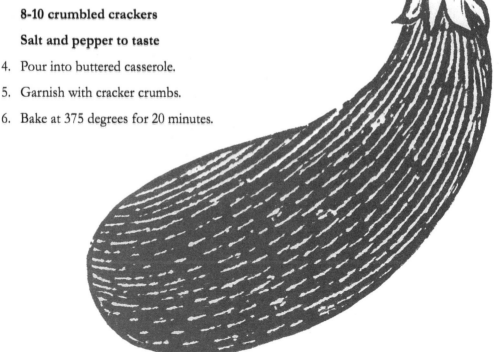

Preachin' On Sunday

Up UNTIL THE TIME I was about eight years old, we lived next door to the parsonage and across the road from the Oakland Methodist Church, a building so run-down that (despite the hard times of the Depression Years) a new brick structure was built, more with faith and prayer than ready cash, to replace the drafty old frame church so well loved and fondly remembered.

Somewhat like the old-time Methodist Circuit Riders, our minister served what is called a "Charge." Four Sundays a month, he alternated preaching mornings and nights at Oakland and Pleasant Hill. On fifth Sundays, he held services at little Canaan Church, down in the Bend of the River near Smithsonia. Except for an occasional young seminary graduate on his first appointment or the preacher sent to us because of his church-building expertise, most were God-fearing country pastors, long on faith but somewhat short on formal theological training. This was a matter of concern to Mother, a Religious Education graduate of Scarritt College.

During World War II, preachers were scarce like many other staples of life. Much was rationed: meat, sugar, butter, gasoline, automobile tires, or anything rubber (Lady's delicates were re-designed and made without elastic). Even churches had a hard time filling their pulpits, which explains how we ended up with Brother Holland, a former Episcopal priest. He must have been desperate for work to come to a country church like ours, and he sure was different from any preacher we'd ever known. He sounded a lot like the British radio newscasters we'd hear talking about the war. Some folks couldn't understand a word he said and figured he must be speaking in tongues. And on top of that, he wore his collar backwards. Having never before been exposed to a clerical collar, I secretly wondered if he slept in it, too. Of course, all manner of rumors and speculation circulated about why he had rejected the Episcopal Church, or worse: why the church had rejected him. And why here, and why us? And on … and on …

Matters were just beginning to settle down a bit (and folks were finding him not too bad a sort) when time came for the church to celebrate the Lord's Supper. Our country church served grape juice and broken soda crackers and called it "Takin' Communion." Row by row, we would file down the center aisle to Miss Sarah's piano renditions of such songs as "Break Thou The Bread of Life" from the old blue paperback hymnal with the shaped notes. That Sunday, as we reverently stood at the altar rail and received the Elements, there were several choking fits, a female gasp or two, and a number of smug male grins before folks filed back to their seats. By the time we took communion again, somebody must have explained a little doctrine to Brother Holland because, so far as I know, that was the first and last time wine was ever served for communion at the Oakland Methodist Church.

And then there was Brother Hancock, a dear old man of God, a retired minister who, in return for the meager day's offering, preached every fifth Sunday, usually the same sermon about Jonah and the whale, delivered in a sing-song style unique to preachers of the old school. The longer he preached and paced up and down, the louder and faster he sang the sermon in his high-pitched voice. When he would run out of breath and gulp for air, his gold watch and chain bounced madly about his vested, rotund chest. Then more dialogue transpired between Almighty God and the reluctant Jonah in the belly of that whale. To the disappointment of all, the old preacher was never known to consult his bouncing watch, and on this Sunday, dinner was always late.

It was a mid-summer fifth Sunday, and the noon-day sun shone down mercilessly on the tin roof. With worn funeral parlor fans, Mothers fanned their fretful children. Daddies just sat there, hunched over, sweating up their shirts and shuffling their feet. The old ceiling fan created little more than noise, and in the hopes of catching a breeze, every window and door was wide open. Nobody ever paid much attention if a dog wandered in or out. Unless, that is, it was fifth Sunday, and the dog was Barney Google, Brother Pruett's very favorite hound dog ….

In the midst of a previous sermon, when Barney had wandered in and made a nuisance of himself, the usually peaceable Brother Hancock had given the pesky dog a good swift kick and sent him flying. Clearly, Barney did not take kindly to this. He still carried a grudge and thereafter positively hated the sight of Brother Hancock. This Sunday, ole Barney Google probably didn't even realize which Sunday it was when he wandered into what country folks called the Church House. But sauntering down the center aisle, he suddenly spotted his enemy. His lope escalated to a fast trot, and a growl rolled through his throat before erupting into a ferocious bark. He bared his teeth, laid his head down low, and moved in on his prey.

Quickly assessing the situation, Brother Hancock brought the conversation between God and Jonah to a screeching halt. Then he uttered a hasty Amen, and attempted a retreat out the back door. Yelling and grabbing for the dog, men in the front pews rushed in to rescue the old gentleman and save him and his one black suit from disaster. Finally, the melee was broken up, the yelping Barney was scolded home, and Brother Hancock escaped with only minor damage to his dignity and his threadbare britches. I will always believe that Barny Google's timely appearance on that particular sizzling summer Sunday, just maybe, may have been the Lord's answer to some weary parishioner's somber prayer.

Some of the preachers of my childhood were so dull and drab that I can scarcely remember them, but Brother Pruett was so colorful and full of fire and brimstone, that I, like anybody who ever knew him, will never, ever forget him. A great gregarious giant of a man, he was endowed with boundless enthusiasm and imagination, and he had a hug or a handshake for everybody he encountered. His gracious, saintly wife went about caring for their large family and serving the Lord in her own quieter way.

Stories told about Brother Pruett were often retold (and most likely embellished) by parishioner and peer, which is how I heard this story. The time was a Sunday morning during World War II, and the place, a small mill-town church served by Brother Pruett. One of the brethren was leading the prayer, and both men, with eyes closed and heads bowed, were down on their knees at the front of the church. As the lengthy, earnest prayer progressed, the plea for peace understandably became the dominant theme, and a number of suggestions were made as to how God might accomplish this. The anguished brother begged, "Oh, God, ki-lll Rudolph Hitler!!"

Affirming his pure and absolute faith in the power of prayer, Brother Pruett, still on his knees, awkwardly made his way over to the praying man and tapped him on the shoulder. In a concerned whisper loud enough for all to hear, he admonished: "Brother, it's A-dolph! A-dolph Hitler! You're gonna get the wrong man killed!"

At our church, Brother Pruett's exceptional number of saved souls seemed to be in direct proportion to how many folks he could load up and deliver to our church from the backwoods of the Bend of the River, crowding them into what he proudly called his Gospel Wagon, a large, hand-me-down farm truck, its tarp-covered bed outfitted with wooden benches.

Strange as it may sound, Brother Pruett could count on a packed house when he preached his annual Temperance Sermon. Perhaps for the sheer drama of it, this event was always staged at night. For preachin' services, little red cane bottom chairs were brought in from the Sunday school rooms so that the children, if they chose, could sit on the front row. For reasons you will soon understand, on this night, I chose to sit close to my mother.

When big Brother Pruett got all dressed up for the occasion in a snug red Devil's outfit (Mrs. Pruett was quite a seamstress), complete with stuffed horns and a swinging knee-length tail, he was indeed a sight to behold. He made his grand entrance down the center aisle, waving a liquor bottle (filled with colored water, I was told) in one hand and carrying at arm's length in the other hand a sturdy home-made, wire-covered wooden cage. Inside the cage, obviously not pleased to be there, was a hissing, striking, writhing rattlesnake. The crowd gasped and gawked, not sure who was more impressive, the huge red devil or the angry rattlesnake. It was never quite clear to me exactly what all this had to do with temperance, but apparently it did. Before the night was over, every man present with bloodshot eyes and tremulous hands marched down the aisle, confessed his sins before God and Brother Pruett, then swore on the Bible to give up liquor forever.

If there was anything Brother Pruett loved as much as preaching, it was hunting and fishing, and he managed to divide his time rather nicely between them. Like the Big Fisherman of the Scriptures, this was all carried on in fellowship with his brethren. When the catch was good, the entire community, saints and sinners alike, were invited to a Fish-Fry, or to another annual event billed as The Varmint Supper. The varmints were any game that could be trapped or shot, and Brother Pruett, with his wife's help, could cook them all kinds of delicious ways. But the climax of this massive cook-out came after any who dared had tasted the Mystery Varmint and had tried to guess what on earth it was. There was always the risk, of course, that after you had eaten it and learned the answer, you might wish you hadn't. One time the preacher played a joke on us all when he revealed it was just plain ole rabbit cooked in some unidentifiable way.

But my favorite Brother Pruett story of all is the time his sermon, from the New Testament, was about John and his exile to the Isle of Patmos. The longer he preached and the more he elaborated, the more enraptured the preacher became. Perhaps he honestly didn't know just how barren and rocky that place was, or perhaps his big heart simply opened up, and he wanted to bestow a few amenities upon John. Whatever the reason, Brother Pruett's preaching was now at fever-pitch. In terms dear to his own heart, he continued: "And as far as the eye could see … there were fields and fields of sagebrush …." Then the preacher paused, momentarily caught up in his own vivid description. He raised his hands high, lifted his eyes Heavenward, and zealously shouted: "MY GOD! What a place to rabbit hunt!"

Frances' Company Spinach

This recipe from the Oakland Methodist Church Cookbook is credited to Frances Pruett Scott who returned to Florence late in life to live near her sister Lucille. Not finding a house to her liking, Frances showed the kind of mettle that would've surely made her parents proud. "Can you believe it?" she laughed, "Here I am, eighty years old and building a house!"

1. Cook slightly and drain:

   3 pkg (10 oz each) frozen chopped spinach

2. Sauté **1 medium onion, chopped,** in **½ stick oleo.**

3. Mix together and pour into 1 ½ quart casserole:

   Sautéed, chopped onion

   Spinach

   1 T Worcestershire sauce

   1 can cream of mushroom soup

4. Sprinkle with **buttered bread crumbs** and **Parmesan cheese.**

5. Bake for 30 minutes at 350 degrees.

Lucille's Squash Casserole

While her father, Brother Pruett, was serving our church, Lucille met and married James Rice, and they lived ever after in a charming country home built on a knoll next to where the old parsonage once stood. True to her heritage, Lucille gave a loving life of service to her church and community. Both sisters were gracious ladies, and, like their mother, renowned cooks.

1. Mix together in a 1 ½ quart casserole:

   2 c cooked yellow squash, well drained

   1 egg

   ½ c mayonnaise

   ½ c chopped nuts

   ½ c finely chopped onion

   ½ c finely chopped bell pepper

   ½ c chopped pimento

   1 T sugar

   Salt and pepper to taste

2. Top with:

   ½ c bread crumbs

   ½ c grated cheese

   Pecan halves

3. Bake at 350 degrees for about 35 minutes.

Broccoli Casserole

I read the recipe section as avidly as I read the rest of the newspaper, and it was here that I discovered this now favorite dish. This recipe is considered a family treasure, and we are warmed by the memories of nieces Kathy and Elizabeth who also love this dish when they used to join us. The wish-we-were-there holiday telephone conversation often included the wistful question: "Are y'all having Broccoli Casserole today?"

1. Cook and drain **2 pkg (10 oz each) frozen broccoli.**
2. Blend thoroughly:

    1 can (10 ½ oz) cream mushroom soup

    1 c grated cheese

    1 c mayonnaise

    2 beaten eggs

    2 T grated onion
3. Place broccoli in buttered casserole.
4. Top with soup mixture, letting broccoli peek through.
5. Bake 20 minutes at 375 degrees.

Dreams Come True

OUR FRIENDSHIP WITH BARBARA AND JIM O'STEEN began when we were students together at Auburn University. Jim had already led quite an intriguing life. While his father was busy with his military assignment to the notorious post WWII Nuremburg Nazi War Crimes Trials in Germany, Jim toured all over Europe by motorcycle.

Jim regaled us with tales of Old Heidelberg and his fascinating experiences there. We spent many an hour listening to Student Prince, our favorite from Jim's extensive twelve-inch record collection, and we'd sing along with the music at full blast. And if Miss Molly Hollifield, Jim's sweet little landlady, had not been so hard of hearing, we might have gotten him evicted.

Jim graduated in Architecture, Barbara in Art, and then for a year they honeymooned in Europe. Before moving to Seattle, Jim stopped over long enough to design our very first home. Years later, we received a letter from Jim (no longer, I regret to say, married to Barbara) from the beautiful island of Tahiti. His exhilaration leapt out at us in his description of the South Sea kind of life he was leading aboard his yacht: He wrote: "We anchored in a turquoise lagoon that was absolutely full of fish and coral of every shape and color. It is like living in an aquarium."

Though unable to accept Jim's invitation to "fly down and join me for a couple of weeks in paradise," we rejoiced that he was able to fulfill his life-long dream to build his own yacht and sail at his own leisure and pleasure the tropical isles of the South Pacific. Few of us ever live to see such dreams come true, and even though Jim would all too soon lose a battle with cancer, I will always consider him one of those fortunate few.

The summer Barbara and the children (David and Shyril) traveled by bus all the way from Seattle to her hometown of Nashville and then on to Florence, she had quite an okra story. Barbara said that when she got South enough, she ordered fried okra at every bus station cafe between there and here. She vowed the deeper South she traveled, the more delicious the fried okra tasted.

I've tried to figure out if this okra-eating odyssey somehow empowered Shyril to fulfill her dream to win an Olympic gold medal, which she did as a member of the 1988 U.S. Olympic Sculling Team. But I suspect that the kind of determination and desire to win taught by her father had more to do with Shyril's Olympic victory than did childhood encounters with Southern fried okra!

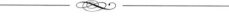

Okra Hors D'Oeuvres

Because our children were allowed to pick and nibble on the fresh fried okra as it was taken from the big black cast-iron skillet (so fresh and hot, in fact, you had to jiggle it around in your mouth to keep it from burning your tongue), it seemed an Olympian task to ever fry enough to make a respectable bowl full for meal time.

However, I will always believe that eaten as it was at our house as an hors d'oeuvre, okra was eaten at its optimum flavor and maximum crispness, with greatest pleasure and fondest memory, kind of like forbidden fruit.

1. Slice **1 lb young, tender okra** crosswise into rounds.
2. Put in paper sack:

   1 c corn meal

   Salt

   Pepper
3. Add okra and shake until well coated.
4. Heat **1 c of hot oil** in skillet.
5. Take okra from sack and remove excess meal.
6. Drop into skillet, and fry until brown and crisp (it cooks quickly).
7. Reduce heat to medium.
8. Remove okra with a slotted spoon, and drain on paper towels.
9. Serve immediately while okra is crisp and hot.

1-800-YEA-OKRA

ONE EVENING AFTER DINNER, a few friends and kinfolks, namely Don Tipper, an attorney friend, and my niece Paige and her husband, en route from one global spot to another, sat around the table re-living events of the recent W.C. Handy Music Festival. We all talked about how enjoyable this year's festival had been, but before long the conversation, as it often does at our house, drifted to food, a topic dear to our hearts and tummies.

Various ones began to compare notes on their favorite foods and how they liked them cooked. Don brought up the subject of okra. Now you have to understand that okra, especially when it is boiled, is a vegetable you either love or hate; there is no in-between. Considering the zeal of okra lovers, I suspect they would lay down their lives for the stuff if put to the test.

When these okra lovers began to wax eloquent, the group quickly split into two camps. While the haters listened in fascination, the lovers began to envision Florence's first Okra Festival, patterned after the Music Festival. Surely, it was suggested, if David could orchestrate such a successful celebration of Jazz, he could do the same for his beloved okra. We discussed and envisioned cook-offs, parades, and okra costumes; we needed to set up a committee, rent an office, and get a phone. Don excitedly pointed out that the Festival could even claim an acronymic phone number, okra being a four-letter word. In the spirit of the moment, David excitedly shouted: "You mean, like 1-800-YEA-OKRA?"

Note: It is hard to believe, but I read about a town in Arkansas that, honest to goodness, has an Okra Festival much like this!

Okra Tomato Casserole

1. Sauté in a skillet in a small amount of **oil**:

   1 thinly sliced onion

   1 c celery, sliced crosswise

2. Add and sauté **2 c sliced okra** a couple of minutes more.

3. Place all ingredients in a buttered casserole, and toss gently:

   Okra, onions, celery

   1 large can of slightly drained tomatoes

   1 c croutons or dry bread cubes

   1 c of cubed cheese

4. Bake at 350 degrees until bubbly and cheese melts.

Slip-Sliding Along

DAVID'S NIECE KATHY TOLD ME about a story Granddaddy Mussleman told her a long time ago when she was a little girl, a story about an even longer time ago when he was a little boy. Never having heard the story first-hand, I cannot vouch for its authenticity, but David says that when he was a child his father told him the story, too.

Granddaddy remembered the time his devilish Aunt Josie lifted him up after supper—he was only a tot—and stood him barefooted in a big bowl of leftover boiled okra. She had herself a good laugh as, still holding on to him, she set his bare feet on the table and watched them slip and slide right out from under him.

And you thought it was tough to eat boiled okra!

Boiled Okra

Cooking boiled okra is as simple as it sounds. For those of us not particularly fond of it, eating it is the hard part. For those, like Dad, who are fond of it, it slides down real easy.

1. Wash **1 lb young tender okra**.

2. Trim ends of okra. If knife cuts through easily, it's tender.

3. Cook in **½ c of water** until fork tender (about 5 minutes).

4. Season with **salt, pepper**, and a dash of **vinegar**.

5. Drain and serve.

Old Fashioned Corn Pudding

Old fashioned corn pudding is a year-round Southern staple.

1. Mix together and cook in a sauce pan, stirring until smooth:

   2 T sugar

   1 ½ T corn starch

   1 ¼ c milk

   2 T butter

2. Remove pan from heat, and then add and mix in:

   3 eggs, beaten

   1 can (16 oz) creamed corn

   ½ t salt

3. Pour into buttered 1 ½ quart baking dish.

4. Sprinkle with a **dash of nutmeg**.

5. Cover, and place dish in pan of hot water.

6. Bake in oven 40 minutes at 375 degrees, or until custard is set.

Fried Corn

1. Shuck **6 ears of fresh corn** (roast'n'ears), removing all corn silk.

2. Firmly hold an ear of corn upright in a large bowl. With a sharp knife, use a downward sawing motion to cut off thin layers of corn kernels from the cob; then cut again. Finally, with same motion, scrape the "milk" and pulp from the cob into the bowl.

3. Heat **2 T bacon drippings** (or butter) in iron skillet.

4. Mix together, and bring to a boil:

   Corn

   ½ c milk

   ½ c water

   1 T of sugar

   Salt and pepper to taste

5. Cook slowly for about 15 minutes, stirring frequently until corn is creamy and thick. Add a bit more milk or water if it sticks.

Christmases Past

FOR YEARS, CHRISTMAS NIGHT AT OUR HOUSE was the traditional time to get together for dinner with my brother Rivers and his wife Judy. By then they had already co-ordinated their schedules and celebrated Christmas with their scattered children. Stacie, the youngest, was usually the only one of my nieces to join us.

However, one bitterly cold Christmas Day, David, our resident Doctor Herriot, got a frantic call from Stacie, a passionate animal lover. Her cocker spaniel Dudley had fallen into Rivers and Judy's icy swimming pool, and (according to Stacie) she had rescued the dripping wet dog just before he went under for the last time. The concerned calls and the veterinary aid and comfort continued until Dudley was nursed back to life and a warmer body temperature. In fact, Dudley, who was driven back to Nashville bundled up next to the car heater, recovered much sooner than did Stacie, who was too shaken by the day's events to stay for Christmas Dinner.

This is the season for remembering Christmases past, when we had a table full at the gracious country home of my childhood. Always included were family members, friends, and anyone we knew who might otherwise have had a lonely Christmas Day. Regularly invited were Daddy's widowed brother (my Uncle Clyde Lindsey), his daughter Betty (who too early had to assume the responsibilities and role as woman of the house), and his sons Louie and Robert (up until they both decided to join the Navy and see the world).

Uncle Clyde still lived in the old home place and farmed much like his father had before him. It was a picture book farm, with little of the modern equipment and technology of my father's farm. My uncle's work horses were huge, docile feather-footed beasts. There were shrieking guineas that by day ran underfoot and by night roosted up in the cedar trees down the lane. He had honking geese and strutting banty roosters whose hens laid the tiniest of eggs. His was the only farm around with a herd of sheep—annual blue ribbon winners—along with his other livestock at the North Alabama State Fair. He frequently went to Mule Day up in Columbia, Tennessee, to trade mules, or sometimes just for the fun of it. My uncle protected himself from the summer sun by wearing his long sleeve shirt buttoned up to his Adam's apple, and a tall, wide-brimmed straw hat that made him appear bigger than life. But my best memory of Uncle Clyde is that he was one of the kindest, gentlest men I ever knew.

I remember a Christmas when one of the invited dinner guests was Mrs. Sol White, a portly widow who lived down the road apiece and whose children lived too far away to come home that year. She was a handsome, buxom woman always outfitted in gloves, lavish jewelry, and a stylish hat. This day, she carried an umbrella, which seemed strange since it was not raining. But once inside, Mrs. White reached down and pulled from the hidden folds of her umbrella gaily wrapped gifts for everybody.

One unforgettable Christmas, when I was about five, Santa left Rivers a note in his stocking that a surprise awaited him in the back yard. We rushed outside, and there between the house and the barn, tied to a fence post, was a beautiful brown and white spotted Shetland pony, soon named Flash. Rivers joyfully leaped on his back and rode him at full gallop, round and round the yard. When my turn finally came, Flash, already tired and always stubborn, expressed his feelings by promptly bucking me off into a big briar patch. I must have been too little to earn his respect. It was my pride and not the scratches and scrapes that hurt, but the harder Rivers laughed, the harder I cried. I would forgive him even now if only my brother would stop laughing about that painful Christmas morning those many years ago.

Speaking of Flash, there is one more story I must tell, but it's not a Christmas one. I vividly remember what a hot summer day it was and exactly what happened. Several kids were out in the yard riding the pony. My cousin Betty decided she wanted to ride, but once she was mounted, Flash (being Flash) refused to move. Betty gently kicked Flash in the flank and politely pulled on the reins, but to no avail. Even with more persistent persuasion, the pony stubbornly stood his ground. By this time, I was so mad at Flash I picked up a pebble from the driveway and threw it at him to make him move. Not a good idea, but did he move! He bucked straight up and took off running. Betty hit the ground, landing on her nose, which turned out to be broken. By then, I was crying real tears along with Betty, but nobody listened when I tried to explain how sorry I was, and that it was Flash I was mad at, not Betty. But the damage was done, Betty's broken nose was all my fault, and the whole world (my parents included) was mad at me.

Nobody gave any credibility to my claim that in that split second after the pebble hit the pony's rear end, before he bucked, Flash tossed his head, looked directly at me, and promised in plain horse language: "Young Lady, you will pay for this!" And sure enough, I did. At the end of the day, Flash was not the only one with a rear end that hurt.

Judy's Sweet Potato Casserole

In addition to being a loving wife to my brother and a very special sister-in-law to me, Judy has many other talents. Their landscaped yard and lush flower beds reflect her gardening skills, and their gracious home reflects her decorating talents. Certainly, everybody in our family can vouch for her cooking skills, especially when she brings this favorite casserole to Christmas Dinner.

1. Mix together:

   3 c canned or fresh mashed sweet potatoes

   ¾ c sugar

   ¼ c butter

   2 eggs

   1 t vanilla

   ½ c milk

   1 c coconut

2. Pour into buttered casserole.

3. Mix together and crumble over potatoes:

   1 c brown sugar

   ½ c flour

   ½ c butter

   1 c chopped pecans

4. Bake at 350 degrees for 25 minutes.

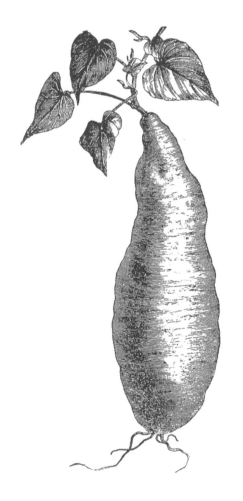

Fried Green Tomatoes

I remember my mother sometimes picking a few green tomatoes to fry. She was fond of them, but Southern though they are, fried green tomatoes were not a staple at our family table. Some folks dip them in what looks like pancake batter, but this is my memory of how my mother fried green tomatoes.

1. Slice **3 or more green tomatoes** ¼ inch thick.
2. Coat slices (both sides) generously with **corn meal**.
3. Sprinkle slices with **salt** and **pepper**.
4. Pour **½ inch of oil** in skillet, and heat until hot.
5. Fry single slices (don't crowd them); then turn with tongs.
6. Drain on paper towels, and serve immediately.

My Brother Was An Only Child (or The Tale of the Tasted Turnips)

As I TELL THIS STORY, you must understand that my brother was an only child, and so was I. Happily, as adults we have achieved a kind of truce, accepting each other as siblings, and even enjoying each other's company. As children, however, the five-going-on-six-year age difference generated at worst combat conditions, or at best an uneasy peace. In retrospect, since my gifted brother left home for college at the tender age of sixteen, I suppose we each had about equal time as only children.

Early on, I took exception to the fact that Rivers, being older and bigger, got to do things I did not. He got to go to the Chicago World's Fair with Mother and Daddy, while I stayed home. Never mind that I was a baby and have no memory of it, I heard all about it! Later, in our newly built home, Rivers' upstairs bedroom —rather, his suite—was finished in knotty pine to match the adjoining family playroom and library, but my request to finish my room in cedar to match my cedar-lined closet was summarily denied. I use these examples simply to illustrate the discrimination I was subjected to as the younger child.

I suspect that Rivers even resented some things about me, such as the fact that I was born into his family and especially the fact that Mother and Daddy decided to keep me. I probably didn't help my case when I besieged him with questions, meddled with his precious model airplanes, or tagged along at his heels like an adoring puppy. It was only my remarkable resemblance to my mother that convinced me that I was not, as my brother insisted when he was fed up with sisters, an adopted child.

But probably the worst thing I ever did to him was what I did to his turnips. I was only about five years old at the time, but that is no excuse. Rivers loved turnips, and if I have any defense, it is simply that I hated turnips. One evening after supper, when no one was looking, I gleefully moved a bowl of leftover turnips from the table to the floor, and offered the turnips to the cat. The cat sniffed the odoriferous vegetable, took one tentative lick, turned tail, and ran.

Had I not bragged that even the cat didn't like turnips, I might have gotten away with it, but my revelation was my downfall. It was long ago, but I do remember that while being reprimanded Daddy's eyes were laughing even when his mouth was trying not to. The tale of the tasted turnips is still a sensitive subject between me and my brother, who may even today harbor the wish that he really had been an only child.

Mother's Sweet Potato Balls
(Momo's Sweet Potato Balls)

Having no turnip recipes, I instead want to share with you this well-remembered fun food from my childhood: fun to wrap the marshmallow up in sticky sweet potatoes, fun to roll them round and round in crumbs, but, best of all, fun to eat.

1. Peel and cook **5 sweet potatoes**, or drain **1 can**.

2. Mash sweet potatoes and add:

   ¼ t salt

   3 T sugar

   ¼ t cinnamon

   A little milk

3. Wrap **2-3 T mashed potatoes** around a **marshmallow**.

4. Roll into a ball.

5. Roll ball in crushed **corn flake crumbs.**

6. Bake in 350 degree oven for about 5-10 minutes.

7. Remove balls with a spatula to a plate.

8. Let cool about 5 minutes before eating.

Mother's Sweet Potato Casserole

This is a good place to include another favorite.

1. Mix together and pour into buttered casserole:

   3 c (4 or 5) sweet potatoes, cooked, peeled, and mashed

   ¾ c sugar

   ¼ c milk

   ⅓ stick of melted oleo

   ¼ t salt

2. Bake at 350 degrees for about 15 minutes.

3. Remove from oven, and top with **marshmallows**.

4. Bake about 5 more minutes until marshmallows are brown.

5. Cool slightly before eating.

The Mussleman Sunday School Class

WHILE I AM CERTAINLY NOT IN THE SAME LEAGUE of Sunday School teachers as President Jimmy Carter (who taught before, during, and after his term of office), he and I do (most Sunday mornings) have something in common. Recently, David and I traveled to Maranatha Baptist Church in Plains, Georgia, to hear President Carter teach. His lesson from the Book of Habakkuk was enhanced by his insight into the Middle East. The day before, he had attended Lady Bird Johnson's funeral in Texas, arrived home at midnight, yet taught his class the next morning. After church and photo sessions, the Carters left for Nelson Mandela's birthday party in South Africa. I guess neither President Carter nor I have learned how to say "no" or how to slow down when we're doing something we love, like teaching Sunday School every Sunday morning.

Nobody remembers exactly when I started teaching the New Life Sunday School Class, but it was more than thirty years ago. We study and discuss (a lot) religious issues as colored by our Methodist beliefs. We are like family and share both the joys and sorrows of each other's lives. We started out as a young adult class, but we have all aged in place (gracefully, of course). I pray that we will grow in our love of God and service to others.

Now let's fast backward to December 3, 2000. David, who has served not only as my advocate but as Devil's advocate as well, rarely misses Sunday School, but this Sunday he felt he absolutely must stay home and decorate the entry to our subdivision, Wildwood-On-Cypress, as he did each Christmas. He figured nobody would notice if he were not there. I went on without him, but everybody noticed he was not there … immediately! Friend and class member Andy Betterton confronted me at the door and demanded to know where David was and why he wasn't here. I couldn't figure out why missing Sunday School (just this once) was such a big deal or an unforgivable sin. But Andy, along with the rest of the class, looked distressed, and I must have looked puzzled because by this time I truly was.

As the class sat quietly, Andy began to explain. This, he told me, was a very special Sunday with a very special surprise. But the problem was that the surprise required the presence of both David and me. As it was, Andy would have to tell me about the surprise that had been long planned and carefully arranged. At the 11 o'clock service, the minister would call David and me forward, present us with a plaque, and announce to the congregation that our Sunday School class was officially re-named and dedicated … the Mussleman Class. I was amazed and humbled, overwhelmed with the magnitude of the honor. I looked around the room at the smiles and tears and love enough to go around. I could tell from their faces, they were all involved in planning the events of the day and in working together to see that it all worked out. But by now time was critical. Moving quickly, Andy set out to retrieve David (amidst the garlands and wreaths) down from his ladder and deliver him ready and dressed for church by 11 o'clock sharp. And that's how it came to pass that the Mussleman Class got its name. Andy managed to get David to church on that very special Sunday, and we had one more wonderful, delicious surprise: dinner after church in Fellowship Hall with friends, family, and, of course, the entire Mussleman Class who were responsible for it all.

I'm not often speechless, but on this occasion I almost was. I probably came off more incoherent than eloquent. In my excitement, I guess I confused "in honor of" with "in memory of" because I remember saying something silly like: "Can you do that, name a Sunday School Class after somebody while they are still living?" Then I followed that statement with the disclaimer, "And I'm not dead yet!!"

I had three opportunities to get it right: at Sunday School, at church, and again at dinner. Hopefully, David and I did somehow get it right. In spite of our undeserved distinction, we were able to express to all our deep gratitude and appreciation for having our Sunday School Class (complete with the name over the door) dedicated in our honor.

Potato and Spinach Casserole

This is such a popular dish with the family that I regret I cannot remember who gave me this recipe. How sad that I can never share with some long lost friend just how many times and on what special occasions we enjoy this dish.

1. Prepare **potato flakes for 12** (follow package directions).

2. As directed, cook **1 pkg (10 oz) of frozen chopped spinach**. The original recipe calls for ½ pkg, but what do you do with the other half?

3. Squeeze out excess liquid from spinach, and fold **spinach** and **2 T finely chopped onion** into potatoes.

4. Pour into 9x13 buttered casserole, and top with **1 c grated cheese**.

5. Bake in 350 degree oven until cheese melts and begins to brown.

Polly on His Heart

Dee and lindsey were barely old enough to remember her, and Matt was not yet born when my mother died, so the children grew up without knowing her, nor she them. Yet, even after these many years, I never sit down to a meal with all the children present without wishing that my mother could have known our very special children. I wish she could have shared with my daddy the deep pride and love he felt for each of them. Daddy would have liked that, too. He was as deeply devoted to Mother as he had been determined in his pursuit of her as his bride.

As an eligible young lady, my mother had been engaged for seven years to a budding Baptist minister, a Mr. Reid, who was destined to become a renowned theologian. The chapel at the university where Lindsey graduated from law school was named in his honor, or as we always kidded our daughter, for her almost Grandfather. Lindsey vowed that whenever she entered Reid Chapel she knew my mother's spirit was there reminding her that if she could hold on to being a Methodist for seven years, then surely her granddaughter could do the same for three years of law school.

We smile over a diary Mother kept in the 1920s during her Scarritt College days.

One Valentine's Day, she noted:

Rivers sent red roses
Mr. Reid sent candy

And on her birthday, wrote:

Mr. Reid sent red roses
Rivers sent candy

All fiercely loyal to Daddy, we wholeheartedly agree we are glad it was he who wooed and eventually won Mother. Think about it: would you want to marry a man you addressed only as "Mr. Reid"?

Before their marriage, while Mother was serving her final appointment as a home missionary in Portsmouth, Virginia, my daddy was busy building their first home in rural Alabama. The lovely bungalow with its wrap-around porch was nestled between the orchard of the old Lindsey home place and the Methodist parsonage next door.

Daddy wrote his bride-to-be this beautiful love letter on a scrap of lumber from their home-to-be and enclosed it in a box of her belongings he apparently mailed to her. Today, as a tribute to the love expressed in this old wooden love letter, and in response to Daddy's request to "preserve this little message from yours truly," this cherished treasure is proudly and lovingly displayed in our home amidst an array of family photographs and precious memorabilia.

Whether Daddy learned strategy and battlefield tactics from his World War I military service (spent entirely in the Quartermaster Corps at an army post in Georgia) or whether he came by it naturally, I'll never know. What I do know is how once and finally for all Daddy bested and out-maneuvered his opponent, the theological Mr. Reid, and won the battle for his lady's love.

As the story goes, one long ago Christmas Daddy and Mr. Reid each gave their mutual lady-love a beautiful silver wristwatch. Mother kept the watch Daddy gave her because (by having the name "Polly" engraved on the back of it) my wise and crafty father rendered his gift non-returnable.

♥ Mother ultimately kept not only his watch but also her love for the persistent man who ever so faithfully engraved forever the name "Polly" … also on his heart.

Dear Pauline
I have packed this
box all by myself.
You will find tears
on the little brown
coat. My heart
aches for you twice
precious.
Pauline, I love you
with all my heart
and soul.
May God of mercy
be ever with us.
May he cause us
to grow stronger
in faith each day
that we are apart.

Will you ever preserve
this little message
from your truly
Rivers
11-27-23
9. PM

Mother's Squash Casserole

This was one of my mother's best company recipes. She always served it in the silver casserole with the embossed hunt scene. As a child, I would trace with my finger the enchanting windmills and woods and horses and hounds captured forever in silver and captured them forever in my memory. Now that the casserole and the recipe are mine, I enjoy the continued tradition of serving my mother's favorite squash recipe in my favorite casserole.

1. In a sauce pan, sauté **1 onion**, chopped, in **1 T of oil**.
2. Add:

    ½ c water

    6-8 yellow squash, scrubbed, scraped, and sliced
3. Cook until tender, drain, and mash.
4. Add and mix well:

    2 eggs

    10-12 crushed crackers

    Enough evaporated milk to make it soupy.
5. Pour into greased casserole, and top with **grated cheese**.
6. Bake 20 to 30 minutes at 350 degrees.

Mother's Stuffed Squash
(Another Great Company Recipe)

1. Simmer **6 whole scrubbed and scraped yellow crookneck squash** about 10 minutes in boiling **water** (or 5 minutes in microwave) until tender but still firm.

2. Cool slightly, and slice in half lengthwise.

3. Using a spoon, carefully scoop out pulp, leaving shell intact: a grapefruit spoon works great.

4. Mash pulp with a fork. Add and mix well:

   6 T cracker crumbs

   1 T oleo

   ½ t sugar

   About 1 T of evaporated milk or cream

   Salt and pepper to taste

5. Stuff the shells with squash mix, and top with **grated cheese**.

6. Arrange in flat dish, and bake 15 minutes at 350 degrees.

SALADS

My Great Culinary Quest and Coup

MY ONLY CONTRIBUTION to "Greatmommy's Famous Fantastic Salad" was to name it because heretofore it was called simply Greatmommy's Congealed Salad. And hers it was because no one else knew how to make it. Mary Ellen the daughter and I the daughter-in-law sometimes found that recipes her mother gave us did not always turn out exactly like hers. The two of us jokingly accused her of altering the details of her recipes, but we privately wondered if that was true!

Since this salad was so delicious, and she was always kind enough to make it for us, one day we asked Greatmommy Mussleman to make enough to serve thirty five. The next evening, when she walked through our front door, and thirty five guests surprised her with a noisy, "HAPPY BIRTHDAY," she realized we had tricked her into making the salad for her seventy-fifth birthday surprise dinner.

After that experience, I decided it was time I learned how to make the salad myself. The next time I asked Greatmommy to make it for us, I asked her to give me her shopping list. Deviously, I converted the list into a recipe. To be certain I had gotten it right, I read the list back to her. Nevertheless, when I delivered the items, she quickly sorted them out and informed me I did not buy the correct amount. Only then did I realize that Greatmommy

did not need to read a recipe, she only needed to see the correct number and sizes of cans and boxes in front of her. Now, you may have heard of "visual learners," but I'll bet you never heard of a "visual cook" before! I rushed home with the visual image in my mind and corrected my recipe, and that Dear Friends and Children is the true story of how I, Mary Ellen, and now you ever got this Famous Fantastic Recipe.

Greatmommy's Famous Fantastic Salad

1. Dissolve in **3 ½ c boiling water:**

   2 boxes (6 oz each) JELLO (Choose your color: lime, orange, or strawberry)

2. Mash with a fork:

   2 pkg (10 oz each) cream cheese

3. Add **hot JELLO**, a little at a time until all of JELLO is blended in. Cream cheese will look a little like cottage cheese.

4. Drain **1 can (16 oz) crushed pineapple**.

5. Add to JELLO and chill:

   Juice plus water to make 3 ½ c

6. When mixture is syrupy, stir in:

   Pineapple

   ½ c chopped nuts

7. Pour into 9x13 dish, and chill until set.

Her First and Last Sweetheart

My GRANDMOTHER'S FULL NAME was Mattie Artemissie Mitchell Cauhorn. She was called Aunt Missie, Cuddin' Missie (Southern contraction for cousin), Nan-Nan by her great grandchildren, Sister by her siblings, and Miz Cow-horn by some folks.

My grandfather was Will John Cauhorn, a prosperous young lumberman with a promising future, I was told, a future cut tragically short with his death during the 1903 Typhoid Epidemic. With four year old Pauline (my mother) toddling at her side and baby Lenice in her arms, my grief-stricken grandmother came back home to Florence to bury her husband beside their infant son Willie, and to make a life and a living for herself and her girls.

When I was a child, Grandmother would point with pride to a tiny spot on the map (somewhere down in Mississippi) named Cauhorn Spur. That spot, named for her beloved Will, marked where abundant timber and a booming lumber mill with its own railroad spur has been lost to time. It can no longer be found on the map. Perhaps someone else's dreams—a farm, a home, a town—are there now, in the stead of my grandparent's lost dreams.

My resourceful grandmother established a boarding house (first on Poplar Street and later on Nellie Avenue) that attracted students from the nearby State Normal School (today the University of North Alabama). I've often wished for some of those boarding house recipes, but I suspect that back then cooking was done more from experience than from recipes, and more by the hired help than by Grandmother herself.

Growing up, I heard many a story of the food and fellowship that abounded there. I met many a "Boarder Alum" who came back to visit "Aunt Missie." As they reminisced, I came to appreciate that my grandmother had the gift, not only of laughing often with others but also that rare gift of laughing at herself.

Grandmother's Nellie Avenue house was across the street from Coffee High School. She hated eating alone, and since there were no school lunch rooms back then, each of her grandchildren (having had a standing invitation for lunch) cherishes the memories of those special times we shared with Grandmother.

Perhaps it was a product of the many years or of the many more nights of living alone, but if Grandmother had a fault, it was that she tended to exaggerate ailments, especially in the middle of the night. Crisis calls, warning us that she might not live to see the light of day, were not uncommon. My daddy never let "Minley" (as he called her) live down the fact that by morning she had miraculously recovered and rarely missed her favorite meal of the day, a hearty breakfast of biscuits, bacon, eggs, and (without fail) honey, fork-mixed-thick and golden with butter.

One crisis late in her life that no one present will ever forget began on a peaceful Sunday afternoon with a frantic telephone call from Grandmother. "COME QUICK!" she gasped, "I've swallowed my teeth, and I'm choking to death!" With Code Blue speed, three generations of family, racing from all directions, converged on her house. While she was both convinced and convincing, there was no physical evidence to support Grandmother's claim that she had indeed swallowed her missing lower plate.

Taking no chances, one family group rushed her to the emergency room, while the rest of us (just in case) stayed behind to search for the missing dentures. When X-rays showed no sign of teeth lodged in her throat, the physician began to wonder whether or not dentures were radio-opaque, and requested that Grandmother hold her uppers under her arm for a test. The X-ray revealed a clear image of teeth under one arm, aimed at her ribs.

At about the same time, news reached the emergency room that the missing denture had been found beneath the chair where their patient had been napping. With the crisis aborted, the attending physician could not resist an opportunity for a little fun. With tongue well in cheek, Dr. Lester Hibbett left a note for the staff radiologist who was off on Sundays. The note, attached to Grandmother's test X-ray, read: "Doctor Deibert: Please help with this diagnosis. Patient complains of a gnawing sensation under her arm."

Though widowed young, Grandmother never re-married. She never complained, but I'm sure her life must have been lonely. As a child, I heard the family tease her about her first sweetheart, a young man named Oscar Wade. Years later, I learned that the two were cousins, and it was the parents (fearing they were too much kin to marry and bear children) who broke up the romance. But Grandmother never revealed such things to me. Oscar Wade became a famous railroad engineer, famous because back in the days when both radio and railroads were big, his route from Chicago to Miami carried him down the track beside WSM, Nashville's popular radio station. There, the engineer regularly greeted the announcer with a few loud blasts of his whistle, and the announcer saluted the engineer over the air waves of the entire South with, "Heeere comes the Pan American! Today … the engineer … is … Os-car Wa-ade … !"

After he was widowed late in life, the devoted old gentleman began to visit Florence, bearing gifts of candy or flowers, to call on Grandmother. We mercilessly teased the family matriarch who would smile and blush like a school girl. Oscar Wade continued to call, even as they both grew frail. Elizabeth McDonald (his niece and grandmother's cousin, kin to us through the Chisholm side of the family) relished her role as Cupid in their late life love affair, and she gladly chauffeured Uncle Oscar back and forth for these special visits.

Grandmother's death at age ninety four ended a beautiful romance, but she went to her grave wearing an orchid corsage sent lovingly by her first … and last … sweetheart.

Grandmother Cauhorn's Strawberry Salad

1. Thaw **1 pkg (10 oz) frozen strawberries**.

2. Drain and reserve strawberry juice.

3. Measure **1 c liquid**, adding water if necessary.

4. Add **16 marshmallows** to liquid, and heat until melted:

5. Add **1 small flat can crushed pineapple, including juice.**

6. Chill until syrupy, and then stir in:

   Strawberries

   ½ c mayonnaise

   ½ c whipped cream or frozen topping

7. Pour into mold and freeze.

8. Thaw about 15 minutes before serving.

Jean Gay's Pickled Peach Salad

Years ago, I was given a delicious but complicated Pickled Peach Salad recipe with hard-to-find ingredients. Even after a trip to multiple grocery stores and at least one gourmet shop, I still found myself making substitutions. Tiring of such efforts, I decided to create my own recipe, using ingredients usually found on my own pantry shelf. Anyway, I never did like the tedious task of cutting up all those slippery pickled peaches.

1. Drain **1 can (28 oz) sliced peaches.**

2. Measure **½ c vinegar** and **juice from peaches.**

3. Add **water** to make **2 c liquid.**

4. Bring to a boil and add:

   Sliced peaches, drained

   ¾ t cinnamon

   ¼ t allspice

   ¼ t cloves

   ½ c sugar

5. Simmer for at least 15 minutes.

6. Remove from heat, and add **1 box (6 oz) orange JELLO.**

7. Stir until dissolved, and then add **1 ½ c cold water** (3 ½ c total liquid).

8. Chill until syrupy.

9. Optional: Add **¼ c orange marmalade.**

10. Rub salad mold with small amount of **mayonnaise.**

11. Pour small amount of JELLO over a few peach slices arranged in the bottom of the mold. Set until firm before filling the mold with the rest of the mixture.

12. Chill several hours until firm. Unmold on glass serving plate.

    Note: spread a few drops of water on plate so you can move the salad and center it.

Family Reunions Then and Now

SOME OF THE FONDEST MEMORIES of my childhood are of the family reunions the Mitchell side of the family (Mitchell was the maiden name of my mother's mother) held every summer, frequently in our pleasant shady yard in Oakland, sometimes at Aunt Ola McCabe's in Killen, and once out at the old Stutts home near Greenhill where we kids waded in a creek. The dates were set a year ahead so out-of-town relatives could arrange their vacations around the reunion. Grandmother's sisters—Aunt Esther from Washington D. C., Aunt Bill from Oklahoma/Florida, and Mother's sister Lenice and her family from North Carolina—stayed about two weeks. Other relatives conveyed from far and near, bearing baskets of fried chicken, homemade rolls, cakes and pies made from scratch, freezers of ice cream, and bowls and bowls of fresh garden vegetables cooked as only Southern cooks can.

It was an all day affair, everybody was glad to see everybody else, and all of us were stuffed full of food. I often tired of the greeting, "My, how you've grown!" but I smiled anyway. Young people are expected to roll their eyes and vow they hate family reunions, but I never did. I loved our family reunions then, and I love our reunions even more now. Family life may be different from yesteryear, but our family ties today are just as precious.

Back then, we were all from intact families, and there was not one divorcee in the entire clan. Today, our family reunions are a little different. We are connected in complex and curious ways. Today fewer families are intact, several family members are divorced, and some are remarried. This means there are step-children, half sisters, in-laws, relatives of relatives, and friends of relatives. Beloved by all, friends Jack (until his health failed) and Sara Voorhies were regulars. There are mixes and matches that we understand but that might be hard for outsiders to fathom.

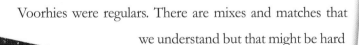

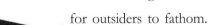

All who come are welcomed, accepted, and loved. It's sort of expected that future spouses are presented at least once at a family reunion before the marriage. At Lindsey Price's wedding, the groom Michael, now official kissin' kin, gave me a big hug and said, "This will be my third family reunion. See you soon!" And sure enough, he did.

Our current Lindsey Family Reunion began twelve years ago when my only brother Rivers and his daughters suggested that our two families get together for a reunion weekend at Doublehead, a new resort that had just opened out on the Tennessee River. That first year and the years following were such delightful events that now we all mark our calendars and at check-out time reserve our block of cabins for next year's Reunion, the weekend following Memorial Day.

We've had various menus for the main meal on Saturday night. We've had galas where everybody cooked their specialties, and we were almost too full to push away from the table. We've had Chicken Stew, Fried Chicken, Barbeque, and Frogmore Stew. However, we really enjoy it when we can arrange for a catered, cooked on-site dinner of Catfish, hush puppies, and all the fixin's.

Days begin early with folks fishing off the piers, rocking on the front porches, migrating from cabin to cabin, and sharing coffee or breakfast with drop-ins. Then there is time to swim, play tennis, ride horses, or take out the jet skis. The little kids always adore the teenagers, and another generation has bonded together and built memories. What I love best is the inter-generational visiting and sharing of dreams, plans, and news, and the swapping of family photos, stories, and genealogy. It's a great time to find out who your family was, who your family is, and, through the promise of the young ones, glimpse who our family may become.

When the evening meal is ready, it is our tradition to form a circle (all forty or fifty of us), join hands, and bless our food by singing the Doxology. Last year, we had waited patiently for David who was late coming in from a veterinary call. When the Amen sounded, David spontaneously raised his hands high and started a ball-game-style "wave" that went round and round the entire circle until laughing we finally dropped hands, cheered, and applauded our own fun. Then we all sat down to feast on the food and to fellowship with our family.

If there are windows in heaven, and if our mother and daddy were looking out to see what their two grown-up children were up to, I'll bet they were happy to see the happiness of our reunion. However, I can't help but wonder if they wondered, "Who are all those people, and where on earth did they come from?"

My Flaming Feminist Aunt

MY LIPS ARE SEALED. I will never disclose exactly which aunt is the star in this story, and you will soon know why. Her children have told me she never told them this story that happened before they were even born. So I am going to tell it to you, just as it was told to me, by my aunt who in the telling laughed so hard she cried.

My aunt and uncle, a fun-loving pair, were not above playing jokes on each other. One hot summer, my uncle, a fine-looking robust man, got in the annoying (to my aunt) habit of doing his yard-work just before supper, and then coming to the table hot, sweaty, and shirtless. Every inch a lady, my aunt objected to this particular breach of etiquette and finally warned him of dire consequences if he persisted in this unacceptable behavior.

I never thought of my aunt as a Flaming Feminist, but I'm told my uncle was cured on the spot when my aunt, exercising her full equal rights, appeared boldly (and briefly, I'd bet) one night at the supper table, just as shirtless as her startled spouse.

Marinated Pea-Bean Salad

This excellent do-ahead salad (a favorite from our Mooreland Hunt days and all those delicious Hunt Breakfasts) looks its tastiest served in a large glass bowl and is easily multiplied to serve an endless number of guests. This recipe serves 10.

1. Combine all ingredients in large bowl, and mix gently:

   1 can (16 oz) English peas, drained

   1 can (16 oz) French style green beans, drained

   1 jar (2 oz) sliced or diced pimentos, drained

   1 c celery, chopped

   1 bell pepper, thin sliced

   2 small onions, thin sliced into rings

2. Heat in a saucepan until sugar dissolves:

   1 c sugar

   1 c vinegar

   ¼ c vegetable oil

   1 t salt

   1 t pepper

3. Pour hot marinade over vegetables.

4. Chill and marinate for 24 hours.

5. Partially drain before serving.

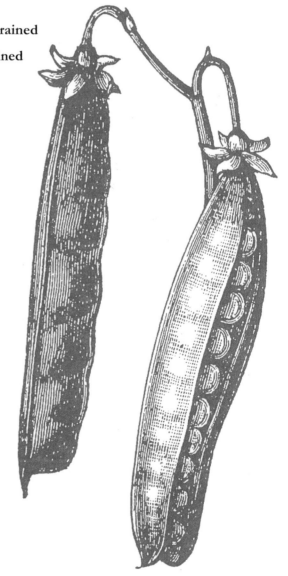

The Troy Connection

EARLY ON, DAVID'S UNCLE PAUL endeared himself to me by singing "O Promise Me" at our wedding, and I forever after loved the sound of his beautiful tenor voice. I also loved his dry sense of humor. After Lindsey's birth, he wrote us suggesting that, since my mother's name was Pauline and his name was Paul, by rights our first-born should have been named Paula. I was reminded of Uncle Paul's wish a generation later when our youngest daughter Laura named her youngest daughter Mary Pauline.

During the years that Uncle Paul and Aunt Lucile lived in Troy, Alabama (both taught at the University), we enjoyed many a visit with them and young Cousin John Paul. That Troy was about halfway between home and the Gulf Coast gave us a good excuse for stop-overs on our way to the beach. The pleasure of our visit was enhanced by their tolerant, enlightened view of life and politics, as well as our mutual love and respect for each other. Dinner was enhanced by the fact that much of it was fresh picked from their garden and always included Aunt Lucile's delicious marinated salad.

Aunt Lucile was a devout Methodist, a devoted Sunday School teacher, and a dedicated teetotaller. She loved to cook and to entertain even after they retired and moved back to Florence when she could have used age as an excuse to do less of such activities. One day, she called to say John Paul was coming for a visit, and she asked David if he could please bring her enough Bourbon to make her son his favorite Lane Cake. David assured her he would be glad to fill her order.

At this point, Aunt Lucile began to describe to him the times he was NOT to deliver the liquor to her. Certainly NOT on Sunday, and also NOT on Saturday afternoon when she would be preparing her Sunday school lesson! Perhaps Monday.

Aunt Lucile's Vegetable Salad

1. In a large glass bowl, alternate and overlap vegetables:

    3-4 tomatoes, sliced (preferably garden fresh ones)

    1 large onion, thin-sliced and separated into rings

    2 bell peppers, cut into rings

    2 ribs of celery, sliced crosswise

    2 cucumbers, peeled and sliced

2. Cover with **2 c cider vinegar,** and marinate for at least 2 hours.

His Not Hers

SOME WOMEN MIGHT RESENT IT when their husbands' recipes are sought after instead of their own, but I ask you: Who's the smarter, she who cooks and chops a pot full of potatoes or she who enjoys watching her husband cook and chop a pot full of potatoes? And, of course, David's potato salad was always made in quantities enough to feed the proverbial army. Or when tailgating outside Auburn's Jordan Hare Stadium or Birmingham's Legion Field, David made quantities enough to feed the hoards of fans with leftovers enough for whoever was our current college student. I wholeheartedly agree with whoever said, "Happiness is like potato salad: when you share it with others, it's a picnic."

One time, I was trying to decide which one of my best recipes to prepare for our end-of-year office picnic, when our secretary, Connie, obviously delegated to break the news to me, gazed shiftily at a spot somewhere near my knees before she gingerly inquired: "Would you mind asking David to make the potato salad?"

Dad's Potato Salad

1. Mix all ingredients together:

   5 lb potatoes, boiled and chopped (may be peeled or not)

   10 whole sweet pickles, diced or grated

   2 T pickle juice

   1 medium onion, grated

   3 or 4 ribs of celery, diced

   1 pt mayonnaise

   2 t mustard

   Salt and pepper to taste

   8 boiled eggs, peeled and chopped (add last)

2. Sprinkle with **paprika** before serving.

Aunt Sadie's Potato Salad

We do not have an Aunt Sadie, nor do we know one. David found this long ago in a recipe book he was reading in a local coffee shop (of all places!), and it has earned our Family's Seal of Approval.

1. Place into a large bowl (in order listed); then repeat layers.

   1 small head of cabbage, grated

   2 onions, sliced thin

   2 bell peppers, sliced thin

   5-6 unpeeled red potatoes, boiled and sliced

2. Sprinkle each layer with **salt and pepper**, spread with **1 ½ c of mayonnaise**, cover and refrigerate 24 hours.

On Passing On

Just as we in the south drawl our words, we tend to draw out events, both happy and sad. Down here, friends and neighbors rejoice when you get born and when you get married. They care when you're sick, and they mourn when you die.

Ours is the kind of Southern Family that has wedding rehearsal dinners at home, and wedding receptions outside under a tent bedecked with ribbons and hanging ferns. We've had political fund-raisers in the front yard, served stew in a big black pot with beer iced down in a wheelbarrow. Other times, seated around our table big enough for twenty, everybody brings a dish and celebrates special occasions, holidays, and birthdays. Between times and on Saturday morning at our house for breakfast, we simply celebrate Family.

Traditionally, church and home have been the center of the universe for Southern Families. Preachers are called back to christen, to marry, and to bury. The word, "Family," always spelled with a capital F, may be broadly interpreted to include close friends, a long-time maid, and distant or even former kin. At each of the children's weddings, our beloved housekeeper Pearl, all decked out in a proud smile and her Sunday best, was always seated with honor, just before the mothers. Down here, extended families are truly extended. Peggy—my brother's first wife and the mother of my nieces Paige, Meredith, and Courtney—explained to a mutual friend that she was always invited to sit with "The Family" at weddings and funerals.

Children of my day were better prepared to understand death as a part of life. As Family, we participated in and were not protected from all the rituals that have to do with dying. We were present before, during, and after the final grave-side service.

My Grandfather Barbee Lindsey, who was living with us when he died, was a kind gentle man with white hair and a soft smile. But being such a young child at the time, I almost remember him more in death than in life. I remember, just barely but vividly, how he was "laid out" at our home. Neighbors, lots of them, sat up all night with the body, as was the respectful custom back then. Throughout the night, I could hear them talking in hushed tones and moving about the house, tiptoeing into the kitchen for food or drink, then out onto the front porch for a breath of fresh air, mindful that the screened door did not slam.

I remember hearing a comment someone somewhere made about a loved one: "We can never forget he died, but we will always remember he lived." What a tribute! Even as we mourn, so much healing happens when the surviving ones can talk about their memories, laugh about the good and the bad times, and share the stories, sometimes never before told, about the departed one who, as our black friends say, "has passed."

This healing often begins in the time immediately following the funeral, after a delicious meal prepared by kind friends and neighbors. This Southern-style Wake usually begins when someone breaks the quiet with, "Do you remember the time … " and continues until all have reorganized their emotions and bonded together into a closer Family unit. As we ponder on what sad or happy occasion may next bring us together, even the sorrow of a funeral does not prevent the occasion from becoming something of a Family Reunion.

Be it a christening, a wedding, or a funeral … a grieving or a rejoicing … a coming or a going … our Southern heritage always requires food.

But times change. These days, less home-cooked and more store-bought food is brought in. Not long ago, we discussed this after a funeral, and we decided it may someday be necessary to address this issue in the obituary published in the newspaper. After the part about "the family requests no flowers" and names a favorite charity, the final line may need to read, "the family requests no Deli Trays."

Note: When you want to "do something" for a family in crisis, and there is simply no time for home cooking, I suggest the loan of a large size coffee maker, complete with coffee, cream, sugar, a gallon of tea, cokes, cups, and napkins. Also appropriate is a ready-to-serve breakfast of assorted sweet rolls, fruits, individual juices, and cereals.

And what can be more helpful than simply a supply of disposable cups, plates, forks, and napkins, plus a box of zip lock bags, rolls of plastic wrap, and aluminum foil for leftovers?

Confetti Salad

As easy as this salad is to prepare, easier than potato salad, confetti salad is still homemade, and it is soon ready to take to a friend.

1. Cook **1 pkg (8 oz) of elbow macaroni** according to package directions and drain well. You may prefer sea shell or curly pasta, but a long time ago we did not have such choices. For enhanced flavor, use macaroni and cheese dinner.

2. Cool pasta, and then add:

   1 pkg (10 oz) frozen peas, slightly cooked and drained

   2 hard boiled eggs, peeled and chopped

   1 jar (2 oz) diced pimento, drained

   1 small bell pepper, chopped

   3 ribs celery, thin-sliced crosswise

   3 sweet pickles, chopped or grated

   Salt and pepper to taste

   ½ c mayonnaise

   (A little **pickle juice**, too, if you like a moister salad)

3. Chill before serving.

SAUCES & SALAD DRESSINGS

Wibs and Wabbits

EVERY RABBIT HUNTING SEASON when Laura was little, Mr. Herbert Pender, an avid hunter and generous friend (who was also the other grandfather of my three oldest nieces), would bring us the Pender family specialty, a big pan of barbecued rabbit. Somewhere along the way, Laura also developed a taste for barbecued ribs, and she frequently told us how she absolutely loved "wibs and wabbits."

There are no longer friends who bring us rabbit, and I doubt if any of us today could eat one even if they did. However, in spite of the likelihood of freezing, raining, and/or snowing weather, Laura still requests and gets, for her February birthday supper, juicy country style ribs coated in Barbecue Sauce, prepared inside in the kitchen by Mom's very own hands and cooked outside on the grill by Dad's very own very cold hands.

Mom's Barbecue Sauce

Over a good slow fire on the grill, this stick-to-the-ribs sauce, brushed onto ribs, chops, or chicken, cooks to a thick juicy outside crust.

1. Mix together in a large pot:

1 bottle (32 oz) ketchup	**2 c brown sugar**
1 T chile powder	**1 T mustard**
¼ c Worcestershire sauce	**¼ c soy sauce**
¼ c Tabasco sauce	**½ c lemon juice**
1 T oregano	**1 T paprika**
4 whole cloves	**¼ t allspice**
1 T red pepper	**2 T black pepper**
2 T salt	***continued*** ☞

120

2. Add and bring to a boil:

   2 sticks margarine   **2 c vegetable oil**

3. In blender, mince **1 large onion** in **1 c water**, and add to pot.

4. In blender, combine and mix thoroughly:

   1 c water   **2 ½ c vinegar**

   4 T flour   **2 c instant mixed baby cereal**

5. Add slowly to mixture in pot, and stir until it thickens.

6. Simmer for 30 minutes or longer.

   Note: This recipe makes about 4 quarts and stores well in the refrigerator for a couple of months.

"The Club" Poppy Seed Dressing

This dressing (reputed to be from Birmingham's exclusive "The Club") is delicious served with any fresh fruit. It also stores well in the refrigerator for quite a while.

1. Mix together in blender:

   1 c sugar   **1 c honey**

   2 t prepared mustard   **2 t paprika**

   ½ t salt   **7 T vinegar**

   2 T lemon juice   **2 T grated onion**

   2 T poppy seed

2. Blend in **1 c vegetable oil** slowly but thoroughly.

3. Store in refrigerator.

Happy Carefree College Days

DURING THE DAYS, or more correctly, during the years we spent in the little town and the big University of Auburn (back then named Alabama Polytechnic Institute), eating out at the Chicken House Restaurant in nearby Opelika was a special treat we shared (when limited funds allowed) with Homer and Wilma Meads. The salmon pink House Dressing was served plain, simple, and delicious over a quarter head of iceberg lettuce. The recipe, we were crisply informed, was not available to customers. But Wilma, a Home-Ec major, and I, not to be outdone, experimented until we came up with what we considered a close copy of the original. At our house, our original recipe has survived well through the years.

Only those who were there can fully appreciate the lasting bond and friendship shared by the fifty-nine men and one woman in the 1958 Veterinary Class who studied and struggled together for those four long years. The spouses who provided the moral and financial support were also a part of this bond, and at class reunions we still are.

In every one of David's Veterinary classes, the same roll was called … Meads … Murphy … Mussleman … but we shared more than an alphabetical proximity to the Meads. They built their house around the corner from us soon after we built ours, and we were classmates and back door neighbors until graduation.

Our barn-red house on the pine-wooded hill was only the first house we built in Auburn. While students there, we built and sold three more. Back then, I doubt if either of us could have spelled (much less defined) the word entrepreneur, but I now know that is what we were. I don't know of any one else who worked their way through college building houses, but with the help of a crew of kindly and versatile old-time country carpenters, and my daddy's good credit at the "First National Bank," that's what the two of us did.

We apprenticed under the carpenters who were patient with our best efforts. Their language was straight out of the rural roots where they lived, halfway between the small towns

of Lochopoka and Notasulga, which were about halfway between the sister college towns of Auburn and Tuskegee. And believe me, that was rural! The carpenter with the hammer would call to the one with the saw, "cut me a 2x4 6 feet, and 5 o' them li'l bitty marks long." Borrowing their words, "They was good people."

They always brought their lunch, packed in brown paper sacks from home, and ate it outside in the shade of our pine trees. Most days, after lunch, lanky old Ike would lean back against a tree, pull out his beloved banjo, and cradle it on his bony overall-ed knees. After a few moments of tuning and caressing, his nimble fingers would soon be flying over the strings. If I was anywhere around, he would dedicate "Wildwood Flowers" to me; to this day, amidst these memories, I love this haunting country melody.

We left Auburn far wiser and richer for having been there. I was graduated with a degree in Sociology well before David, and I worked awhile in the Registrar's office at the student wife rate of fifty cents an hour before moving on to earn my teacher's certificate. Ironically, I got a job teaching Civics in Phoenix City, the notorious Alabama mill town that sat across the Chattahoochee River from Fort Benning and Columbus, Georgia. Alabama's Attorney General-elect had been murdered because of his promise to clean up the town's gambling and corruption, and martial law had been lifted only a short time before I began teaching there.

I had a class load of 200 students and commuted sixty miles a day in a student wife car pool. I was astounded when some of my students, products of growing up during that difficult era, challenged me to explain just why it was that, if you did not use your vote, there was anything wrong with selling your vote.

By the time David was graduated with a degree in Veterinary Medicine, our firstborn daughter Lindsey had joined the family, which included our first black cat, Thomas, and our first boxer, Sis. Shortly before Lindsey's birth, Sis upstaged and outnumbered me five to one with her first litter of pups. Many years and five children later, I have now come to realize what I did not recognize then … that this surely must have been for me an omen.

"Chicken House" House Dressing

1. Blend together:

   ⅓ **c catsup**

   ⅔ **c mayonnaise**

   1 t Worcestershire sauce

2. Chill and serve over a slab of iceberg lettuce or a tossed salad.

The Mystery of the Dented Spoons

ONE DAY, PUTTING AWAY THE SILVER, I noticed that the bowl of one of my sterling teaspoons was dented; then I discovered that the bowls of all of the spoons were dented. I was further distressed when interrogation of the children turned up no clues (although I could think of many possibilities) as to how the spoons got that way.

In keeping with family tradition, the case was placed on the supper-time agenda for further discussion. When we sat down to eat, Dad, as was his custom when the noise level required it, called the family to order. This night, he underscored his efforts by soundly rapping on the table with, of all things, his spoon.

Suddenly David stopped, spoon mid-air, his mouth mid-open. His face paled and then turned red. A knowing silence settled over the table as six pairs of eyes accusingly confronted the culprit. In that brief moment, frozen in time, we all as one realized that the mystery of the dented spoons had been solved.

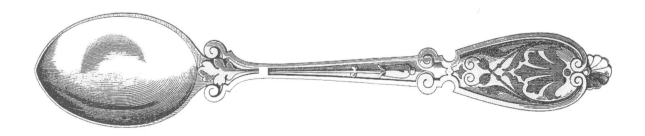

Quick Sauce For Vegetables

This universal dress-up/cover-up is good to crown any green vegetable, especially broccoli, a family favorite. Guests will never suspect how simple this sauce is to make, but if they ask, I would in the gracious manner of Southern cooks share my original recipe with them.

1. Melt (in microwave is easiest) **2 T margarine**.
2. Blend in **2 T lemon juice** and **6 T mayonnaise**.
3. Serve over **green vegetables**.
4. Sprinkle with **paprika**.

Dreams and Realities

MOST PEOPLE WHO ARE NOT DREAMERS do not understand people who are. And they don't understand that the business of fulfilling dreams is hard work. And that it takes persistence, patience, time, and more hard work. And even when some dreams do not come true, we dare to dream our impossible dreams. That is what it took (and more) for David to develop Wildwood-On-Cypress Subdivision on Cypress Creek, a dream that began in 1964.

That was the year we bought 200+ forty-foot lots in old, platted Park Ridge Subdivision from Slick Van Sandt, who also lived on the creek and who had acquired them, lot by lot, on the Courthouse steps for taxes. Every lawyer in town vowed it was impossible, but thirty years later we purchased the final 523rd lot, giving us clear title to this virgin wooded peninsula surrounded by creek and parkland. Our own lawyer, Bert Haltom (a Federal Judge by the time we finalized the transaction) sent us the first tall stack of abstracts with an aspirin taped on top.

Indeed, tracking down third generation lot owners, scattered from one end of the country to the other, was a headache. Lot acquisition became my avocation and, before it was over, my vocation as well as a great adventure. I have never been able to part with the hundreds of letters and documents it took to finalize the purchases. The story is history. These speculative lots were auctioned off in Chicago in 1922 when Henry Ford was trying to buy Wilson Dam

125

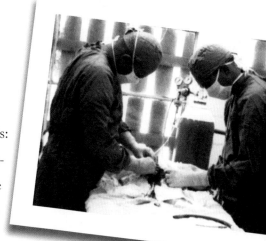

and make the Shoals area his Detroit. But the problem was this: The U.S. Government and Mr. Ford never could reach an agreement. Today, many crumbling sidewalks and even a few rusting fire hydrants still edge area cotton fields, a testament not only to Mr. Ford's failed dreams but also to the failed fortunes of many land speculators. In spite of difficult-to-deal-with lot owners, near disastrous (20 percent) interest rates, legal roadblocks, and political detours, our dream did with David's determination and ingenuity become our reality.

Perhaps fulfilling one dream enables one to risk another. David had several years back sold his veterinary practice to pursue other interests, but he retained both his license and his love for his profession. Thus, he established the Emergency Veterinary Clinic, and yet another dream became reality. David is renowned in Northwest Alabama for his veterinary skills, compassion, and especially for the kind notes he writes, without exception, to every client who enters his office. Of course, our family Dr. Herriot could write his own sure-fire best seller if he were ever to compile some of the warm, very human, sometimes sad, and sometimes hilarious (but always entertaining) dramas that unfold when animals, their owners, and a caring veterinarian of the old school come together in emergency situations.

Buttermilk Sauce

This easy-to-make sauce can be served over vegetables, with Eggs Benedict, or in lieu of the harder-to-make Hollandaise Sauce.

1. Blend in a double boiler:

   2 T butter   **2 T flour**

   ¼ t salt   **¼ t pepper**

2. Add **¾ c buttermilk** and cook until thick, stirring constantly.

   (If you prefer a cheese sauce, add ½ c grated cheese.)

3. Blend in **2 T mayonnaise** while still hot.

Shrimp Sauce

You will notice an absence of exact measurements for this recipe because, to be perfectly honest, there are none. Use whatever proportions meet your needs, and please your taste buds.

1. Mix together (to serve 4)

   About 1 c catsup

   A big spoonful each of horseradish and lemon juice

   A dash or more of Tabasco

   If there is a difference of opinion (as there is at our house) about how hot to make the sauce, provide a choice. Make 2 separate batches, labeling one Hot (add additional Tabasco) and the other Not-So-Hot.

FRUITS

The Last Mussleman Log

GRANDDADDY CARL MUSSLEMAN, Uncle Paul, Aunt Ellen, and a sister named Augazelle who died at age eighteen were all born and raised in the family log home built generations ago by Henry (1791-1856) and Catharine(1795-1858), the first Musslemans who migrated from Lancaster County, Pennsylvania and settled out here in North Alabama near Bailey Springs and Shoals Creek.

One day, Aunt Ellen shared with me a touching story. When Augazelle died from what in those days they called "Blood Poisoning," she was engaged to be married. How sad that today's wonder drugs were not available then. Afterward, Aunt Ellen (herself still a child) tearfully and lovingly packed away her sister's wedding gown in a trunk in the attic of the home where both were born. The trunk was eventually moved to Aunt Ellen's attic, but is now in the possession one of her two daughters, Kaye or Linda, where the dress surely remains forever pristine and virginal.

Years ago, the Mussleman home place was sold to Junior Kennedy, who eventually razed the old house to make way for a new one. Most of the salvaged logs became Noona Kinnard's new log home on Shoals Creek, where they will last for many generations more.

When we built our previous home, I sought out and found for our den mantle (literally) the last oak log from the old home place. When I called Junior, he remembered dragging a log out to a shed in the pasture to use for a step. "You'd be most welcome," he said, "to come and get it." "I'd be much obliged," I said, and I truly was. Granddaddy's father (by trade a carpenter and at one time the head-master for the neighborhood school) was graduated from the State Normal School in 1893. He was also, I am told, the one the community always leaned on, turned to, or sent for whenever anyone needed help. They say a mile long funeral procession was the final tribute to a man fondly known far and near as "Uncle Dee." His name was David Crider Mussleman, as was his father's name before him. Our son Dee, the third David Carl/the fifth David C. is named after his father/grandfather but called after his great-grandfather.

I felt a rush of excitement when I discovered that the original David C. married Isabella Price in December 1851, exactly 100 years before the fourth David C. and I married in December 1951. When I would run my hand over our cherished old mantle, hewn by the hands of a long ago Mussleman, I sensed a profound bond of kinship with those who were our children's ancestors.

Aunt Ellen's Fried Apples

Mary Ellen loved serving this recipe given to her by her namesake Aunt Ellen. It would be fitting indeed for the third and fourth generations of Ellens—our Janna Ellen and her Sydney Ellen, and Mary Ellen's Elizabeth Ellen and her Meredith Ellen—to include it in their repertoire of recipes. When I asked Aunt Ellen for what I presumed was an old family recipe, she laughed and admitted that she had found the recipe in *Southern Living Magazine*. In honor of this dearest of all ladies, no matter where or when she got it, in my book this recipe carries her name.

1. Peel and slice **6 or 8 apples**.

2. Heat **1 bottle (16 oz) of White Karo syrup** in large skillet.

3. Add apples and **"a big chunk of butter."**

   (Aunt Ellen asked, "You won't write it down that way, will you?")

4. Bring to a boil and stir.

5. Cook quickly, reducing heat "a little."

6. When syrup thickens and apples are transparent, remove from pan.

7. Pour syrup over apples and serve warm.

Stove Top "Baked" Apples

1. Adapting Aunt Ellen's recipe, you can also "bake" apples on top of the stove.

2. **Cover the bottom of a skillet with a little water**, and add:

   ¾ bottle of Karo syrup

   A few drops of red food coloring

3. Halve **5 or 6 tart apples**. Remove seeds with knife, and core with a melon-baller. I prefer the peeling left on!

4. Bring syrup to a boil, and add halved apples. Use enough to fill skillet with a single layer. (You may crowd them a bit as they shrink with cooking.)

5. Cook slowly, and turn two or three times until apples are transparent.

6. Remove to a shallow serving dish, and pour warm syrup over apples.

Aₛ A CHILD, I MUST CONFESS that I never once said, "When I grow up I want to be a politician." But I did grow up to be one. On the other hand, I did not become a detective, a missionary, or a truck driver as, at various times, I vowed I would.

Many people have asked me (and I've even asked myself), "Why on earth would you/a nice lady like you/anybody ever want to run for public office?" My knee jerk response was, "Why not?" I was never reluctant to stand up for what I believed, and one thing I believed was that, as a woman, I had an equal right and enough book sense, common sense, and gumption to be a good politician.

As I became more and more interested and involved in the life and the leadership of church and community, involvement in politics was a natural progression. My interest in city government was piqued when I was an early female appointee to the Florence City Zoning Board. (I would go on to serve on many other boards, the most recent one as Chair of the Civil Service Board.) When our city changed to a Mayor Council form of government, the mayor's race was wide open. Like many others, I put my hat in the ring. I discovered that I enjoyed campaigning, knocking on doors, meeting people, confronting issues, making speeches, and learning about the world of politics and government. Not unexpectedly, I did not win that race. How-ever, when I later sought

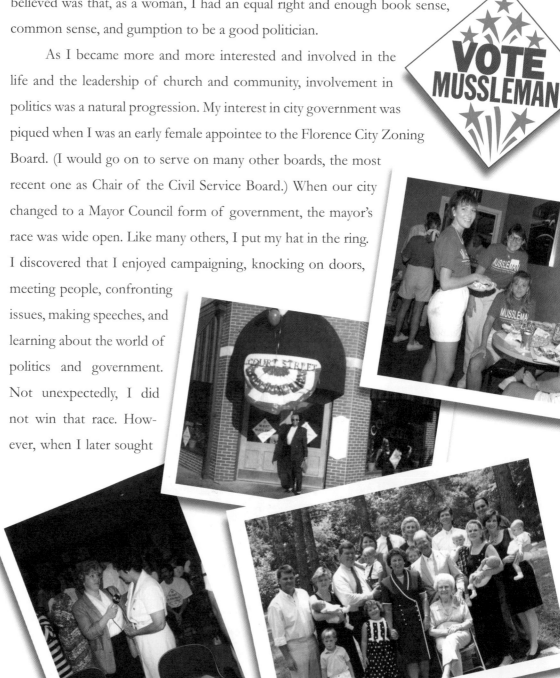

and won the District #5 position, I became the first women elected to the Florence City Council, serving my fellow citizens for eight years.

One of my proudest moments came the morning after that first election. David and I found ourselves driving down the street behind a truck loaded with workers from the Florence Electricity Department (where David, nicknamed "Flookie," had worked as a young man). Spotting us, one of the long time workers cupped his hands and yelled from the back of the truck, "Hey, Flookie! Tell your old lady I'm proud of 'er!"

I'm sure that at first, they weren't real sure how to deal with me (The Woman). However, I was truly blessed by the fact that Mayor Eddie Frost, Council President Steve Pierce, and my male counterparts treated me with respect and eventually accepted me, if not as "one of the boys" at least as a bonafide council member. Of course, the gloves were off when it came to defending my position against such issues as selling off dedicated park land to private investors, or supporting our model recycling program, or certification for the city landfill. During Council Sessions, we voted on such issues as multi-million dollar budgets, bond issues, health insurance, board appointments, and city planning. I could hold my own as well as the rest of them, but after battling over the issues, we usually forgave and forgot.

I determined that most issues could best be handled with a sense of humor. Our first overnight trip was to our state capitol in Montgomery. Another new Council member seemed to be somewhat uncomfortable sharing the elevator of an out of town motel with me (The Woman). With confirmation of a private room in hand, I broke the awkward silence with a big smile and assured him, "It's okay, George, I don't think we have to share a room this time."

Politics is a tough teacher. One of the lessons I learned early on was that no matter how conscientiously I considered or how carefully I researched my vote on an issue, any vote (yes or no) risked alienating as many citizens as I satisfied. I learned what an honor and responsibility it is to be an elected official. I thoroughly enjoyed my time in politics, and found it to be one of the most fulfilling and enriching experiences of my life. While in public office, I met a fascinating array of folks … warm, caring, salt of the earth folks, decent, concerned citizens. I also met the other kind … the self serving, the looking for a hand out, or the trying to get a hand in your pocket kind. And rest assured, any decent, honest politician (yes, they do exist) had jolly well better be able to tell the difference!

Baked Fruit Compote

This colorful fruit dish is great for a wintertime buffet or for a holiday dinner.

1. Blend together in a mixing bowl:

   1 can (16 oz) of applesauce

   ¾ box brown sugar

2. Add the following **cans (16 oz each) of drained fruit:**

   Peaches   **Pears**

   Apricots   **Pineapple chunks**

   Purple plums

3. Pour into a 9x13 baking dish.

4. Sprinkle with **1 roll of crushed round crackers**, and dot with **butter**.

5. Bake at 350 degrees for 30 or 40 minutes.

6. Serve Warm.

Mixed Fruit Bowl

Any assortment of fresh and canned (drained) fruits will do.

1. Use some combination of the following:

   1 can pineapple chunks

   1 can pears, sliced

   1 can sliced peaches

   1 can fruit cocktail

   3 thick-sliced bananas

   Any fresh fruits in season such as grapes, berries, melons, or strawberries

2. Add **1 can of cherry pie filling**, and blend together.

3. Chill and serve in a large glass bowl.

Jewel's Breakfast Pizza

When someone celebrated a birthday at Florence City School's central office, where my office was, one of the nicest gifts was this delicious dish prepared by Jewel Gooch, one of our secretaries who was such a good cook that she ran a catering business on the side.

1. For Pastry, cream together:

   ½ c butter

   ¾ c sugar

2. Add **1 egg**.

3. Mix in:

   2 c self-rising flour

   1 t vanilla extract

4. Roll into a ball, and chill.

5. Pat out chilled pastry in a greased pizza pan.

6. Bake 10 minutes at 350 degrees.

7. Cream together, and spread on cooled pastry:

   8 oz cream cheese

   ½ c sugar

8. Arrange on top of cream cheese:

   2 sliced apples   **2 peeled oranges cut in pieces**

   1 sliced banana   **1 c strawberry halves**

   1 c nuts   **1 c red and green seedless grapes**

   2 sliced kiwi fruit

9. For glaze, mix in a saucepan, and cook over medium heat:

   ⅔ c sugar   **1 c orange juice**

   2 T corn starch   **¼ t salt**

   3 T coconut flavoring

10. Spread cooled glaze over fruit, chill, and serve.

The Christmas Babe

THE SOUTH IS KNOWN FOR ITS UNIQUE TRADITIONS, and it didn't take long for our family of five lively and imaginative children to establish unique ones of our own. Family gift-giving traditions (established by David and me even before we were married) have long proved curious to non-Musslemans. Let me explain.

One Valentine's Day during our courting days, David declared his love for me with a dozen long-stemmed red roses, while I, knowing his taste for the finer things of life, expressed my love (and amused his army buddies) by mailing him a case of pickled pigs feet. No wonder friends regularly inquire, "What did you get for Christmas/Valentine/Birthday THIS year?"

One very special Christmas, the children's gift to me was a beautiful kid: a baby goat. It was the perfect gift, and I was delighted. She was allowed to spend Christmas Day in the house where she was cuddled and cradled in someone's arms most of the day. It was easy to chose a name for this goat. In the spirit of the season, she would be called Babe.

Our first goats were: Walter, who loved to charge young Matt, stop suddenly, and then gently butt heads; and Walter's shy spotted wife Inky and their baby Flower who was born in our back yard. Later goats lived mainly at the barn, where they doubled as family pets as well as calming companions to our thoroughbred horses.

In the summer, our goats were sometimes sent forth to eat the hillside between house and creek, where they were contained by an electric fence. Disasters were bound to happen and did when some animal or somebody bumped into the fence, or a careless dog mistook a metal fence post for a fire plug. Most victims of the fence tended not to be repeaters, especially the dogs.

Then there was Pickin' Willie. His goatee (yes, that is the correct term for a goat's beard) made him a look-alike to a bearded friend named Bill who also picked a mean banjo. On one occasion, a goat (so new he wasn't even named yet) became so ill he required David's best veterinary skills (and our best TLC) to snatch him back from death's doors. Him we named Lazarus.

We loved our goats, but I blame one of them for one of life's most embarrassing moments. As we greeted my daddy and his new wife at the front door, a sociable goat nosed his way through the back door, unobserved. With a brief, "Baaa," the goat (how do I describe it?) naughtily nudged brand new step-mother from the rear. Maybe it's not fair to blame it all on the goat, but our in-law relationship did seem to go downhill after that!

Cranberry Sauce

No matter how many salads or other cranberry sauces may be on the holiday dinner menu, Laura always requested this one and even as a little girl prepared it herself. We still serve cranberry sauce in the same cut-glass bowl it has been served in at every Thanksgiving and Christmas dinner since I was a little girl.

1. Measure into saucepan:

   1 c sugar

   1 c water

   1 pkg (12 oz) fresh cranberries, picked over and washed

2. Boil gently 10 minutes, stirring often.

3. Cool, pour into holiday bowl, and chill before serving.

Fresh Fruited Cranberries

This recipe from Aunt Lucile Mussleman is another favorite Southern way to serve New England cranberries.

1. Grind coarsely:

   1 lb fresh cranberries

   3 lb cooking apples

   Rind of 2 oranges

   3 oranges

2. Measure and add ¾ **c of sugar for each cup of mixture.**

3. Store in refrigerator.

DESSERTS

Ambrosia

The Ambrosia Mother always made at Christmastide (back when oranges were a very special treat) is a dear childhood memory. But today, ambrosia reminds me most of my daddy. In his latter years, he loved to stay busy with his hands and knew that none of us had time for the peeling and cutting up of so many oranges. During the citrus season, there usually was a bowl of coconut-topped Ambrosia waiting in Daddy's refrigerator, a bowlful of this delicious dessert. He knew how much Janna and Laura loved Ambrosia, but of greater importance, the making and the sharing of Ambrosia met Daddy's abiding wish to do a kindness for others.

Dada's Ambrosia

1. Peel **8 oranges**.
2. Remove seeds and cut in chunks.
3. Add **1 can (16-18 oz) of crushed pineapple**, juice and all.
4. Fold in **6 or 8 oz of flaked coconut**, reserving a little.
5. Garnish (just like my Daddy did) with reserved **coconut and maraschino cherries**.

Just Like Mom's

WE WERE ON OUR WAY BACK from a Mussleman family get-together at the white-sanded beaches of Alabama's Gulf Shores. The several carloads of us rendezvoused in Montgomery one last time before going our separate ways. After a week at the beach, all were tired of seafood and hungry for our favorite country restaurant food. We pushed tables together to make one big one and ordered from a mouth-watering menu of fried chicken, country ham, chicken n' dumplin's, pinto beans, turnip greens, fried okra, hot biscuits, corn muffins, and frosty mason jars of iced sweet tea.

We were a chattering, cheerful bunch, but above the din, I overheard Janna and Laura, down at the other end of the table, discussing how blackberry cobbler, this restaurant's house special, kindled warm childhood memories. I smiled fondly at my girls. My chest swelled momentarily with pride when one said to the other, "This blackberry cobbler is sooo good … it tastes just like the ones Mom used to … " (but I got my come-uppance with the rest of the sentence) " … buy."

In a momentary lapse of memory, I had overlooked the fact that home-baked though they might have been, my best cobblers (with butter and sugar added) had indeed been store bought (from the frozen food section). Oh, well. So much for Mom's home cooking.

Apple Crisp

This recipe for Apple Crisp, first discovered in a 1950s Auburn Cookbook (a great buy at fifty cents a copy) is kissing kin to cobblers but is easier to make.

1. Place **4 c sliced apples** and ¼ **c water** in a deep dish pie pan.
2. Sift together in a bowl:

¾ c flour	**1 c sugar**
1 t cinnamon	**½ t salt**

3. Cut in **1 stick margarine** to resemble coarse crumbs. Sprinkle crumbs over apples.
4. Bake at 350 degrees for 40 minutes, and serve with cream or ice cream.

   Note: Do NOT use lite or low calorie margarine.

Peace on Earth, Even In the Kitchen

THE PRODUCTION OF BOILED CUSTARD is more fun as a two-person job, but after all, most things are. One scalds and stirs the milk while the other separates the eggs, beats the whites, and does all the rest. Now guess who is the one, and who is the other. Next, guess whose Mother was at home furrowing her brow and lamenting, "Bless his sweet heart, poor lil' ole' David is working his fingers to the bone, having to make all that boiled custard all by himself."

Poor lil' ole David had furthered this fantasy by conveniently dropping by his mother's house on the appropriate night, sighing mightily, and reckoning how he'd better get on home and Make The Boiled Custard.

The two of us have become so specialized I doubt we could ever switch roles, with David scalding and stirring and me separating, beating, and doing the rest. So why switch? The system works, and annually we improve our time. Last Christmas Eve, it took less than one hour from egg-breaking start to bowl-licking finish.

Our system of checks and balances works, too. We each tenderly and lovingly supervise the other with such tactful remarks and helpful suggestions as:

D: "WATCH OUT! You're getting YOLKS in the WHITES!"

JG: "Don't let the milk BOIL!"

D: "I don't guess you remembered to buy extra vanilla, DID YOU?"

JG: "If you don't turn the heat DOWN, it's going to BURN!"

JG: "QUIT SCRAPING THE BURN OFF THE BOTTOM OF THE PAN!"*

However, every delicious spoonful of Boiled Custard is worth whatever the risk may be … to marital bliss, holiday harmony, and peace on earth … even in the kitchen.

*Andy Betterton, our friend who's just like family, lovingly refers to the little brown flecks (a by-product of scraping the burn off the bottom of the pan) as "character flakes," and each year inquires if they are present in the custard (which, of course, they always are). However, Andy prefers to conduct his own personal taste-test just to be sure.

Mussleman Boiled Custard

1. Heat **1 gal whole milk** in your largest pot, STIRRING CONSTANTLY until scalding hot. (Don't let the milk BOIL!)

2. Separate **12 eggs**. (Don't get YOLKS in the WHITES!) Put whites in largest mixing bowl.

3. Blend together in smaller bowl:

   12 egg yolks, beaten until thick and creamy

   2 ¼ c sugar

   ¾ c corn starch

   Thin with: **1 c milk**, or enough that it pours easily

4. Add yolk mixture slowly to hot milk, STIRRING CONSTANTLY.

5. Cook until mixture thickens and coats a spoon. (Turn heat DOWN enough so it won't BURN on the bottom of the pan)

6. Beat until stiff **12 egg whites** and **½ t cream of tartar**.

7. Add and beat until glossy:

   2 c sugar

   2 oz vanilla

   (Be sure you have plenty of vanilla: buy an extra bottle!)

8. Slowly pour 2 c of hot mixture into bowl of whites, stirring constantly.

9. Remove pan from heat, and add whites to hot yolk mixture.

10. Blend in whites with a large whisk until creamy.

11. This recipe doubles in bulk to make about 2 gallons, and will require a BIG pot. (The only big-enough-pot we have is the 18-quart heavy-duty family canner we inherited.)

    Note: Of course, if you are not having our usual twenty-three or more for dinner, you may choose to make a more reasonable amount and cut the recipe in half.

Hand-Wringing Time in Atlanta

When David's sister Mary Ellen moved away to Atlanta, she gathered up all her favorite family recipes to take with her. Because her mother had misplaced her cherry pudding recipe, Mary Ellen got a copy from Granny Mussleman.

Some time later, Mary Ellen decided to treat new-found friends in her new-found bridge club with the dessert. She bought enough canned cherries to double the recipe. But alas, instead of pudding, she ended up with a syrupy mess. Assuming that she had somehow misread the easy-to-make recipe, she went back to the store and once more bought cherries enough to double the recipe. Again, instead of pudding, she produced a syrupy mess.

Time was now short, and Mary Ellen's temper even shorter. Wringing her hands, she rushed to the phone and called her mother. Still unable to locate her recipe, her mother hurried out to buy cherries and try to figure out the problem. From both ends of the line, the bad news was the same: that recipe did not work. I never did know what the problem was, but by the next day and another trip to the store, Mrs. Mussleman had figured out the error and had made the proper corrections. This was, however, too late to save the bridge club, all of whom commented on (if not complimented) the interesting and … uh … different … cherry sauce Mary Ellen served over ice cream that day.

Furthermore, I'm told it took the southeastern market quite some time to recover from the sudden puzzling demand for canned tart cherries.

Cherry Pudding

1. Drain **1 can tart cherries** and reserve juice.

2. Separate **2 eggs**.

3. Mix together in pan, and cook over low heat until mixture thickens:

   3 heaping T flour blended into cherry juice

   2 beaten egg yolks

   ½ c sugar

   A pinch of salt

   continued

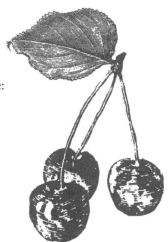

4. Remove from heat, beat together, then fold into cooked mixture:

    2 beaten egg whites

    ½ c sugar

5. Line dish with **vanilla wafers**, and layer cherries over wafers.

6. Pour cooked mixture over cherries.

7. Chill before serving.

Lucy

I have no idea who Lucy was or why this sauce is named Lucy, but David remembers it as manna from Heaven when served over a piece of plain yellow cake from the kitchen of his childhood next door neighbor and kin, Aunt Esther Harrison. I wonder if her son Hap remembered, or if he ever learned to make it, or if any of his children have ever tasted Lucy?

1. Scald in pan:

    2 ½ c milk

    ½ c sugar

    ⅛ t salt

2. Add slowly, stirring constantly:

    2 T corn starch dissolved in ½ c cold milk

    1 t vanilla

3. Bring to a boil.

4. When Lucy coats spoon, remove pan from heat.

5. Pour warm over **plain yellow cake**.

Hand-Cranked and Other-Cranked

I DON'T KNOW HOW MANY ice cream freezers our family has worn out through the years, and I couldn't even guess how many dozens of eggs and gallons of milk have gone into heaven only knows how much homemade ice cream, but I can assure you, lots.

Years ago, all ice cream freezers were hand cranked, and making homemade ice cream was a big social event. The women cooked and poured the custard, rich and thick and golden, into the tall round container. Then the men took over, placing the container in the wooden bucket and filling the bucket with layer after layer of ice-and-salt and ice-and-salt. The men spelled each other as the cream began to freeze, and the task of cranking the freezer became harder and harder. Folks congregated on the porch, rocked in a creaking swing, or spilled down into a shady yard. The hungry, impatient children circled, ready to fight over who got to lick the dasher.

As much as he hated the extra work, Granddaddy Mussleman swore that ice cream cranked by electricity never tasted as good as ice cream cranked by hand. All things considered, he just may have been right.

Easy Homemade Freezer Ice Cream (Basic Mix)

1. Mix together, and pour into freezer container:

    2 cans evaporated milk   **2 eggs beaten**

    2 ⅓ c sugar   **2 T lemon juice**

    2 t vanilla

2. Add **whole milk** to fill-line in container. When using fruit, add milk to fill line after adding fruit.

3. Freeze according to freezer instructions.

    This easy recipe is great as plain vanilla or with any one of these fresh fruits added (plus enough additional sugar as needed to sweeten fruit):

4. Optional: Add **2 c of sliced strawberries,** or **6 peeled and mashed peaches,** or **2 c of any fruit in season.**

Strawbanapple Ice Cream
(A Three Fruit Medley)

1. To basic mix add:

   1 c sliced strawberries

   3 mashed bananas

   1 small flat can crushed pineapple with juice

   Additional sugar as needed to sweeten fruit

Banana Pudding Ice Cream

One time, David and I had a terrible disagreement over which flavor ice cream to make. Guess who won. Guess whose freshly-baked, warm-from-the-oven banana pudding … meringue and all … got dumped into the ice cream mix. I almost cried. I admit the resulting Banana Pudding Ice Cream was indeed delicious, but never again did I allow one of my precious puddings to be cannibalized by an ice cream freezer. Through the years, David has mellowed on this issue, but I have not. We now agree: The following ingredients make excellent Banana Pudding Ice Cream.

1. Added to the basic mix:

   6 mashed bananas

   ½ c sugar

   6 or 8 (a handful) of coarsely crumbled vanilla wafers

Who Am I?

THESE ARE EXCERPTS from a paper Laura wrote about her family when she was in the eleventh grade. Mrs. Judy Berry, her English teacher, wrote a sweet note and a grade of 98 on her paper.

"When answering the question, "Who am I?" the thing that answers this question is my family. I would not be who I am without them.

My parents have given each other and all of the children in my family an infinite amount of love. They have taught us that color, religion, wealth and all these things do not matter. It is who you are on the inside that counts.

My two brothers and two sisters are also some great people. We are all very close and I love each of them dearly. We are all alike in lots of ways, but thanks to my parents, each of us is free to be what we want to be. Just because one of us succeeds in something does not mean the other has to do the same. All my parents ask is that we do our best in everything we do and to be all we can be!"

How David Learned His Lesson

OUR STRAWBERRY-LOVING FAMILY used to annually make a trip to Lutts (pronounced "Loots"), Tennessee, a small pastoral community twenty five miles north across the Natchez Trace from us. There, acres of strawberries, some laid off in stringed squares, stretched as far as the eye could see. Geese, I am told, do not eat strawberries, and that is why they were made guardians of their own strawberry patches where they ate weeds instead. Does this explain the term, "silly goose?"

Back then, Lutts was a commercial strawberry center, and on certain days berries were picked in the field with the caps already removed, a luxury that eliminated the worst work of "putting up strawberries."

On the way to Lutts one spring day (David and I agreed), if the berries were available already capped, we would buy ten crates; if not, we would buy only half as many. To our disappointment, they were not picking berries capped that day, but when David saw all those luscious ripe red strawberries, he could not contain himself or his enthusiasm. He insisted we buy ten crates anyway. Knowing all too well how much work that many strawberries entailed, I insisted we limit our order as agreed. David badgered, beseeched, and bargained. David said, "No problem. I love to cap strawberries, and I will personally cap all ten crates by myself." I said, "Fine. No problem. Be my guest." And graciously (but smugly), I accepted his offer.

Poor David: He capped strawberries and capped strawberries and capped strawberries. We ate strawberries and ate strawberries and ate strawberries. He generously bestowed berries (uncapped, of course) upon family, friends, and (I suspect) total strangers. Thanks to David, who learned his lesson, we enjoyed fresh frozen strawberries all winter long. But we never, ever bought that many strawberries again.

Strawberry Squares

1. Stir together and spread in a shallow pan:

    1 c sifted flour

    ¼ c brown sugar

    ½ c chopped walnuts

    ½ c margarine, melted

2. Bake at 350 degrees for 20 minutes, stirring occasionally.

3. Sprinkle ⅔ of crumbs in 9x13 pan.

4. Combine and beat at high speed to form stiff peaks, about 10 minutes:

    2 egg whites

    1 c sugar

    2 c sliced strawberries

    (or 10 oz frozen strawberries and reduce sugar to ⅔ c)

    2 T lemon juice

5. Fold **1 c cream whipped or 1 ½ c Cool Whip** into strawberry mixture.

6. Spread over crumbs in pan, and sprinkle with remaining crumbs.

7. Freeze 6 hours or overnight.

8. Thaw about 15 minutes before serving.

9. Cut into squares.

The Never-Ending Romance

THE EVENING WAS DELIGHTFULLY COOL and crisp there in the village of Hunstanton By-The-Sea. The sea was the North Sea in County Norfolk on the eastern shore of England. Mr. Cademy, the Methodist rector and his wife, ever the gracious hostess, often invited David and me after we had attended Vespers, along with our other church friends, the Kings and the Watsons, to their manse for high tea. We had early on found a church home at the beautiful little Methodist Church nearby. As the organist played, a young boy provided the power, rocking back and forth on the church bench beside her. I still have my cherished copy of the English Methodist hymnal. These dear new-found friends, all old enough to be our parents, had adopted us as their own during the tender first year of our marriage, which we spent far, far from home. We were too happy to ever be homesick, but we did look back with a certain sense of amazement on how we came to be in this lovely picturesque part of the world.

It was 1951, and David was a Sergeant in the National Guard (Dixie Division) and was activated to military duty during the Korean Conflict. He had received his orders to Europe, a far more desirable assignment than war-torn Korea. He sent me this news in a twelve-page letter just before I headed home from college for Christmas. But even more exciting, he asked me to marry him right then and there before he left.

Now that I am a parent, I realize how justified our parents would have been had they disowned us both on the spot, or had at least suggested a Court House wedding when we insisted on hastily activating our plans to marry right away so as to honeymoon in Europe.

Somehow, love prevailed. A mere ten days later, on December 29, 1951, Florence First Methodist Church was filled with guests, invited by word-of-mouth, telephone, and letter. I was as amazed as everyone else that in so short a time we actually planned and pulled off such a beautiful affair.

The altar was banked with evergreens left over from the hectic holidays and sprayed white by a contingency of loyal friends the morning of the wedding. I marched down the aisle in a satin wedding gown borrowed from my sister-in-law Peggy Lindsey and in a veil borrowed from my friend Peggy Price. My favorite cousin and only attendant, Serrill Stuart Arello, wore a dress she had worn in an out-of-town wedding. I was certainly wearing something borrowed, and I think something blue, but (except for my burgundy wool going-away outfit, with rhinestone buttons and my classy white felt hat) I had precious little time to buy much of anything new.

So began our marriage and its never-ending romance. David shipped out to Europe; I was left behind to complete my semester of college, with plans to join David ASAP. He endured the seasickness and discomfort of a no-frills troopship, while I (following him three months later to England) enjoyed the grandeur and luxury of the historic HMS (His/Her Majesty's Ship) Queen Mary.

I will never forget my first view of the Queen Mary as I arrived by taxi from Grand Central Station to the New York pier of my departure. Her magnificence and her mammoth size were absolutely unbelievable. She was more than 1,000 feet long, with twelve decks of varying heights; her three huge and tall smokestacks proudly wore the colors of the Cunard Line. Finally, all 1,927 passengers boarded, and the last "All Aboard!" sounded. We cast off amidst the music of bands, the blasts of the ship's three steam type whistles, and the noise of well-wishers on the pier, waving and wishing us "bon voyage." Not one soul was there to see me off, but I stood at the rail, smiling and waving as if there were. We sailed out to sea, watching the New York skyline and the Statue of Liberty (her torch held high) fade away into the distance. I realized that this five day voyage was only the beginning of a new life's journey for me.

I had heard that Tourist Class (where I was booked) was as luxurious as was First Class on lesser ships, and I believe it. We had crystal chandeliers, polished brass, and teak wood, too. We never felt confined or "cabined." We had stewards who turned down our beds each night, food was served as elegantly as any I had ever seen (even though sea sickness did take its toll), and every guest was invited to sit a The Captain's Table for dinner. He surely must have been A Captain, not THE Captain.

It did not take long for the several young military wives to find each other and hang out together for the entire voyage. We explored the ship, peeped through the grilled doors at First Class opulence, and took in all the festivities and fancy food that seemed available around the clock. Our excitement increased with the passing of each day of our journey. By the time we landed at the Port of Southampton, all passengers aboard (even those traveling on to Cherbourg, France) crowded on deck, all vying for space at the rail. Again, there were bands and whistles and masses of people cheering and greeting us. But this time, there was someone there waiting for me. As I searched the crowds, I began to worry and wonder: "How will we ever find each other?" To this day I cannot tell you how we did. I guess love has its ways. But suddenly we found each other, and from that moment neither lost sight of the other. David was waiting when I stepped off the gangplank, and we fell into each other's arms, newlyweds happily reunited, laughing, crying, hugging, and kissing there on the docks of Southampton. Finally, it was time to collect my on-board luggage and steamer trunk. So began our new life together on that enchanting British Isle, which then as now seems more fantasy than reality.

After an overnight stay in London at the lovely White's Hotel, we traveled by train to the quaint seaside village of Hunstanton and to our upstairs flat at 22 Cliffe Parade. It had an immense bay window overlooking the gray Wash of the North Sea. The cracked walls were mute testimony to the fact that even this rural-most part of England had not escaped the bombs of World War II. The east coast had been on the German Luffwaffe's route home from such strategic destinations as London and Coventry, and left-over bombs were indiscriminately dumped on the countryside.

Framed in our window between the street and the beach below the cliffs was the neatly manicured village bowling green, bordered by exquisite flower gardens and daily frequented by white-clad gentlemen playing at bowls. Tourists in the summer and villagers in the winter walked the craggy beaches inhabited year-round by gregarious seals. The locals vowed the friendly creatures, if encouraged, would follow you home, but I never saw one do so, and I was never sure whether or not they were putting me on.

I had barely arrived and been carried over the threshold of our first home before our downstairs neighbor, Mrs. Curson, came bearing gifts … two fresh-laid hen's eggs. It was not until we ourselves had experienced England's still rigorous post-war food rationing that we appreciated how dear a gift this was.

Mrs. Curson immediately took me under her wing, and every Tuesday she and I, like two cheery adventurers, boarded a double-decker bus to Market Day in the nearby town of King's Lynn. As the bus slowed on the curve passing Sandringham Castle (the death-place of the then recently deceased King George), we always strained for a glimpse of royalty. Seeing none, Mrs. Curson would regale me with favorite tales of royalty she had sighted. When I was later able to share all the details of our being within smiling distance of the elegant Princess Margaret and the regal Queen Grandmother (both with their beautifully British peaches and cream complexions), she was almost as excited as I was. We explored King's Lynn's narrow cobbled streets and its historic nooks and crannies. We had a standing invitation for tea with the friend whose chickens had laid my gift eggs. We weekly purchased the few fresh eggs she could spare, carefully cradling them in newspaper nests in our shopping bags. David and I later moved to a more spacious flat at Corner House, so named because it sat on the corner that separated New from Old Huns'ton, but I never missed going to Market Day with my dear old neighbor and friend.

I learned to shop like a regular British housewife, riding my bicycle to the village Baker or the Greengrocer. In fact, we lived on the local economy, without PX or commissary privileges until I was finally approved as a dependent. We shopped for food daily, for like many Brits our window sill was our only refrigerator. I got used to un-sliced, un-wrapped bread and carrying my own shopping bag for my purchases. I accepted the fact that there was always a cat asleep in every fish market window, but I could never bring myself to buy one of those pitiful, fully-feathered, glassy-eyed chickens hanging by their feet in the front of the markets.

The Cademys, Kings, Watsons, Mrs. Curson, and her daughter Joan all helped me celebrate in true English style my twenty-first birthday, which to our English friends was a major rite of passage. Then, when my mother and daddy, to our great pleasure, later came to visit us, these same friends entertained them royally and proved beyond all doubt that British folk are a warm, gracious, generous lot, and (in spite of reports to the contrary) are marvelously full of good humor. They sent us back to America with treasures from their homes as love gifts and memories that will live forever in our hearts.

By this time, we had become the proud new owners of the sleekest, shiniest, smoothest-running automobile I have ever, even to this day, laid eyes on: one of only 200 1938 MG limited TA custom-made four-seater editions ever produced, and ours (even then) was a collector's item. This classic black convertible with its DRO 497 license plate was in mint condition. It had been lovingly stored during World War II, awaiting the return of its owner. Sadly, a casualty of war, he never returned. The next owner was a Captain Hurry, a dapper young man who sped about town with his red hair and his tartan scarf flying in the wind. He mourned but acquiesced when his wife demanded a more sensible means of family transportation for their two babies. It is the only automobile I've ever loved, and I expect Captain Hurry and I, as long as we both shall live, will always regret having parted with the world's classiest automobile.

We spent our last night in England, a bitterly cold December one, as guests of the Watsons at their Bed and Breakfast Inn. They tucked us in under a mountain of eiderdowns with a clay bed-warmer at our feet. The following morning we were treated like royalty to tea served in bed, but the magic spell was broken when David's cup suddenly tipped over. Tea spilled everywhere and splashed all over everything. As we mopped up, the four of us laughed so hard we cried, then we later cried again as we bid each other our final fond farewell.

Being older and wiser, they (more than we) must have realized how final was this farewell. We vowed to keep in touch and write, and for years we did. With youthful hearts full of dreams and plans, we vowed to meet again someday. But it's sad to say, in the course of things, by the time we returned years later to England, our old friends were no longer there to greet us. As with us all, our promises are so easily overtaken by life's realities. Even our beloved church was boarded up with a sign telling us that if we needed a vicar to contact one in the neighboring village of Ipswich.

On that long ago December morning, we pulled away from the curb in our beloved MG loaded down with all our possessions. Our final view … our final memory … of the Watsons was of the two of them, standing together as one, smiling and waving to us, bracing themselves against the bitter winter winds blowing in from the cold, cold white-capped North Sea.

Trifle

The first time I ever tasted Trifle was at high tea (which is actually a kind of light early supper) at the Cademys. This recipe is a combination of Trifles I have known and tasted through the years … both there and here … from Mrs. Cademy's (laced with raspberry jam) to Martha Daniel's Punch Bowl Cake, and including Hannah Brown's authentic English Trifle (laced with the kind of spirits Mrs. Cademy would have never considered).

1. Prepare according to package directions. Chill until syrupy:

   6 oz of strawberry JELLO

2. Add to JELLO:

   1 pkg (16 oz) frozen (or fresh) sliced strawberries

3. Line trifle bowl (or large glass bowl) with **thinly-sliced pound cake**

   (For a fancier look, use sliced jelly roll)

4. Mix **½ c red wine** with **¼ c raspberry jam**.

5. Drizzle on sides and on bottom layer of cake.

6. Prepare according to package directions:

   1pkg (6 oz) and 1 pkg (3 oz) vanilla pudding (instant or regular pudding).

7. Slice **5 or 6 bananas**.

8. Drain **1 can (16 oz) pineapple chunks.**

9. Layer in this order: JELLO, pudding, bananas, pineapple.

10. Repeat, ending with pudding.

11. Garnish with **whipped topping** and **cherries** or **strawberries.**

12. Chill before serving.

CAKES & ICINGS

The Walstons

AFTER WE REDISCOVERED AND REUNITED with (through an obituary notice) our Walston kin, I looked forward to the holiday greetings sent by cousins Amelia Walston and her brother Robert. For more than 40 Christmases, Robert sent cards reflecting his photographic hobby, with a photograph of some picturesque church and its brief history. One year, he featured historic Canaan Methodist Church, built sometime before 1840 on land donated by our common ancestor, Edmund Noel, who was born in Virginia in 1793.

While my niece Paige was living in England, her research of family history led her to a churchyard cemetery near Chipping Camden in the lovely Cotswolds. She was especially intrigued by Penelope Noel, who "dyed a mayde" at the age of twenty two, and who is sculpted with ribbons twined in her long ringlets. According to Paige (and including her editorial commentary):

> "Poor Penelope's family were Royalists during the English Civil War and her brother served with Valiant Prince Rupert of the Rhine and went into exile during Cromwell's Protectorate. Penelope's father died, no doubt of a broken heart, during that sad, Presbyterian time. Penelope passed from this Vale of Tears in 1650, leaving behind a mother and two married sisters, Juliana and Sophiana, all who are immortalized in gargantuan marble statues, plaques, reliefs and cenotaph, there in the village church, shedding copious tears over all the deaths. Penelope dyed during the Darkest Dayes of Cromwell's control, believing that all was lost for the Royalist Cause, her brother and the Noels of Chipping Camden."

The history of Canaan Church does not compare in antiquity to that of its sister church in England, but this lovely little church, tucked away on an Alabama country road amidst green fields and a stand of aged oaks, has its own place in U.S. Civil War history. It is one of the oldest local churches still in use today.

In the bitterly cold winter of 1865, the Union Army, under the command of General James B. Wilson, encamped 22,000 cavalry troops (one of the largest military encampments of the entire Civil War) at Gravelly Springs, not far from Canaan. Virtually all barns, churches, and out-buildings were torn down to build barracks and stables for the Union Army. Though seized by the military, little Canaan Methodist Church was somehow spared, and Yankee troops were billeted there.

Benches I sat on as a child were still pock-marked with bullet holes, and there were traces (still visible on the walls) of the old slave gallery. I remember going there to Fifth Sunday Preaching and afterward Dinner-On-The-Ground beneath the aged oaks. Exceptionally fertile bottom land on the Colbert Reserve—known since pioneer days as the Bend of the River, good cotton land—stretches as far as the eye can see until its banks slope gently into the Tennessee River.

A few years ago when my daddy read the obituary of Banks Walston (Daddy's mother was a Walston), he promptly wrote to a mentioned survivor and reestablished contact with this branch of our family with whom he had through the years lost touch. Amelia and Robert's invitation to the 90th birthday party of their sister, Cousin Kathouise of Birmingham, provided my first opportunity to meet these long-lost, new-found cousins. To our amazement, Daddy and Kathouise compared memories of playing together as children, more than eighty years past, at the old home place. I cherish the picture taken of them that day in front of a beautiful cherry chest, hand-hewn by their common grandfather. Later, Amelia and Robert traveled to Florence and helped us celebrate my daddy's 90th birthday.

We share a rich Methodist heritage with these gracious delightful cousins. Robert retired after many years as Bursar for Birmingham Southern College, a Methodist college that is now our daughter Laura's alma mater. He would drive across town to attend McCoy Methodist church next to the campus, slipping out in time to pick up Amelia at her First Methodist downtown church. Another cousin, an earlier Robert Walston, was the Methodist minister who officiated at my parent's wedding on December 22, 1924.

Under the 1991 Times Daily headline, "Stranger's Gift Shocks Members of Small Church," a story unfolded about a Mr. Robert Walston LeMay who was born in 1898 at Oakland, Alabama, and who was baptized there at the country Methodist church of his childhood (also of mine). The congregation collectively gasped in astonishment, and many shed tears of gratitude and joy as the generous Mr. Lemay observed, "the Lord has been gracious to me … ," and presented the little church a big check for $50,000.

Mr. LeMay pointed out that his middle name was that of the Reverend Walston, who had served Oakland Methodist Church back in the 1800s. It appears Mr. LeMay (whom I never met) is distant kin, and that he may have been named for either my cousin Robert, my great-grandfather John, or my great-uncle James, all Walston kin and all Methodist ministers of that period. The name Walston is one I carry with great pride. Long after my daddy's death, I enjoyed the continued friendship with dear Robert and Amelia and our other Walston kin.

Amelia's Wondrous Christmas Cake

Amelia, who lived to celebrate her 100th birthday, always sent her own holiday greetings that were usually expressed in poetry, as was this special recipe:

A Wondrous Christmas Cake

Stir 'til very soft and dreamy
One cup of Christmas light,
Pour the milk of kindness in,
To make it snowy white;
Never spare the sweet tidbits
Of gentle love and caring;
Add as much as you can spare
Of giving, listening, sharing.

No need to brown or bake,
No need to frost or ice,
Just share your wondrous
Christmas Cake,
Give everyone a slice!

Wishing you a warm and sharing holiday!

Methodist Carrot Cake

This is such an all-time old-time favorite, I would be disloyal if I failed to include this in a family collection. Years ago, our associate minister's pretty young wife Jane introduced this cake to us with,"Y'all will never guess what's in this cake!" And sure enough, we could not, and did not.

1. Mix together by hand:

2 c flour	**¼ t salt**
2 c sugar	**3 c grated carrots**
½ - ¾ c vegetable oil	**4 eggs**
2 t cinnamon	**1 t soda**

2. Add:

   ½ c nuts

   ½ c raisins

3. Optional: After trying another carrot cake recipe, our Janna suggests adding **1 small can of drained pineapple** to this recipe.

4. Bake in 9x13 pan or 2 cake pans at 350 degrees for 25 minutes.

Cream Cheese Icing

1. Mix together slowly, beat until fluffy, and spread on cake:

   2 small blocks of cream cheese (room temperature)

   ¾ stick of oleo

   1 lb box confectioners sugar

   1 t vanilla

   Note: If icing is too stiff, add **a few drops of milk.**

Breaking and Entering

DAVID'S MOTHER AND FATHER MARRIED when she was only sixteen, and he was ten years older. His mother, Ruby Mae Pierce Mussleman, the oldest of four children (Ruby, Allen, Grace, and Virginia) was only nine years old when her mother died. I once asked Mrs. Mussleman what her father (who at one time was County Sheriff) had said when she wanted to marry at such an early age. She remembered his somewhat sad acknowledgment of all the family responsibilities that had befallen her, so he reckoned she'd been grown up long enough, and gave her his permission and his blessing.

David's Granny Mussleman gave Ruby, her new daughter-in-law, this special coconut cake recipe, and it has continued to hold its own as a cornerstone of Mussleman family tradition. David's daddy Carl used to always grate the fresh coconut, and being the inventor that he was, he toyed with creating an electric coconut grater but never quite perfected it. Today, that step is bypassed with frozen grated coconut, a progress Granddaddy Carl surely would have applauded. He did invent for Greatmommy Ruby's convenience an electric clothesline that allowed her to hang up and take in her laundry from the comfort of the back porch. However, I seriously doubt if today's generation—who has never cracked a coconut nor hung out laundry on a line—could appreciate the genius of Grandaddy's coconut grater or his clothesline.

Though I tried this recipe many years ago and turned out a reasonable facsimile, Lindsey is the family member who (having actually apprenticed under the master herself in this cake-making ritual) has assumed the official role of Family Coconut Cake Baker. Greatmommy was a blessing to us all these years, but for many more reasons, of course, than just for all her years of coconut cakes. She delivered her cakes well ahead of time for both Thanksgiving and Christmas, all wrapped and ready for the freezer. In fact, they were so thoroughly wrapped in so many layers of waxed paper and foil that, in order to get down to the cake itself, I feared I might get charged with breaking and entering!

Greatmommy's Coconut Cake

1. Cream together:

   1 c butter or margarine

   3 c sugar

2. Add:

   1 c milk

   1 t salt

   4 ½ c sifted flour

   2 ½ t baking powder

3. Fold in:

   6 beaten egg whites

   1 grated coconut or 1 pkg frozen coconut

   1 t vanilla

4. Pour batter into 3 round cake pans or 2 pans (9x13).

5. Bake at 350 degrees for 25-30 minutes.

6. Ice with coconut icing.

Coconut Icing

Cook to a soft boil in a saucepan:

   2 c sugar

   1 c milk

   1 t salt

1. Add **2 T butter** (do not use lite or reduced fat), and stir until melted.

2. Beat, cool slightly.

3. Add **1 ½ pkg frozen coconut**.

4. Spread on cake.

5. Sprinkle **½ pkg coconut** on top and sides of cake.

6. Wrap carefully, and store in refrigerator or freezer.

Susan's Coconut Cake

Both the Keith family and this cake Susan Keith made for my daddy were big favorites of his. Katie and Matthew, the Keith children that Laura so loved to baby-sit, were favorites of hers. Observing their busy son in action, we jokingly remind the parents that we forewarned them that any Matthew we've ever known, including ours, has been just as delightfully mischievous as their Matthew has turned out to be.

1. Prepare as directed, and bake in 9x13 glass baking dish:

   1 pkg yellow cake mix

2. Remove from oven, and punch holes in cake with a fork or, as the original recipe suggests, "with a wooden spoon handle."

3. Bring to a boil, simmer 1 minute, and pour hot over cake:

   1 ½ c milk

   ½ c sugar

   ½ pkg frozen coconut

4. When cake has cooled, spread over cake:

   8 oz whipped topping

5. Sprinkle remaining coconut over topping.

6. Keep cake refrigerated. Serve from the dish it is baked in.

Summer Sherbet Cake

This is a delicious way to cool down in the heat of the summer.

1. Slice in half horizontally **1 round frozen Angel Food Cake.**

2. Spread softened **lime sherbet** on top of bottom layer.

3. Place top layer over sherbet.

4. "Ice" the top and sides of cake with softened **raspberry sherbet.**

   Note: It may be necessary to return the cake to the freezer during the spreading, as the sherbet melts rapidly.

5. Wrap cake, and store in freezer.

   Note: Any combination of sherbet flavors may be used.

6. Garnish cake with **twists of lemon and a few leaves of fresh mint, or with any sliced fresh fruits** or **berries.**

Flower Garden Cake

This cool, do-ahead, Southern summer-time treat stores well in the freezer, ready to be served at a moment's notice.

1. Drain and set aside **1 can (16 oz) crushed pineapple**.

2. Save **1 c juice** (add water, if necessary, to make 1 c).

3. Separate **6 eggs**.

4. Mix together and cook over low heat until mixture coats spoon:

   ¾ c juice

   ¾ c sugar

   Juice of 2 lemons

   6 egg yolks, beaten

5. Soften **1 ½ envelopes of plain gelatin** in remaining ¼ c juice.

6. Stir into hot mixture until dissolved.

7. Add crushed pineapple, and set aside to cool slightly.

8. Beat together until stiff, and add to yolk mixture:

   6 egg whites

   ¾ c sugar

9. Fold in:

   1 medium Angel Food Cake, torn into small pieces

   1 c nuts, broken into pieces

10. Pour into greased tube pan.

11. Chill for several hours, or store in freezer.

12. Unmold, and frost with **whipped topping**.

13. Garnish with **cherries, fresh mint leaves, a few twists of lemon, or any appealing fresh fruit.**

The Old Three-Cornered Cupboard

My MOTHER ALWAYS made her holiday fruit cakes the week before Thanksgiving, at which time we were allowed to eat only one of the cakes. The others were soaked in respectable Methodist grape juice, wrapped in linen towels, and stored in the three-cornered china cupboard for Christmas eating and gift-giving.

How I wish I knew more about the old cupboard, a treasure from Daddy's side of the family. Daddy, who was born in 1893, remembered it from his childhood as being the top part of a larger piece of furniture (old even then) in their high-ceilinged dining room, so it certainly is certifiably antique. The broken corner of one of the glass panes adds to its authenticity, so when it someday becomes yours, Dear Children, whatever you do, do not replace it.

What long-forgotten family stories we could learn if only our old cupboard could talk! I wonder what more it could tell us about such ancestors as Major John Lindsey, my fifth (or is it five times removed?) grandfather who was a soldier in the Revolutionary War. According to my cousin, author, and City Historian William Lindsey McDonald (from whom I've learned so much family history), the Major was severely wounded by a sword in hand-to-hand combat. After the war, he wore a silver cap over his wrist where his hand had been amputated, and he was thereafter known as "Silver Fist Lindsey." Later commissioned a deputy by the U.S. Government, he was involved in negotiations that led to the 1816 Treaty (which, I'm told, bears his signature) with the Cherokee, Creek, Choctaw, and Chickasaw Indians. Chief George Colbert represented the Chickasaws and was granted a Reserve of sixteen square miles on the north side of the Tennessee River. Records show that the Walstons (my daddy's mother's family) purchased a large tract of this land directly from Chief Colbert.

According to my daddy, the Lindsey family was one of those forever torn asunder by the Civil War. Brother in Confederate grey fought against brother in Union blue. Lindseys from both sides are buried in a Civil War Cemetery up in Pulaski, Tennessee. After the war, the Union survivors settled just over the Tennessee line, less than fifty miles away from the Rebel survivors who limped back home defeated to North Alabama. In Daddy's lifetime, he sought out and met some of these cousins, but one of my brother's dental patients who is married to a Tennessee Lindsey is as close as our present day family has ever come to being reunited with theirs. Then there's the connection that my mother-in-law's step-mother (whom we never knew) was a Lindsey from that part of Tennessee. Even in the South, that would be farfetched kin.

After the War, in 1876, Philip Lindsey filed the following claim against the Federal Government for items confiscated or destroyed by the 200 Union soldiers encamped that winter at his farm, near Gravelly Springs.

5,100 pounds of salted pork (from smokehouse)	$667.00
50 bushels of corn (from crib)	$ 50.00
500 bundles of fodder (from barn)	$ 15.00
3 stand of beehives	$ 50.00
100 pounds of honey	$ 20.00
40 gallons of molasses (taken away in canteens)	$ 40.00
50 pounds of potatoes (dug from garden)	$ 25.00
1,000 pounds of cotton (burned on-site)	$300.00
1,000 newly cut fence rails (burned on-site)	$ 30.00
1 Clay Bank 3 year old mare($ he had turned down)	$200.00
Slaughtered a milk cow and two heifers	$000.00
Slaughtered all the hogs on the place	$000.00

However, according to Cousin William, because his Great-great Grandfather (my Great-great Uncle Philip) had owned slaves and because his three sons had fought in the Confederate Army, his claim (like most claims of this nature) was repeatedly denied. As soon as the courts turned him down, he simply resubmitted his claim. It is documented that in 1891, the persistent, stubborn Rebel was finally successful in winning a partial claim against the U. S. Government. Sadly, he died before he actually received the money.

But I have my own, more precious, more recent family memories. Though it must have surely faded through the years, I never open the doors of the beloved three-cornered cupboard that now graces our dining room but what I still savor, though ever so faintly, the unmistakable, unforgettable aroma of my mother's fruit cakes.

Mother's Fruit Cake

Since none of our children enjoy fruit cake enough to eat it, much less make it, I include this recipe for historical purposes only.

1. Mix together:

   ¾ **c melted margarine**

   1 ½ t soda in ¾ c hot water

   1 ½ c sugar

2. Slowly add **3 c plain flour.**

3. Add **3 eggs** and blend thoroughly.

4. Add the following, mixing by hand:

   2 c nuts

   1 lb jar prepared mincemeat

   1 lb raisins (If you like a light color, use white raisins)

   ½ lb mixed peel

   1 lb chopped dates

   ½ lb candied pineapple, cut in pieces

   ½ lb candied cherries

5. Reserve a few nuts, pineapple, and cherries to decorate top of cake.

6. Pour into pans of your choice and decorate. (Any type or shape pan as deep as a loaf pan will do. Even coffee cans, in my day, were often used.)

7. Bake in a slow oven at 275 degrees for 1 to 1 ½ hours or until cake pulls away from the sides of the pan.

8. Wrap cakes in wax paper, then in a linen towel (like my mother did).

9. Store in a cool place for at least 2 weeks (preferably in a three-cornered cupboard).

10. Keep cakes moist by pouring a little **spirits of your choice** over the top of cake.

Anne's Chocolate Sheet Cake

In consideration to chocolate lovers, I include this easy to make, richly flavored cake. Because it is so delicious, it appears in lots of cook books, often bearing the name, I assume, of the last person to pass it on. It was given to me as Gloria's Cake, but since my friend Anne passed it on to me, let's give her the credit.

1. Sift together in a mixing bowl:

   2 c plain flour

   2 c sugar

2. Mix in a pan, stir, and bring to a boil:

   1 stick oleo

   ½ c shortening

   4 T cocoa

   1 c water

3. Stir into flour and sugar.

4. Add and mix with beaters until smooth:

   ½ c buttermilk

   2 slightly beaten eggs

   1 t soda

   ½ t salt

   1 t vanilla

5. Pour into 2 cake pans or 1 pan (9x13).

6. Bake at 350 degrees about 25-30 minutes.

Chocolate Icing

1. Bring to a boil in a pan, and remove from heat:

   1 stick oleo

   4 T chocolate

   6 T milk

2. Add and beat until thick:

   1 box confectioners sugar

   1 t vanilla

   1 c pecans

3. Spread on cake.

Jes' Lak Miss Lizzie

My GRANDMOTHER, Lizzie Walston Lindsey, died when my daddy was sixteen years old, so I was never to know her. However, she left a legacy of goodness and kindness, a woman, I'm told, who was always there as a source of strength and service to any who needed her. As a teenager, I was astonished when I had stopped at a country store and an aged black lady I'd never seen before (and who apparently had never seen me before) stared at me in wide-eyed disbelief, threw up her hands, and declared: "Lawdy … Lawdy … if you ain't jes' lak Miss Lizzie!"

I was astonished because no one had ever said that to me before, and even I could tell I looked "jes' lak" my mother, Pauline. Daddy must have chosen a wife whose appearance and character closely resembled that of his own beloved mother, and his daughter is proud of the birthright left her by these two exceptional women.

My paternal grandparents, Elisabeth (Lizzie) Webb Walston and Henry Barbee Lindsey, are buried in the old family cemetery that sits atop a hill that once overlooked the

Walston Plantation. It is today a serene and peaceful place. Breezes whisper gently as ghosts through the old pine trees standing there. Now serving the entire community, it still carries the name, Walston Cemetery. One of the oldest tombstones there is of an earlier Elizabeth Walston, born 1780 … died 1830. Tradition says that when the *Yankees swept through North Alabama during the Civil War, the family silver was safely hidden in the aged vault that stands today, weathered and grayed, at the old cemetery.

When I was a child, rumors abounded that somewhere on the Walston farm, gold had been buried and was there still, waiting to be recovered by some lucky treasure hunter. I would from time to time hear whispers about mysterious maps and tales supporting their authenticity. Daddy didn't put much stock in such tales, but three quarters of a century after the Civil War, others apparently did. Periodically and persistently, the light of day would reveal a night's worth of holes dug deep by unknown vandals who had no regard for the fences they cut or the crops they destroyed. What secrets these treasure hunters knew or thought they knew, what prompted them to dig where they dug, or whether they were ever rewarded for their efforts, we were never to know.

Commonly known as the Walston Place, it represented what was left of the rather large former plantation, with the deed signed by Chickasaw Chief George Colbert himself and carved out of the Reserve granted him by the U.S. Government through the Treaty of 1816. I do not know the details, but like many Southern families after the Civil War, the Walstons lost their land. It was with great pride that Daddy was able to purchase several hundred acres of the original land, restoring it to rightful family ownership.

The farm was blessed with a cold, clear spring that meandered through it. Rimmed with watercress, the spring bubbled up out of the ground, sending bits of golden sand dancing merrily up to catch the sunlight. Its waters eventually pooled into a shaded mysterious place known as the Blue Hole. Here, t'was said, a team of mules … wagon, driver and all … had long ago disappeared forever into its deep, evil waters. Some said it was quicksand "what got 'um." Some said "somethin' jes retch up n' pull 'um under." In spite of good fishing there, many farm hands persisted in their fear of the place and doggedly refused to go near the Blue Hole.

I loved to play at the hilltop site of the old Walston home, also known as The Anchorage. I dreamed of the grand days that might have been mine as a hoop-skirted lass. I imagined the sounds of carriages approaching and the laughter of company coming. I skipped along overgrown pathways, explored the crumbling remnants of the slave-made brick foundation, and picked bouquets from tangled bridal wreath and root-bound clumps of double buttercups. For me, being there was a very special time, and I never left without feeling the overpowering presence of my past.

*Back then, folks in the South spat the word, YANKEE, more than spoke the word. Mother's dear friend Nellie Shannon, a product of a loyal Southern home and as gracious a Christian lady as you'd ever meet, told as fact that she was grown before she learned DAMNYANKEE was not, as she had been raised to believe, one word.

From the Good Old Days

In ANY COUNTRY KITCHEN of my childhood, there were almost always left over biscuits, corn bread, and slabs of plain yellow cake. The cake was served with fresh fruit and cream whipped by hand, with pudding, JELLO, or just plain with a glass of foamy farm-fresh milk. The mid-day meal was called dinner, and enough was cooked to "make out" supper that night. In the summertime, it was a blessed relief not to have to fire up the big wood-burning cook stove again for supper. We all teased Mother about the wood cook stove she insisted on installing right beside her modern electric range in our new home. However, through the years, when bad weather caused the inevitable power outages, and we found ourselves with no central heat and no electric range, we were grateful she had held onto some of those good old ways from the good old days.

The convenience foods and prepared mixes we depend upon now were unheard of then. In season, folks ate from the bounty of their gardens. The rest of the year they ate from the smokehouse (ham and bacon), from the cellar (Irish and sweet potatoes, turnips and onions), and from the pantry (home-canned fruits, vegetables, pickles, and jams put up in sparkling Mason jars during the summer). Any hens who got lazy with their egg laying were fair game for the dinner table year round, but fresh pork was available only after hog killin' in the first cold spell of Fall.

I include this plain yellow cake as a tribute to days gone by and as a reminder that even in today's kitchens cakes can come from places other than boxes.

Plain Yellow Cake

1. In a mixing bowl, beat for 2 minutes:

½ c shortening	2 ¼ c sifted flour
3 t baking powder	1 t salt
1 ½ c sugar	¾ c milk

2. Add, and beat for 1 minute:

2 eggs	¼ c milk
1 t vanilla	

3. Pour into greased 9x13 pan.

4. Bake at 350 degrees for 25 minutes.

The Almost Perfect Kitchen

YOU KNOW, LIFE PROVIDES US MANY OPPORTUNITIES to learn humility. Pride doth indeed goeth before a fall. In planning the house we were building, I took special delight in designing the family kitchen.

I considered lighting, traffic flow, and storage needs. There were cabinets for everything from iron skillets to Christmas china, and a pantry big enough to store food enough to last through a blizzard or a house full of company. To be sure that everything fit, I measured over-sized cooking pots and serving pieces. I computed my arm length and adjusted shelf-levels to my diminutive height. I planned space to accommodate any size gathering, even an intimate window-seated nook in the sunny bay.

I was confident that, for us, I had designed the perfect kitchen. Until, that is, the first time I started to make Seven Minute Icing in my perfect kitchen. That's when I discovered a terrible error. There was no electrical outlet close enough to the stove to plug in the mixer. So what did I do whenever I made this icing? I dragged out an extension cord, plugged it into the nearest faraway outlet, stretched it half-way across the kitchen, and hoped that nobody clothes-lined themselves during the next seven minutes!

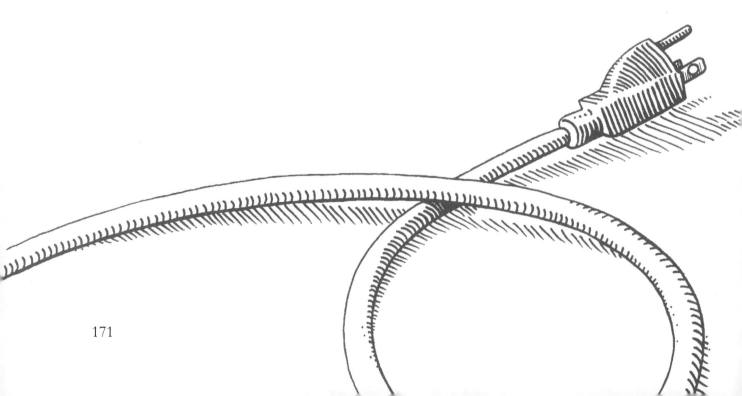

Seven Minute Icing

This icing recipe is one Matt especially loves with Devil's Food Cake. David declares that cake with this icing always passes the twenty-four hour test, meaning that at our house a really good cake will not last one minute/one hour longer than that! This icing is easy to make but requires strong wrists, since it must be beaten continuously with a hand held mixer for seven minutes.

1. Bring water to a boil in bottom of double boiler.
2. Add together in top of double-boiler, and beat 6-7 minutes at highest speed with portable mixer until soft but firm peaks form:

   2 egg whites   **¼ t cream of tartar**

   6 T cold water   **1 ½ c sugar**

   1 t vanilla   **Dash of salt**

3. Spread on Devil's Food Cake.

Red Jelly Icing

Serve this variation of Seven Minute Icing on special occasions (like Valentine's Day) when you want to celebrate with color. The flavor will come from the kind of jelly you choose.

1. Mix together in top of double boiler:

   ½ c red jelly   **¼ c sugar**

   1 egg white   **1 t syrup**

   Red food coloring

2. Beat continuously about 5 minutes until soft peaks form.

   Option: Use mint jelly and green food coloring. If you like, add a drop or two of mint flavoring.

One Minute Chocolate Icing

I discovered this recipe a few years ago in a collection of recipes written in my mother's hand. Frankly, I cannot remember her making it, but I have found it to be the best no-fail, cooked chocolate icing ever. This is one of those recipes where exact measurements and careful timing are essential. Don't be mislead by its liquid state at the end of the cooking time. Work quickly. It cools and hardens FAST.

1. Mix together in a sauce pan, and stir constantly.

   ½ c cocoa

   6 T margarine

   1 ½ c sugar

   ¼ t salt

2. After it comes to a boil, cook exactly 1 minute.

3. Beat, cool slightly, and spread on white, yellow, or chocolate cake.

Burnt Sugar Icing

I well remember this icing my mother used to make and how delicious it was. It can be used on any yellow cake.

1. Mix together, and heat in a sauce pan:

   1 ½ c sugar

   1 c buttermilk

   ½ t soda

2. Slowly melt **½ c sugar** in a cast-iron skillet.

3. When sugar burns to a light brown syrup, pour into mixture in pan.

4. Stir and cook over medium heat until icing makes a soft ball when dropped in cold water.

5. Add **½ c butter or margarine**, and stir until melted.

   Note: If icing seems too hard, add a little cream.

6. Spread on cake.

PIES

Ahead of Her Time

MOTHER LOVED TELLING ABOUT, and I loved hearing about, the childhood summers that she and her little sister Lenice spent back and forth between the neighboring farm homes of their Mitchell and Cauhorn grandparents. Whether they traveled there by horse and buggy or by train to the nearest depot just over the Tennessee line, getting there was part of the fun. Nearby, there was always a nurturing network of aunts and cousins from both sides of the family, all close to Mother in age. Grandmother's youngest sister Willie T. was only two years older than mother, and they were more like sisters. Summer times (riding horses, romping in the hayloft, picking orchard fruit and garden vegetables, gathering eggs and feeding the farm animals) were happy times.

Mother spoke lovingly of her Grandma Cauhorn, whose voice still bore the traces of her English birth. True to her heritage, she adored gardening. As a bride, she began her plantings: walnut trees, a plum orchard on one side of the house, an apple orchard on the other side, and every season thereafter a yard full of beautiful flowers.

But according to my mother's journal, it was Grandma Mitchell, "with her sweet devotion to family and God, her good humor and bravery in the face of hardship," who Mother loved next to her own mother, and of whom she wrote, "A nobler soul never lived."

Grandpa Mitchell was for twenty years Tax Collector for Lauderdale County, which in those days involved some door-to-door calling. I somehow got the idea that Grandpa had a way with the ladies and may have had some sort of arrangement ('in lieu of taxes'), but such matters were never openly discussed, at least not in front of us children.

Early on, my mother was an achiever, a leader, and a scholar. She was actively involved in church and school activities, busy with art, piano, and elocution. At graduation, she was awarded the coveted Turris Fidelis Award, given then by the State Normal School (now the University of North Alabama) to the student with the highest academic standing. Later,

Dr. Willingham, the school president, called Mother in and asked: "Would you be willing to take a teaching place away from where the electric lights shine?"

So it was that Mother began her teaching adventures at a little place called Hollytree, and would later move on to such Alabama communities as Myrtlewood and Paint Rock. Room and board at $15 to $20 a month was pre-arranged with a respectable family by the Board of Education that hired her for $60 to $80 a month. One summer, she taught in a place so remote it could only be reached over a rough mountainous trail, either by horseback or by the logging wagon that carried the logs out and the mail in each day. The only schooling these children received was during this two month session, and Mother said she'd never seen students more eager to learn. She boarded with an elderly one-armed preacher who still believed the earth was flat, and his wife who served greasy fried chicken, thick, heavy biscuits, and left-over pie for breakfast. The wife fretted all summer over her petite boarder who seemed such a picky eater. Mother was unaccustomed to such fare and reported that she was starved half to death by summer's end.

During these years, Mother felt more and more called to become a missionary to Japan. This decision was somehow interwoven with her grief over a young man killed on the final day of World War I, and her seven-year on-again, off-again engagement to her first school principal. By then he, in preparation for the ministry, was enrolled in a Baptist seminary, and she, in preparation for the mission field, had accepted a scholarship to Scarritt, a religious college located now in Nashville but then in Kansas City. Apparently, distance made neither the hearts grow fonder nor their divergent theologies more compatible. By the time Mother had completed her studies, their engagement had ended.

That previously mentioned network of aunts and cousins close to Mother's own age had always been an advocate of my daddy, regularly feeding him insider information and covertly encouraging him in his courtship of Mother. Free of previous entanglements, she finally fell in love with my father who had for so long loved her. So it was that Mother became a home missionary in Portsmouth, Virginia, where until their marriage she served instead of a missionary to faraway Japan. Even as a young child, I was aware of my mother's intrigue with the Orient long before I was aware of the reasons behind it.

When my twenty-four year old mother and my thirty-one year old daddy married, the word obey, by mutual consent, was omitted from their marriage vows. When reminded of it, Daddy always chuckled, but the character of their relationship was thus cast. Mother had a good business head, and she and Daddy together shared the responsibility for family and financial decision-making. Early in their marriage, a banker, making it perfectly clear that he preferred to deal with the man of the house, declined to finalize a business transaction with Mother's signature. Daddy indicated who he preferred to do business with by promptly transferring all funds and business to another bank. I doubt if the banker ever saw the humor in it, but years later Daddy chuckled about that, too.

Having such liberated privileges as her own checkbook and her own automobile, Mother enjoyed an independence well beyond that of most wives of her day. Furthermore, there was never any doubt whatsoever that whenever and wherever she lived out her calling to do the Lord's work, Mother did so with Daddy's blessing.

The summer I was born, Daddy completed his master's degree from Peabody College and became principal of a vocational high school in Eva, a lovely little community near Camden, Tennessee. There, unlike teachers in Alabama who were paid during the Depression years with Script (a promissory note from the government), he was paid with real money, U.S. dollars. As a child, I recall someone's comment about how fortunate I was that both my parents had master's degrees, but of course I did not appreciate how true or how uncommon it was in those days.

By the time I was four, we had moved back home to Alabama, and when I turned six, Mother resumed her teaching career. To make sure I got a good foundation in our poor county school, she became my first grade teacher at Oakland Elementary School where my father was Principal. Wolf, my faithful little fox terrier, followed me to school each day and lay quietly at my feet, unless Buzzy Fulmer (next door in Daddy's sixth grade class) performed on his harmonica or some budding soprano hit a high note. At this point, Wolf raised his nose and howled until the music stopped. Star pupil though he was, I doubt if the County Board of Education ever authorized the good grades that appeared on a report card issued to a student named Wolf Lindsey.

Mother was also an artist, her early years devoted to watercolor and her later years to oil and canvas. From time to time, she would become involved in such creativities as painting ceramic plaques or designing sea shell jewelry. Miss Pauline's hand-painted wedding gifts were cherished treasures throughout the community. She also loved to sew and was as likely to create from a sketch as from a pattern, and more than likely to put the final stitches in my clothes as I was walking out the door.

We found time to pick blackberries that cascaded over the pasture fence, wild flowers wherever they grew, and vegetables from the bountiful garden that sweet, humble Lula—the wife of Cute (his real name) Ellis Jackson, our long-time sharecropper—raised for us on the halves. Mother also found time to cook and to can, but housekeeping sometimes seemed to pale in priority to more enjoyable activities.

There was always time for storytelling, and what a wonderful storyteller Mother was … favorites such as Br'er Rabbit or Tikki-tikki-timbo, ghost stories, and tales rich in the dialects of our South. And what fun we had reading from the wealth of books in our home library. Included were the special birthday and Christmas books sent to me all the way from Portland, Maine, by my namesake, Miss Henrietta Lang Gay, retired Scarritt College Librarian. She wrote me beautiful, loving letters, but she died while I was a young child, and I never had the opportunity to meet her. With no nearby playmates, books were my best friends.

I am certain that the happiness of my growing-up years contributed to my desire to come back home and raise our young children with my parents (already loving grandparents) close at hand. That we did, but in all too short a time after our return, Mother had surgery, and the prognosis was not good.

For the final two years of her life, with the growing awareness that her illness was terminal, Daddy rarely left Mother's side, devoting himself totally to her. When she was able, they visited and traveled, savoring their time together. Whenever she was receiving treatments at Nashville's Vanderbilt Hospital, Daddy was there with and for her.

Daddy accompanied Mother on one final trip, a very special one, to her beloved Lake Junaluska, a Methodist Retreat nestled in the Smoky Mountains of North Carolina. She drew peace and strength from the huge lighted cross overlooking the tranquil lake embraced by the nearby mountains. There, she met a young woman who was struggling to answer the call to Christian ministry. Even in her weakened condition, Mother lovingly counseled and encouraged her. On her return home, Mother continued to pray for and write to the young woman. Finally a letter arrived with the good news that the young woman had decided to become a missionary, crediting and thanking Mother for her role in that decision. My mother approached the end of her life on earth with a deep faith and the conviction that the Lord had sent her on one final mission … and that the mission had been accomplished.

A devout Methodist, Mother was active in the local district and conference leadership of her church. By the time I was six, I probably had attended more Missionary Society meetings than had many members. Until her health failed, Mother was the teacher of the Ladies' Sunday School Class at Oakland Methodist Church, a class that in her memory bears her name. Daddy frequently taught the Men's Class. Living a full life of service to all who knew her, mother was also leader, mentor, and role model to the women of her church and community. I took all this for granted and was years older and wiser before I began to appreciate that she was also that, and more, for me. She was a woman ahead of her time, a woman who gave her daughter the liberating encouragement to reach for and achieve whatever her goals might be. How proud my mother would be of all that women in general (and her daughter and grand-daughters in particular) have been able to accomplish in today's world!

Who she was can be seen in who her daughter has been:
- Wife, mother, and grandmother
- School Teacher
- Sunday School Teacher
- School Social Worker
- First woman elected to the Florence City Council
- Founder of her own business
- Writer

Who her granddaughters are:
- Wives and mothers involved in church, careers, and community
- Yale Divinity School Graduate
- Librarian
- Travel Agency Executive
- City Administrator
- Registered Nurse
- Attorney
- Pharmaceutical Representative
- Elementary School Teacher

Yes indeed, proud she would be.

Mother's French Coconut Pie

1. Beat **3 whole eggs** slightly, in a bowl:

2. Add **½ stick melted oleo, 1 t vanilla, 1 c flaked coconut**

3. Pour mixture into **unbaked deep dish pie shell**.

4. Bake 10 minutes at 450 degrees on lowest oven rack.

5. Bake until set, about 30 minutes more at 350 degrees.

6. Cool before serving.

Lemon Cake Pie
(Custard on Bottom, Cake on Top)

Another of Mother's favorite pies, this recipe was given to her by her friend Mrs. Ruth Tonn, who was the mother of my friend Gene. He and I both played clarinet during our years together in the award-winning Coffee High School Band. While I no longer play my cherished clarinet, I could never part with it or with the memories it holds. Directed by our beloved Mr. Mac (Floyd McClure) and assisted by a mascot named Fido, we band members forged forever kinds of friendships. I and Skippy McClung (then a drummer in the band but now a retired school principal, of all things!) have maintained this forever kind of friendship through these years. With a standing invitation from us, he flies in from the Washington D.C. area every year for great Handy Festival visits.

1. Break **2 eggs**. Separate yolks from whites, and set aside.

2. Cream together **1 c sugar, 1 T oleo, 2 T flour**

3. Stir in **2 beaten egg yolks, 1 c milk, 1 lemon (juice and grated rind)**

4. Fold in 2 stiffly beaten egg whites.

5. Pour into **un-baked pie crust,** and bake at 300 degrees until brown.

The Meringue That Tattled

ALTHOUGH DAVID LOVES to make chocolate pies from his Granny's recipe, I always dread the occasion. Why, you might wonder, would any wife dread her husband's pie-making? Let me explain in terms that you can probably understand. When he uses twelve eggs rather than three, simple arithmetic should help you figure out that the problem is multiplication. As delicious as David's pies are, it takes all available pots, pans, bowls, sinks, ovens, and wives to accommodate the excess and restore order to the kitchen.

Had it not been for David's enthusiasm for pie-baking, the story I'm about to tell would never have happened. The picture-perfect products of one of David's pie-making orgies were left on the kitchen cabinet to cool. We had retired for the night, forgetting that Paddy the Irish Setter and Rachel the Bloodhound were napping blissfully in front of the still warm fireplace, until we heard a terrible commotion from that part of the house.

Within moments, Paddy, as was her habit whenever she wanted to tell us something important, whined mightily and scratched frantically on our louvered bedroom door, plucking it like strings on a banjo with her toenails.

We came rushing out to find the remains of two or three pies upside down on the kitchen floor. Paddy began to whine again (the lady who doth protest too much?) in an obvious attempt to establish her own innocence and to blame it all on poor Rachel. In characteristic confusion, Rachel danced around the room, her long bloodhound ears flopping and her droopy eyes beseeching, acting as she often did in the midst of chaos, like the sky was falling.

Indeed, Paddy (being the smarter of the two) just might have pulled it off and committed the perfect crime had it not been for the tell-tale evidence: big dollops of meringue conspicuously clinging to the whiskers of the obvious guilty party, Irish Paddy.

David and Granny's Chocolate Pie

FILLING

1. Cook over low heat, stirring constantly:

   ⅔ c sugar   5 T flour blended into ½ c milk

   3 T cocoa   3 beaten egg yolks

2. In another pan, heat **1 ½ c milk** to scalding.

3. Pour scalded milk slowly into chocolate mixture.

4. Continue cooking until thick.

5. Add **1 t vanilla**.

6. Cool and pour into baked pie shell.

MERINGUE

1. Beat **3 egg whites** until stiff.

2. Add:

   ½ c sugar   ½ t cream of tartar

   1 t vanilla

3. Top cooled pie filling with meringue.

4. Bake at 350 degrees until meringue is lightly brown.

5. Cool before serving.

To Mary Ellen, With Love

MARY ELLEN WAS ONLY THIRTEEN years old when her brother David, whom she adored, and I were married. Having no sister myself, it was fun to finally have one, especially one who included her new sister-in-law in just a little bit of that adoration. Even devoted sisters, however, can be confronted with difficult decisions. There's a story about the time young Mary Ellen was dispatched to Trowbridges (a favorite local ice cream parlor), all by herself, to bring back two ice cream cones, one for her and one for her brother. But as children sometimes do, she lost control of the cones, and one scoop of ice cream toppled to the sidewalk. She momentarily stared down at the puddle of melting cream, and then headed to the car where her watching family waited. Handing the empty cone to David, she candidly announced, "Here, your ice cream fell off."

She grew up to be a charming, beautiful woman, who, like her brother, zestfully embraced life and all its wonders. And the two of them could get carried away about any number of things. Like for instance, Tabasco: the more the better. They had this on-going contest to see who could eat the hottest food. The only rule seemed to be that the loser was the one who teared up the most and quit first. And neither of them, I might add, liked to lose.

And then, they were both diehard Auburn University football fans. It was back sometime in the '70s, and Auburn fans everywhere were fired up, screaming for another victory over its in-state arch-rival, the University of Alabama, in the season-ending match that was always a thriller. We were in a real quandary because the local cable TV that carried the Auburn-Alabama game was not available at our house, and acquiring everybody tickets for the game at Birmingham's Legion Field was virtually impossible. Then somebody came up with the brilliant idea to rent a room at Howard Johnson's Motel, where they did have cable TV and game coverage.

So the Mussleman family could all watch the game together! But you need to understand who, and how many, the all were. They were Greatmommy and Granddaddy; Mary Ellen and her first husband, Clifford Farmer, and their two (Kathy and Elizabeth); and Dad and I and our five (Lindsey, Dee, Matt, Janna, and Laura). That's thirteen in all, and all in one motel room for at least four solid quarters of football mania. We brought in food and drink by the sacks full. The grown-ups took turns taking the children over to the HoJo restaurant for another one of their twenty eight flavors of ice cream, all the while trying not to miss a single play of the game.

It was not a good day for our team, and it didn't get better. When Auburn failed to rally in the final minutes of the game, the frustrated Mary Ellen could take no more. She burst into tears, slammed into the bathroom, locked the door, and stayed there long after the post-game coverage had ended and everybody but Mary Ellen was ready to check out and go home. In the end, we were just glad we did not have to drive home from Birmingham in the same car with her! Of course, Mary Ellen did recover and could even laugh about it, but we never let her live down the time she locked herself in the bathroom at Howard Johnson's and refused to witness Alabama's victory over Auburn.

Because she so deeply loved her family (especially her daughters Kathy, Elizabeth, and Suzanne), it is impossible for me to separate the word love from the name Mary Ellen. And this love spilled over to include her two successive dachshunds, Bitsy and Claire. I've never known anyone more foolish about her dogs than Mary Ellen. Given the good life she provided her pampered pups, it's no wonder they each had such long, happy lives. Janna's love for Riley, her dachshund, rivals that of her aunt and namesake, and when I see her romping about with her dachshund, it is like seeing Mary Ellen herself. It is our Laura, however, who resembles Mary Ellen enough to be daughter rather than niece, and who explodes into a room with the same joy and noise level so characteristic of her aunt.

I've often wondered if there was not some common genetic cord that bound them together and led David to choose a career in Veterinary Medicine and Mary Ellen to love her animals the way she did. And if there was, it was certainly a powerful one, for that same cord runs strong in every last one of our children.

Because Mary Ellen always spent Thanksgiving here in Florence with us, this was our favorite time of the year. Knowing her excitement about being here added to our excitement about getting ready for her, her family, and all the festivities that go with the holidays. Whether she was living in Atlanta or Louisville, Mary Ellen was never too far away to want to know everything that was going on in the family. She rejoiced in any good news, or was concerned about any that was not. The children knew that during her visit their aunt would find some special time for each and every one of them, to listen, to encourage, and to show them how much she cared.

That first unbearably sad Thanksgiving that Mary Ellen was no longer with us, our grief was still too recent and raw to feel much of anything but loss. But we knew that Mary Ellen would have been the first to insist we keep our Thanksgiving just as it has always been, and we have learned to approach this time of year with the kind of joy that she so well taught us. As deeply as we will always miss her and as surely as she will always be a part of our lives, it is with thanksgiving that we celebrate having known and loved her, and she us.

When I think of Mary Ellen, I remember her exuberance, her quest for happiness, and her wish to be ever youthful. The year she was to celebrate her fiftieth birthday, she talked a lot about how much she dreaded growing old. She thought fifty sounded awfully old, she did not feel or look fifty, and she most assuredly did not want to be fifty. The accident that took her life the month before her birthday stopped time and age for her, sparing her from that dreaded fate of growing old. There is a certain sense of peace in my heart that the memory of Mary Ellen I treasure is of a Mary Ellen who is ... free-spirited ... full of life ... and forever young.

Mary Ellen's Derby Pie

This rich, full flavored, traditional Louisville pie is one Mary Ellen always served during Kentucky Derby Week.

1. Melt ½ **c butter** and cool.

2. Stir butter into **2 lightly beaten eggs**

3. Add and mix well:

   1 c sugar

   ⅛ t salt

   ½ c sifted flour

4. Fold in:

   1 c semi-sweet chocolate bits

   1 c chopped pecans

   1 T bourbon

5. Pour into **unbaked pie shell**.

6. Bake at 350 degrees for 30 minutes (or until top looks shiny).

7. Set aside for several hours.

8. Slightly reheat pie before serving. Top with **whipped cream**.

COOKIES & SUCH

How Old Ironsides Got Its Name

THERE WERE NEVER ANY BETTER GOOD NEIGHBORS than the beloved Virginia Ray or, as my children early on called her, "Gingeray" and her husband W.R. They were next after us to build a house on the creek, bringing more children to the neighborhood.

I really had a great story to share with the Rays the summer they returned from their Fourth of July trip to Boston. Through the good offices of their nephew Steve, a U.S. Naval Admiral and at that time Commandant of Annapolis, they were among the select few invited aboard the historic U.S.S. Constitution for its once-a-year Independence Day voyage around Boston Harbor, and they themselves became part of history.

When I told David about where the Rays had gone and why they had gone there, the two of us began to discuss and debate the ship's history. David pulled out the encyclopedia and became enchanted with his new-found knowledge, especially the story of how the ship came to be called "Old Ironsides." He seized every opportunity to tell this amazing tale, and one July evening an array of dinner guests provided him with a new audience.

Present at our table were a Yale professor, who questioned but was too polite to dispute, plus an assortment of friends and family who collectively accounted for more than sixty years of advanced education. Degrees ranged from sociology to geology, from law to foreign language, from music to veterinary medicine.

To verify his story, David read to us straight from the World Book: "A sailor is said to have been shot from the British guns, bouncing off the Constitution's sturdy sides, and exclaimed that the ship had sides of iron." We laughed and joked about hardheaded sailors, speculated on how and why a British sailor ever happened to be shot out of a cannon anyway, and discussed suitable headgear for such sport. Don Tipper suggested it would be a long time before that sucker took a nap in a cannon again. Then, of course, we each had our own clever versions of what said sailor really said as he flew through the air and/or as his head hit the ship.

186

The non-disputatious and kind Professor Willie Ruff was already back in New Haven before we discovered that David had made one little error and misread one little word. "A sailor is said to have BEEN shot … " is not correct. Read correctly, the encyclopedia states, "A sailor is said to have SEEN shot from the British guns bouncing off the sturdy sides, and exclaimed that the ship had sides of iron."

Rest assured we will never let David forget the time he misread history to us. And one can't help but wonder how many wars have been waged, friendships lost, hearts broken, or the course of history changed by just one little misread, misheard, misunderstood word.

Gingeray Brownies

This well-worn recipe, recopied every time the existing one became too smudged with chocolatey little fingerprints to read, has served the children from kindergarten through college. If all the brownies ever made by our family from this recipe were laid end-to-end, I would not even hazard a guess as to how many times they would encircle the globe.

1. Mix together slowly by mixer or by hand:

   1 ½ c flour

   2 c sugar

   1 t salt

   1 t baking powder

   ⅔ c oil

   ¾ c cocoa

   4 eggs

2. Fold in **1 c nuts**.

3. Spread (mixture will be thick) in greased 9x13 pan.

4. Bake in oven for 25 minutes at 350 degrees.

5. Cut while warm and store in covered container.

O, Tannenbaum

FROM THE TIME when our now grownup five children were young children, going after the Christmas tree was a cherished family tradition. But today, with the convenience and beauty of artificial trees, it is only the memories that warm our hearts.

The woods that were ours were full of evergreens, so when the children were young it was not unusual for us to have shopped early and picked out our Christmas tree by the end of summer. The decision was never an easy one. The girls liked cedars, the boys liked pines, one liked the fullness of this tree, and another liked the tallness of that one. Choices were carefully thought out and fiercely fought out, but when the final votes were counted, the decision stood.

The one qualification we all insisted and agreed upon was that in the old house the tree must touch the beamed ceiling, and in the new one built next door, the tree must reach into the second level of its two-storied living room. One year as we watched the White House Tree Lighting on television, we realized that we may have committed a faux pas of national magnitude, for the Mussleman's inside tree stood taller than the President's outside tree.

A couple of weeks or so before Christmas, our family and its entourage of friends, neighborhood children, and dogs would ceremoniously tramp through the woods to chop down a tree for ourselves and for anyone else needing one. Too heavy to carry far, we would lash the tree(s) on top of the jeep or station wagon and merrily make our way back home.

After fortifying ourselves with a cup of hot cheer, the real work began. Out came the ladders, hammers, saws, wire, and wood to erect the tree (tree holders did not work for the likes of our tree). Down from the attic came all the boxes full of holiday ornaments, strings of lights, garlands of holly, and my cherished collection of crèches (nativity scenes) that it took to decorate, from top to bottom, both house and tree. The delightful discovery of a child's homemade ornament or some treasure from a Christmas past evoked all-but-forgotten memories. Without fail, someone had to be dispatched to search for more of those tiny tree lights from shops that had long since sold out of all but the white ones or the colored ones (whichever were in fashion that year).

At last, the heavy wooden cross-pieces holding the tree were draped and covered with sheets. Gaily wrapped gifts mysteriously appeared, and the house lights were dimmed. Then with the touch of a switch, the room filled with twinkling, sparkling lights.

There was a momentary hush as we, like the awestruck shepherds of old, gazed up, up, and up in wonder, and we could almost hear the angels singing. The joy of the season came upon us. The cares of the day, the weariness of our momentous task were suddenly forgotten, and all of us were overcome with an abiding sense of joy … of peace … and of good will.

And with every year and every tree, the child within each of us would agree … "THIS year, THIS tree is the most beautiful, most perfect tree of all."

Krispies

1. Beat **2 egg whites** until stiff.
2. Blend in and beat until glossy:

   ⅔ c sugar

   1 t vanilla

   Pinch salt
3. Fold in **1 ½ c corn flakes**, slightly crushed, and **½ c pecans**.
4. Drop by teaspoon on greased cookie sheet, and top each with a **maraschino cherry.**
5. Bake 20 minutes, or until lightly brown, at 325 degrees.

   Variations: Color green, and flavor with mint. Substitute 1 ½ c coconut for corn flakes. Substitute brown sugar for white sugar, and maple flavoring for vanilla flavoring.

Christmas, a Tradition

By Lindsey Mussleman

(Printed in the Florence First United Methodist Advent Booklet 1987)

"TRADITION" COMES FROM THE LATIN root meaning "to hand down." If there is but one word that sums up Christmastime to me, it is tradition.

Tradition is a vital aspect of Mussleman family life, especially at Christmas: It's scouting for the largest Christmas tree we can find to rise to the two-story ceiling of my parents' home and then decorating it with ornaments that date back to when there were fewer than five children; it's watching Mom and Dad make boiled custard late on Christmas Eve; it's listening to Luciano Pavarotti sing "Jesu Bambino" from St. Peter's Cathedral; it's the gathering of the family around the Christmas breakfast table to share memories after each has made his/her edible contribution; it's sneaking to a needy family's home while the children are at play on Christmas Eve to leave "Santa Claus" and Christmas goodies. In years past, it was all five children crowding into one bed on Christmas Eve trying to figure out why Mom and Dad were making us stay there until "morning light" and then why they were so tired when they finally got up. It was opening Christmas gifts on Christmas morning. And they were not always your "run of the mill" presents. Like the goat Mom got which she promptly and appropriately named Babe (in a manger), or the autographed Art Buchwald book Dad got. I doubt any tops last year's present to each child from Mom: a family recipe book ... complete with the history of each recipe ... from Mussleman Scrapple to Lindsey Chicken Stew.

Other traditions center around First United Methodist Church: the Christmas Eve Communion Service where old friends are just getting in for the holidays; choir Christmas caroling on Rogers' corner, the hospitals and nursing homes; and the Christmas Cantata climaxed with Handel's "Hallelujah Chorus."

Christmas traditions are an important part of my Christmas memories. Within our family these traditions grow from Mom's having given us "roots" and Dad's having given us "wings." With such a foundation, hopefully, the next generation will be built.

Sorry Cookies

It's a complete puzzle to me why these delicious blonde brownies that make such great companions to our brunette brownies are called "sorry," because they certainly are not. I quizzed the school teacher who gave me the recipe, who admitted that she had found the **Sorry Cookie Recipe** on the side of a brown sugar box, and she had not a clue as to why. Perhaps they were baked by someone who wanted to say, "I'm sorry," to someone; perhaps they were intended as an apology, not to describe these delicious cookies.

1. Mix well:

    1 box brown sugar

    3 eggs

2. Add:

    2 c biscuit mix

    1 c coconut

    1 c pecans

3. Pour into 9x13 pan.

4. Bake at 325 degrees for 30 minutes.

5. Cut while warm and store in covered container.

Lemon Pie Bars

This old favorite is especially elegant on a party table.

1. Combine and crumble into 9x13 pan:

    1 ½ stick of oleo

    1 ½ c flour

    ½ c confectioners sugar

2. Bake 20 minutes at 350 degrees.

3. Mix together, beat slightly, and pour over hot crust:

    3 eggs

    1 ½ c sugar

    3 T flour

    2 T lemon juice

4. Bake 20 minutes longer at 350 degrees.

5. Sprinkle with confectioners sugar, and cut into bars.

Janna and All the "W" Girls

MISSISSIPPI UNIVERSITY FOR WOMEN (commonly known as "The W") is located in Columbus. Its lovely campus, deeply steeped in tradition, is graced by historic buildings, beautiful old magnolia trees, and even more beautiful young women. When the courts struck down their female only status, all the old "W Girls" (assuming no self-respecting male would want a diploma with women on it) closed ranks, descended upon the Mississippi State Legislature, and won the battle to retain the word "Women" in their school's name. Janna, as President of the Student Government Association her senior year, joined them, traveled back and forth to the capital at Jackson, and turned out to be one of the prettiest, most effective lobbyist of all! However, the "W Girls" must have assumed wrong; in spite of their best intentions, Mississippi University for Women, one of the oldest and last remaining female colleges in the country, is today undeniably and successfully co-ed.

Peanut Butter Ritzies

We were introduced to this great treat when we visited Janna at Parent's Day at the "W."

1. Spread **peanut butter** on **24 Ritz crackers**.
2. Top with another cracker to make a sandwich.
3. Melt **12 oz white chocolate** in microwave or on stove top.
4. Dip sandwiches in melted chocolate, turning to cover completely.
5. Cool on waxed paper or wire rack.

Kissin' Kin

HAVING LONG SINCE LOST Granny Mussleman's teacake recipe, I was delighted to discover Aunt Myrt's (and maybe Granny's) in a cookbook from their home church at Killen. Aunt Myrt was Granny's older sister who, along with her school teacher sister Bess, moved in with and helped raise the many young children of their other sister, Laura, after she died. I knew this story, but I did not know that Granny's sister was named Laura when we named our Laura, but it was special to discover that hers is a family name.

It was not until those children were grown that their father, to everybody's delight, married his sister-in-law, Myrt. And that is how Betty Gautney Holt's aunt also became her step-grandmother, who was our friend and Dad's cousin. Betty married Don, who at that time was the senior Holt of the law firm: Holt, McKenzie, Holt and Mussleman. The Mussleman is our daughter Lindsey.

Dad's second cousin Bessie, one of Great-Aunt Laura's children, grew up and married my second cousin Stanley, who was Great Aunt Ola's eldest son, which makes us, as we Southerners say, double cousins.

It is not uncommon for families down South to become convoluted kin the way our families have. Though not related, my Grandmother Cauhorn and Dad's Granny Mussleman had been childhood friends. They both were born and raised in the east end of the county, out near Greenhill and Cowpens Creek, Tabernacle Church and Tabernacle Cemetery where Grandfather Cauhorn and other kin are buried.

After Dad and I were married, our two grandmothers eagerly renewed their old friendship, once traveling together down to visit us at our Auburn home. Uncle Paul, on his way back from Florence to Troy, delivered them to our door; then they cheerfully boarded a Greyhound bus for the long ride back home. Both were then well into their seventies, and Grandmother, whose digestive system required considerable coddling, was amazed at Granny's constitution that allowed her to eat, even at night, such unbelievable foods as onions and cucumbers.

My memory of that visit is one of much happiness and laughter and good food: Granny's tea cakes and her delicious apple dumplings, along with her efforts in vain to teach me another art I never mastered, that of making apple dumplings, yet another recipe long lost. Or did I in a fit of frustration conveniently misplace it?

194

Aunt Myrt's Tea Cakes
(and maybe Granny's)

1. Cream together:

   1 c sugar

   1 c margarine

   1 c shortening

   Add and mix together:

   1 egg

   1 t salt

   1 t soda

   1 t cream of tartar

   1 t vanilla

   2 ½ c plain flour

   Roll in small balls.

   Mash flat with hand or fork.

   Bake at 325-350 degrees until tea cakes are tan in color.

EGGS & CHEESE

Disruptive Dogs and the Sunrise Service

FOR MORE YEARS THAN I CARE TO COUNT, we hosted the Methodist Youth Easter Sunrise Service at our home on Cypress Creek. Our neighbors, the Rays, founded the Sunrise Service years before, and we inherited it from them. Grownups who began the tradition as youths now attended as parents with their children.

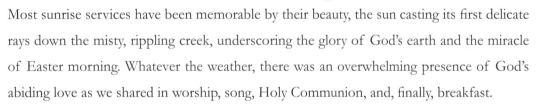

No two Sunrise Services were ever alike. There have been mornings so bitterly cold that all exposed fingers, toes, and noses turned blue, and kids raced back inside to jostle for warmest spot in front of the fireplace. There have been times when the rain, having washed pure the morning, ceased just in time for the services, providing us with early Spring's most perfect setting. Most sunrise services have been memorable by their beauty, the sun casting its first delicate rays down the misty, rippling creek, underscoring the glory of God's earth and the miracle of Easter morning. Whatever the weather, there was an overwhelming presence of God's abiding love as we shared in worship, song, Holy Communion, and, finally, breakfast.

One year a formation of our native mallards swam devoutly down the creek in perfect harmony with the minister's Amen. I wish I could say that through the years our dogs were as reverent as our ducks, but I regret to say they were not.

One particular year, whichever of the next door Wade Labradors was in residence joined our dogs in greeting the guests and managed to cajole someone into throwing a stick into the creek. Those nice enough to play this game received a good Methodist sprinkling when the Lab returned for more and enthusiastically showered them with creek water. Not being a Methodist, whichever Lab it was called attention to his wish to retrieve throughout the service by leaping, again and again, noisily into the creek.

However, given the firm Wesleyan upbringing of our own dogs, there was absolutely no excuse for their behavior. During the days of Paddy the Irish setter and Rachel the

Bloodhound, the two would regularly (and without any provocation that we could see) start a dog-fight. Like seasoned gun slingers, they would begin with a stilling, chilling stare-down. The hair on the back of their necks would stand up, followed by their slow approach toward each other, all the while growling obscenities, perhaps about the other's mother. Shortly thereafter, at some invisible signal, one almighty fight-to-the-finish would erupt. To put it mildly, all hell would break loose.

My professional social work theory was that jealousy was the root cause of this anti-social behavior and that their noisy argument had something to do with who was really TOP DOG. Whatever the cause, we found that there were briefer fights and fewer torn ears for Dr. David to repair if we in the family simply walked away and ignored their inappropriate behavior. This, however, was a little difficult to do in the middle of the Easter Morning Sunrise Service. After being dragged off in disgrace, the canine street fighters were finally and forever banned and banished from Easter mornings when they chose the very same moment to commence their fight that the minister reverently requested, "Let us bow our heads for a moment of silent prayer …."

In brown-eyed innocence, Paddy afterward looked beseechingly at us, vowing to us that it was not her fault. However, considering that Maggie later replaced Rachel as the family Bloodhound, and the dog fights continued as before, we now look back and realize, "May you rest in peace, Paddy, m'girl … but you lied to us."

Cheese Fondue

This was always a favorite of the Easter Sunrise Breakfasteers.

1. Line buttered 9x13 baking dish with **6 slices of bread.**
2. Top bread with **8 oz grated sharp cheese.**
3. Mix together and pour over cheese:

   5 eggs, beaten   **1 large can of evaporated milk**

   2 ½ c of milk   **Salt and pepper to taste**
4. Cover and refrigerate overnight.
5. Bake at 325 degrees until set (about 45 minutes), and serve at once.

Italian Strata

There are many variations of Fondue, but this unique blend of tomatoes and oregano is especially tasty for company brunch.

1. Cut **6 slices of bread** with donut cutter.

2. Reserve donut rings and holes for topping.

3. Use bread scraps and enough additional sliced bread to line bottom of buttered 9x13 baking dish.

4. Top with **8 oz grated mozzarella cheese.**

5. Spread on top of cheese:

   1 can (3 oz) mushrooms, drained

   1 medium onion, thin sliced

   Optional: 3 oz thin-sliced pepperoni

6. Beat together and pour slowly over bread:

   5 eggs

   1 can evaporated milk

   2 ½ c milk

   1 t oregano

   ⅛ t garlic salt

   Salt and pepper to taste

7. Arrange donut rings and holes over egg mixture.

8. Drain **1 can (14 oz) of Italian tomatoes.**

9. Cut tomatoes in half, and arrange inside donut rings.

10. Sprinkle with **Parmesan cheese.**

11. Garnish with **sliced ripe olives.**

12. Bake at 325 degrees until set (about 45 minutes). Test center with knife. If it comes out clean, strata is done. Serve at once.

The Great Mac and Cheese Debate

My MOTHER ALWAYS MADE SPAGHETTI AND CHEESE, but no one (least of all me) makes better macaroni and cheese than Greatmommy Mussleman. It is not surprising when two siblings disagree, but isn't it a genetic irony that when they were little, Lindsey (named for me and my side of the family) preferred macaroni, and Dee (named for Dad and his side of the family) preferred spaghetti whenever this great dish was on the menu?

Greatmommy tried her best to keep up with whose turn it was for which, and on one occasion she served a combination of macaroni and spaghetti and cheese. Maybe we should use both ingredients and change the name to Spa-roni and Cheese or Mac-ghetti and Cheese. However, this sibling disagreement is long forgotten, the merits of one pasta versus the other is no longer an issue, and now, without exception, we are happy with macaroni and cheese.

Greatmommy did a superior job of teaching, and Dee did a superior job of learning the fine art of making this family favorite. So now, it is Dee who the grandchildren (and the grownups) beg to "fix the macaroni and cheese." The only difference is that now it takes two casseroles instead of one to feed our gathered family.

Greatmommy's Macaroni and Cheese

1. Cook according to directions, and drain **16 oz macaroni or spaghetti**.
2. Add:

   2 c grated cheese (reserve some for topping)

   (Chef Dee reports he usually doubles the amount of cheese)

   3 beaten eggs

   ½ stick melted margarine

   ¾ can evaporated milk

   Salt and pepper to taste
3. Pour in large (9x13) buttered casserole.
4. Top with reserved cheese.
5. Bake at 375 degrees until bubbly.

David's Cheese Grits

Grits are to the South what hash browns are to the North. No breakfast is considered complete without grits, and they are so delicious and so currently in fashion that they can even be served to company and for any meal!

As you can guess by the name of this recipe, David is the undisputed chef de cuisine of grits at out house.

	SERVES 6	SERVES 12	INGREDIENTS
1. Boil:	4 c	8 c	water
2. Slowly add:	1 c	2 c	quick grits
3. Stir and cook down until grits are very thick.			
4. Add:	4 oz	8 oz	grated sharp cheese
5. When cheese melts, add salt to taste and:			
	½ c	1 c	buttermilk
	½ t	1 t	crushed red pepper
	½ stick	1 stick	oleo

6. Continue to stir, and cook down a few more minutes until grits are creamy and smooth. Add water if they get too stiff.

Grits Casserole

1. Grits casserole can be prepared the same way as David's Cheese Grits, but serve them en casserole with **2 beaten eggs**, a dash of **garlic** stirred in, and topped with **cheese**

2. Bake in oven for 20 minutes at 350 degrees.

SOUPS

The Great Cypress Creek Rescue

OUR CHILDREN'S GROWING UP MEMORIES will certainly include our dear friends and neighbors, the Hendrix family, and, among other things, the role they played in the drama of the Great Cypress Creek Rescue. It all began with the fun we used to have canoeing down the creek at flood stage. The leisurely trip normally took more than two hours, but the rushing current would telescope the trip into a wild ride taking a fraction of that time. What we did not then appreciate but now do is what dangerous folly this was. Fortunately, we learned our lesson before tragedy became our teacher.

Understand that at flood stage large trees along the creek bank become partially submerged, and their branches sway crazily with the force of the muddy waters that erase the shoreline and lap at the yards between house and creek. One such Sunday afternoon, David, Lindsey, and Dee in one canoe and friends Bill and his brother Jim in the other put in upstream, with our house on the creek as their mid-point destination. But Bill never made it. After the brother's canoe capsized, Bill washed ashore, walked home, vowed never again to set foot in a canoe, and, so far as I know, never did. The surviving canoeists arrived at our house and rearranged themselves, with Lindsey and Jim in one canoe and Dee and David in the other, before embarking on the downstream leg of the journey to the Tennessee River.

About that time, Dee and David spotted the family ducks struggling in turbulent waters across the creek and tried a mid-stream correction in order to rescue them. This was, to say the least, a terrible tactical blunder. Standing between the Hendrix and the Ray's house, I watched helplessly as their canoe yawed and crashed broadside against a huge tree, now in the middle of the rushing flood waters. The canoe bent like a match stick and folded itself around the tree trunk. Miraculously, David held on to Dee, and they both clung to the safety of the tree limbs, a couple of hundred feet offshore.

Moments later, Lindsey and Jim's canoe also capsized, and they became stranded in a network of trees downstream past the McIntyre's. This frantic Mother was soon joined by the rest of the neighborhood, except for Charles Hendrix who, oblivious to us all, was noisily mowing on a riding mower the part of his lawn above the flood; he neither saw nor heard the unfolding drama.

Lindsey and Jim, closer to shore and in calmer waters, were able to carefully work their way to land, safety, and Mom's welcoming arms. Poor Lindsey had the additional burden of calming the nervous Jim who, as soon as the fear of drowning was past, remembered his fear of snakes and was nearing hysteria as he approached the bank in waist high water. At this point, he almost lost it. Rather, we almost lost him. Jim began suddenly to flail about in the water, screaming that he had been snake bit. It took a while to get him untangled from a piece of submerged barbed-wire fence, then more time to calm and convince him that he had only been barbed wire scratched and not, as he feared, snake bit.

As we formulated plans for David and Dee's rescue, we kept up steady tree-to-shore communication above the roar of the creek and the Hendrix' lawn mower. We yelled encouragement back and forth, joking in our efforts to keep spirits up and fears down. I even laughingly inquired if they wanted me to call the Rescue Squad. Somewhere along the way, old friend and popular radio personality Jack Voorhies appeared (arriving too late to accept his invitation for a canoe trip) and eased things for us all with his famous wit and his booming, reassuring voice.

By this time, curious Stanley Hendrix, in Curious George style, was reconnoitering the area by swinging treetop to treetop from the near-shore trees. In fact, David alone, by a combination of swimming and tree-topping could have made it to shore, but this would have been too risky with eleven year old Dee in tow.

Our first rescue attempt was not a bad try. We tied a long rope to the small Hendrix fishing boat, hoping the current would carry it out to Dee and Dad, and we could pull both safely back to shore. Unfortunately, before it could reach them, boat, rope, and all were gobbled up and disappeared into the swirling waters.

For our next act, we brought in more rope, tied it to the Hendrix' rubber dinghy weighted down with volunteers Barbara Hendrix and nine year old Mark, and launched them to retrieve Dee. This effort ended abruptly when, bobbing like a cork, the dinghy capsized and sunk. The would-be rescuers ended up in the treetops and the number to be rescued was back up to four.

Poor Barbara, who happened to be wearing a wrap-around skirt when she answered the call of the sea, had the additional problem of maintaining her modesty. The sight of his family literally up a tree finally caught the attention of Charles who abandoned his lawn mowing and joined the Rescue Team.

Eventually, we used up all our ingenuity, rope, and anything that floated in our failed rescue efforts. The four to be rescued waited bravely, perched there in the trees, looking like giant orange life-jacketed birds. But time was now truly becoming critical. This situation had become frightening and serious. Darkness loomed, and my anxiety edged into raw fear.

Looking back, I realize this was the first time we who so loved our placid, rippling creek and perceived her always as a trusted friend had ever considered how dangerous an enemy she could become. We would never stop loving the creek, but we now saw the treacherous side of her nature. We now knew we must take more seriously her capricious behavior and beware of her quick tempestuous moods.

Finally, we did what we should have done in the first place. We summoned the Rescue Squad. Virginia Ray made the call, and when she explained that people were stranded in trees in Cypress Creek and requested their services, she had a hard time convincing them this was not a prank call. On arrival, the Rescue Squad, already begrudging and skeptical, asked where the launching ramp was! Obviously, they did not know that the normal non-flood depth of Cypress Creek was no more than three to four feet. Not until they almost capsized and were forced to fall back and call for heavier equipment did they appreciate the seriousness of our family's plight and the danger of their mission. They then successfully did what Rescue Squads are supposed to do: rescue.

At last, the Great Cypress Creek Rescue was over. The chilled, weary but rugged adventurers were safe. Our prayers answered, we greeted them with open arms, warm blankets, and very grateful hearts.

By the next day, her anger spent, the Creek's mighty rushing flood waters had receded sufficiently for us to walk along her muddy banks, survey the nightmarish scene, and harvest the yards of tangled rope, wrecked canoes, boats, dinghies, and the Ray's kayak I forgot to mention, all hanging peacefully and benignly from the tree branches well above our heads.

Downstream and days later, we even recovered W.R. Ray's cherished fraternity paddle that had been sacrificially placed in service that fateful day.

There is one final chapter to add to this tale. Late in the day, the day after the Great Rescue, David, Matt, and I embarked on a different kind of rescue. I do remember (as I crawled into our one rescued and remaining seaworthy canoe) muttering to myself: "After the agony of yesterday, I do not believe I am really doing what I am about to do … " But this was important. O'Mally and Guinevere, our still un-rescued family ducks, had just been sighted downstream, forlorn and stranded near the bridge. In fairly calm waters, off we went.

After we slipped, slid, and coaxed, and they squawked, honked, and flapped, we got ourselves and our beloved ducks loaded into the canoe. David paddled. I calmed Guinevere. Matt hugged O'Mally. Mission accomplished, we floated happily downstream toward our pick-up point. Above us on the 1920s one-way steel bridge, we noticed a car loaded with people slow to a stop. We could see the people climb out of their car, craning their necks, pointing, and looking down curiously at us. I felt like I had been cast in a scene from the movie *Deliverance*. Drifting down through the warm spring evening were snatches of their conversation:

"Look … man … red beard … ?
paddlin' … creek …
barefooted woman …
li'l boy … orange … jacket … ?
holdin' … "

"Wha'd You Say?"

"I SAID, Do you see that crazy man with a red
beard paddlin' down the creek with a barefooted
woman an' a li'l boy in a orange life jacket holdin'
sump'un … looks like uh … uh … "

In an amazed tone, the voice came through to us, loud and clear, "Well, I' be
damned. If he ain't a-carryin' uh DUCK!"

Barbara's French Market Soup Mix

Soup Mix (Dried Beans)

1. Mix together:

1 lb navy beans	1 lb pinto beans
1 lb great northern beans	1 lb green split peas
1 lb yellow split peas	1 lb black eyed peas
1 lb lentils	1 lb baby limas
1 lb large limas	1 lb black beans
1 lb dark red kidney beans	1 lb barley pearls
1 lb garbanzo beans or soy beans	

2. Package in 2-cup packages.

Barbara's French Market Soup

1. Wash **2 c beans** (French Market Soup Mix).

2. Cover with water and soak overnight.

3. Drain beans and pour into large pot.

4. Add:

2 qt water	1 ham hock
1 large onion, chopped	¼ c lemon juice
1 clove garlic	1 chile pepper
Salt and pepper to taste	

5. Cook slowly for 1 ½ hours or until beans are tender

6. Add **1 can (25 oz) of tomatoes, chopped,** and simmer 30 minutes, stirring frequently. Makes 2 ½ quarts.

Old Man Rivers

WHEN I WAS A CHILD, Daddy always got away with crumbling up his crackers in his soup and turning Mother's reproachful look into a twinkle by distracting those of us who, having witnessed such manners, might have repeated them. In an excited voice, Daddy would say, "Did an airplane just fly by the window?" or "Look at Wolf!" But no airplane appeared, and our dog Wolf, upon hearing his name, would knowingly roll his eyes and go back to chasing rabbits in his sleep.

When we turned our attention back to the table and realized we had been foxed one more time, we all smiled at Daddy who was happily eating his soup, garnished with freshly crumbled crackers.

What I did not then know but do now is that my daddy, Rivers Malone Lindsey, was named (as was also an uncle of his) for a family friend, Dr. Richard Henderson Rivers, who served as the president of LaGrange College in nearby Colbert County from 1854-1855. Decisions then made by Dr. Rivers have had a significant impact on local history. Amidst controversy and in search of a better location for a college, he marched all the students and faculty (except one as the story goes) across the Tennessee River, and moved the campus to Florence. He still served as president when the college was reincorporated in 1855 as Wesleyan University, the antecedent of the present University of North Alabama. Dr. Rivers led an interesting life as a gifted preacher, musician, and believe it or not, an advocate for women's rights. Dr. Rivers was thrown from his buggy and crippled for life on the way to a country church service conducted by his preacher-friend and my great-grandfather, John Walston, who at that time served on the University's Board of Trustees.

Most of the faculty and students left the classroom for the battlefield and marched off to the Civil War. Dr. River's presidency ended in 1861 after the outbreak of war, and the commencement exercises were cancelled. The one surviving building, historic Wesleyan Hall, was used on separate occasions by soldiers from both sides as they fought back and forth across North Alabama and the streets of Florence. One tale says that a U.S. General used Dr. Rivers' office as his headquarters; another says it was instead the General's horses that were stabled there.

As a young child, I was not much of a historian and obviously not much of a musician either. Convinced that the marvelous melodious *Showboat* song, "Old Man River," was written about my daddy, I was proud that they had so honored him but was puzzled that he was referred to as 'old man.' He was not at that time old, and in those days when you called anybody 'old man' somebody, it was not complimentary. Furthermore, I thought that if they were going to write a song about my daddy, they could have at least spelled his name right, R-i-v-e-r —S!

Homemade Vegetable Soup

While all the neighborhood children, including ours, were growing up, I could always count on young Mary Ellen Hamlin to appear at my kitchen door and, with only cursory coaxing, sample my soup. Her Scandinavian taste buds must have been tempted by the cabbage and okra, a Southern touch I learned from my mother.

1. Cook a **meaty soup bone** and/or a **couple of lb stew meat** in **half a pot of water**, until tender, for at least two hours.

2. Add and cook about 30 minutes:

4 large potatoes, chopped	**2 onions, diced**
6 carrots, diced	**3 ribs of celery, sliced**
1 pkg (16 oz) frozen limas	**1 can (28 oz) tomatoes**

3. Add and cook about 20 minutes:

   1 pkg (10 oz) frozen cut okra

   1 small head of cabbage, sliced

   1 can (16 oz) of whole kernel corn

   ¼ lb spaghetti, broken into small pieces

4. Add **salt, pepper,** and **hot sauce** to taste.

5. Simmer (the longer the better) until ready to serve.

The Cypress Bend Place Neighborhood

IN THE NEIGHBORHOOD where our children grew up, there were six families: the Hamlins, Wades, Musslemans, Hendrixes, Rays, and McIntyres, with twenty children in all. To say the least, it was a lively full-of-fun-and-games neighborhood. Pets ranged from dogs, cats, goats, and ducks to horses and snakes (sometimes kept in the Hendrix bathtub). Once, we were loaned a jack-ass named George who arrived in a purple horse trailer pulled by a purple Corvette! Children could move from yard to yard or to the creek and still be in sight of a parent. Young Matt and his buddy Donna McIntyre spent many of their daylight hours playing happily together outdoors. Janna and Laura loved playing "school" or what they called "David and Jean Gays." Lindsey and Dee spent most of their time at our twelve stall horse barn across the road, riding and training their hunters and jumpers, teaching riding lessons and mucking stalls. Cypress Bend Place was a great place to raise a family!

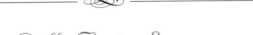

Dolly Parton Soup

I'm told Dolly never heard of this soup, never served it, and has no idea why somebody named it for her. If anybody ever named such a tasty, nutritional, low calorie soup after me, I'd be awfully honored. But then, Dolly is famous for bigger things than soup.

1. Bring to a boil and simmer until vegetables are tender:

4 c water	1 can (28 oz) of tomatoes
1 large onion, chopped	1 bell pepper, chopped
1 c celery, sliced	Salt and pepper to taste

2. Optional: Not in Dolly's recipe, but I sometimes add:

   ½ small head of cabbage, sliced or

   5 oz pkg of chopped frozen spinach

   1 T soy sauce

   ¼ t crushed red pepper

Savory Sauerkraut Soup

Soups are lots of fun to improvise and play around with. I like to create recipes with foods that are commonly stocked in my pantry or freezer and are easy to prepare, like this one. I hope you enjoy the texture of my soup and have fun eating a bowl full!

1. Heat **1 t olive oil** in sauce pan.
2. Sauté **1 small chopped onion** in oil.
3. Add:

   1 can (14 oz) chopped stewed tomatoes

   1 can (10 oz) tomato soup

   1 can water

   1 can (14 oz) drained kraut

   ½ t sugar
4. Stir several times.
5. Cook slowly until onions are well done.
6. Season to taste and serve.

My Soup Therapy Theory

THIS GREEK SOUP made from chicken stock is a long time family favorite. The children request it in both fair health and poor. It tastes just right when you've been sick and decide you do, after all, want to live but could use a little help getting there. I was fascinated with recent research that verified what mothers for centuries have known: Chicken Soup does indeed have therapeutic value. But what the research failed to mention was how important it is that the mother who makes the soup serves it with her special caring touch and a side order of love.

Greek Soup

This is a marvelous way to use leftover chicken broth. Our old friend Bo Brice introduced us to this savory soup he made as the first course of a farewell dinner party for the Northcutts, so long ago hosted by us and the Brices.

1. Bring **3 c chicken broth** to a boil.

2. Add to broth **1 c instant or ½ c regular rice**, and cook according to package directions.

3. When rice is done, mix together:

   2 beaten egg yolks mixed with ½ c water

   2 T lemon juice

   Salt and pepper to taste

4. Pour slowly into broth, stirring constantly.

5. Bring to a boil (being careful not to let soup actually boil).

6. Add **½ lemon, thinly sliced.**

7. Simmer until ready to serve.

   Note: You may also choose to add some of the chicken (boned) used to make the broth.

APPETIZERS & DIPS

No Bah Humbugs

PEPPER JELLY IS THE SPECIALTY David so greatly enjoys making for friends at Christmas time. Let me assure you that I do not object to the Christmas spirit: I believe in it! I do not object to his making jelly for friends *for* Christmas, but I have been known to object to making jelly for friends *at* Christmas.

I wish David could understand that cooks are supposed to make pepper jelly in the summer when peppers are at their maximum flavor and minimum price. Or the reason he must go door-to-door and store-to-store in seeking out the canning supplies is because holiday stock has long since replaced summer stock! I wish he understood that even if it is his project when he dons his apron, he might as well be in his scrubs and the kitchen might as well be his surgery with his scalpel and blade demands for spoon, sugar, and jars. It takes all of us and all we can do to get him and all of his jelly project out of the way for the real Christmas cooking.

If it were not for David's childlike delight in such activities, I might be tempted to shout, "BAH, HUMBUG!" But if I haven't done so after all these years, I probably never will. Considering how his positive enthusiastic beat-of-a-different drummer approach to life has taken away so many Bah-Humbugs from my life, I take this opportunity to express a warm and loving "thank you" to my husband and assure him there will be no "Bah Humbugs" from me.

Perhaps it is even time for me to withdraw objections to his Christmas-time jelly making. And, just perhaps, next year, in the true Christmas spirit, I could roll up my sleeves and help him get all that delicious sticky stuff cooked, poured up into jars, and then help deliver Pepper Jelly with a Ho, Ho, Ho! to friends.

Dad's Pepper Jelly

1. Mix together and boil for 2 minutes:

   1 c bell peppers and ½ c hot peppers, chopped

   1 c vinegar

   5 c sugar

   Green or red food coloring

2. Remove from heat and add **1 bottle Certo.**

3. Pour hot into jars and seal.

4. Serve pepper jelly over a block of cream cheese, with plenty of party crackers nearby.

Cauliflower Dip

There is no better dip for fresh vegetables in the whole world than this old standby. I well remember the first time we ever tasted this dip at a lovely party hosted by our friends from Sunday School, the Bensgtons; and that was the first time I had ever experienced the then unheard of custom of eating raw vegetables as hors d'oeuvres.

1. Mix together:

   1 carton sour cream

   ½ c catsup

   ½ pkg dried onion soup mix

2. Chill and serve with vegetables as an appetizer.

   Note: In addition to florets of broccoli and cauliflower, serve sticks of carrots and celery, try crisp green beans, fresh asparagus, and even purple-edged slices of young turnips.

Spinach Balls

This recipe makes several dozen and stores well in the freezer.

1. Mix together:

   2 pkg frozen chopped spinach, cooked and drained very dry

   2 c herbed stuffing (the packaged kind)

   1 small grated onion   **5 beaten eggs**

   1 stick melted oleo   **1 t garlic salt**

2. Form into bite size balls, and place on cookie sheet.

3. Bake for 20 minutes at 350 degrees.

Sausage Balls

1. Mix together with your hands, until well blended:

   3 c Bisquick mix

   1 lb hot sausage

   1 lb grated sharp cheese

2. Shape into small balls.

3. Bake at 350 degrees until brown, about 10 minutes.

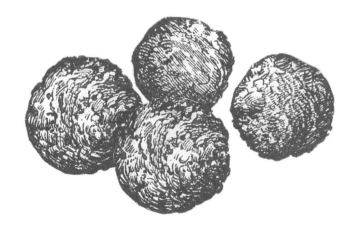

Handy Street Strut

THIS POEM IS DEDICATED TO NANCY GONCE for her great community spirit, and especially for her years of service as the W.C. Handy Music Festival Coordinator. It is written in the spirit of Jennie Joseph's poem, "Warning," which we have together enjoyed.

In Florence, Alabama, in a special little town,
Some folks got together and said, let's mark it down,
Let's have a Festival, a Street Strut, music everywhere, fun.
Let's honor blues, jazz and Mr. Handy, our native son!

We'll all hold hands, listen to the music, pat our feet,
We'll have concerts in the hall, we'll dance on Mobile Street.

I might as well tell you now, so as not to later shock you,
Nancy and I may join the Strut with great dispatch,
Wearing hats that neither suit nor match,
A big red hat with purple, a bright green hat with blue.

Or wear toenail polish that doesn't match our sandals.
Or even carry purses that have no handles.

Take heed, that as old women we shall both, if we wish,
Swing our shiny beads in ways that are quite outlandish.

We will paint our lips and shake our hips and you can bet
That we'll throw kisses to people we've never even met.

We will wave at all the children there with dancing feet,
As we strut our way downtown on crowded Court Street.

We'll twirl our umbrellas, we'll strut around Wilson Park,
To the beat of all that jazz, as friends join us on our lark.

So as not to surprise you later
And you think we've forgotten how
We should take a little time to practice our shenanigans
Today. Right here. Right now.

All this, we as old women can do,
Only if our lives become less hectic and busy,
Either before, during or after dementia,
Before we get hopelessly mixed up and dizzy.

Then only if we two together can schedule a time,
To commit these delightful absurdities
and still keep this poem in some sort of rhyme!

Nancy's Marinated Broccoli

Through the years, whenever Nancy shares her Marinated Broccoli with me, it is a very special treat.

1. Cut **1 bunch fresh broccoli** into florets.

2. Blend well, and pour over broccoli:

   ½ c vinegar   **1 t onion salt**

   1 t garlic salt   **1 t oregano**

   ¼ t thyme   **½ t pepper**

   ½ t dry mustard

3. Cover and marinate overnight.

Crab Spread

Serve this refreshing before-dinner appetizer with crackers.

1. Blend together:

   1 pkg (8 oz) cream cheese, softened

   1 T Worcestershire sauce   **1 T lemon juice**

   2 T mayonnaise   **2 T grated onion**

2. Shape into a round in the middle of a serving platter.

3. Spread a generous amount of Seafood Sauce on top of mix.

4. Place on sauce **1 can (6 oz) of crab meat, drained and flaked**.

5. Sprinkle with **fresh or dried parsley**.

6. Cover and refrigerate for several hours.

7. Serve with crackers.

Shrimp Dip

1. Mix together until smooth:

   1 bar (8 oz) of cream cheese

   1 c mayonnaise

   1 t lemon juice and a dash of Tabasco

2. Add:

   ½ lb fresh shrimp, boiled, drained, and chopped

   or 1 can (7 oz) shrimp, boiled, drained, and chopped

   1 c of celery, finely chopped

   2 T onion, minced

3. For full flavor, refrigerate over night. Serve with crackers.

Artichoke Dip

This dip is served hot and is especially good served with toast tips or crackers on a cold winter's night.

1. Mash with a fork **1 can (14 oz) of Artichoke hearts,** drained.

2. Add and mix:

   1 c mayonnaise

   1 c fresh Parmesan cheese, grated

   ⅛ t garlic

   Dash of lemon juice

3. Bake in a serving dish, for 10 minutes at 350 degrees.

Hot Broccoli Dip

1. Sauté **1 chopped onion in ¼ c butter**.

2. Add and simmer over low heat:

   1 pkg (10 oz) of frozen broccoli, cooked and drained

   1 roll of garlic cheese or 8 oz sharp cheese grated

   2 cans cream of mushroom soup

3. Add just before serving:

   1 can (8 oz) sliced mushrooms, drained

   1 c toasted slivered almonds

4. Serve hot in dish with warmer.

5. Serve with corn chips or crackers.

Of Friends and Foxes

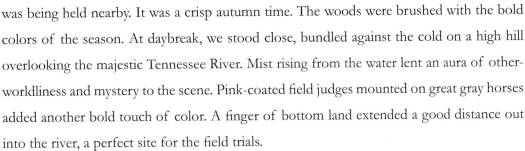

OUR FRIENDSHIP with Ralph and Raymond, the Graham twins, began in high school, and with Pat, in college. Pat and Ralph were dating, David and I were dating, and we shared many good times together.

Pat's father was an avid fox hunter, and one very early morning, the two couples of us went out to watch the National Field Trials for fox hounds that was being held nearby. It was a crisp autumn time. The woods were brushed with the bold colors of the season. At daybreak, we stood close, bundled against the cold on a high hill overlooking the majestic Tennessee River. Mist rising from the water lent an aura of other-worldliness and mystery to the scene. Pink-coated field judges mounted on great gray horses added another bold touch of color. A finger of bottom land extended a good distance out into the river, a perfect site for the field trials.

In boots and heavy jackets, old men and young men lovingly worked their hounds, talking to them and sharing with them visions of blue ribbons that danced in their heads. The hounds bounded about and bayed, straining for the scent of the fox they knew would be released to test their skills.

With the crack of a gun that echoed up and down the river, the field trials commenced. We watched, enchanted, as the scene was acted out below us. Again and again, the freed fox darted in and out of cover (or covert to the purist). In pursuit, the hounds, true to their breeding, could be seen working to perfection, eager for the kill. Excitement mounted for both man and beast. Finally the fox came into full view at the tip of the peninsula. The hounds began to close in. The fox stood still … poised … listening. He looked back toward the sound of the hounds, now at full cry. He casually looked across the water at us. After a final moment's calculated hesitation, he jumped into the river, head held high, bushy tail afloat, and swam swift and straight to our shore. The four of us quietly cheered for the fox as he slipped silently into the safety of the surrounding woods below us and was seen no more. On the far shore, the howling whimpering hounds tracked and paced in frustration and circled in confusion. And as nature would have it, the sly fox had once again out-distanced, out-witted, and out-foxed his pursuers.

Never could we have guessed what parallel roads we were to travel. David and I married one December, and Pat and Ralph married the next; we had five children, and they had four; David with his private pilot's license and Ralph as an Army helicopter pilot shared a passion for flying. While Pat and I still share a love for cooking and recipe swapping, our abiding friendship is founded on far more than that. Both families became involved in a life of horses: they into dressage and eventing, and we into hunting, jumping, and steeple-chasing. It was on Cyd (the horse our son Dee first loved, trained, and owned) that their son Jim began his blue ribbon career. Jim eventually became a world class horseman and a member of the prestigious U.S. World Cup Equestrian Team. At a later time, we visited Jim in England, where he was training with Mark Phillips (Princess Anne's then husband) and the U. S. Olympic team.

Never could we have imagined all the wonders that life held in store for us when we four stood on that high hill overlooking the Tennessee River, watching the drama played out by horses, hounds, and one crafty fox in that long ago crisp autumn dawn.

Pat's Mushroom Crescent Snacks

1. Brown in **2 T butter, 12 oz fresh mushrooms**, and **2 T finely chopped onion**.
2. Stir in and cook until liquid evaporates:

    1 t lemon juice

    1 t Worcestershire sauce

    ¼ t garlic powder
3. Press **1 can (8 oz) of crescent rolls** in 9x13 pan.
4. Cover with **8 oz cream cheese**.
5. Spread mushroom mixture over cream cheese.
6. Sprinkle with **¼ c Parmesan cheese**.
7. Bake at 350 degrees for 25 minutes.
8. Cut into bite size pieces, and serve warm.

BREADS

Aunt Linnie and Her Promises

AUNT LINNIE HADDOCK, Granddaddy Barbee Lindsey's only sister, had been a nurse when nursing was a questionable profession for a lady, and a divorcee when divorce was a scandalous predicament for a lady. On top of that, she maintained her auburn hair color, long past her prime, by means which in those days gave tongues another reason to wag.

I so vividly remember Aunt Linnie. She was always well-corseted and wore rustling taffeta dresses with lace collars. Her eyes crinkled shut when she threw back her head and laughed a sort of joyous cackle. Unruly wisps of hair regularly escaped from the bun on the back of her head.

I always considered her a tragic figure because her first husband, for reasons I was never to know, not only walked out on her but carried their two young sons with him. I will never forget the radiance of her face the day she was finally reunited with one of her adult sons, Homer, and met her grandchildren for the first time. For reasons I could neither fathom nor forgive, the other son, a successful pharmacist in Texas, refused any contact with his mother, and Aunt Linnie grieved all over again for the lost son she was destined never again to see.

Her second husband's main occupation seemed to be rocking in one of the two swings that flanked each end of the long front porch. He was a rotund man who migrated seasonally from one swing to the other, catching the sun in winter and avoiding it in summer. Their income must have come from the furnished apartments Aunt Linnie rented in their big rambling home. Tenants moved in and tenants moved out, often in the middle of the night, often leaving behind unpaid rent and a few treasures: an assortment of cheap jewelry, trinkets, junk, a silk lamp shade, high-heel shoes, once a lady's buxom dress form, and (back then a big fashion item) hats be-ribboned and veiled, lavishly decorated with flowers or even fruit. Such abandoned items were saved and stored in a little room off the back porch that she called her "Do-hicky," maintained solely, I assumed, for my playhouse pleasure. I would entertain myself there for hours, the time marked by the chiming of the four-faced courthouse clock that towered over the roof tops a few blocks away.

220

How times have changed the face of downtown Florence! Back then, there was a mule barn bustling with activity and a mossy watering trough near the intersection of Tombigbee Street, the street my aunt lived on, and Court Street, our town's main thoroughfare that stretches all the way from the college down to the river.

On Saturdays, Aunt Linnie would give me a dime for the matinee (a double feature complete with a Tom Mix serial) and a nickel for popcorn at the Majestic Theater. To get there, I had to push my way through a sea of laughing, chattering country folk, mostly black, who came in droves, mainly in mule-drawn wagons, to town on Sa'diddy.

A victim of progress, the old neighborhood is gone now. Sprawled in its place is a bland, gray high-rise apartment complex, all concrete and glass and modern. But that's not what I see when I pass where that corner was. I see the corner the way it used to be, and Aunt Linnie's familiar front porch. And if I listen quietly for a moment, I hear the rustle of taffeta, a faint joyous cackle, and a distant clock tolling the hour.

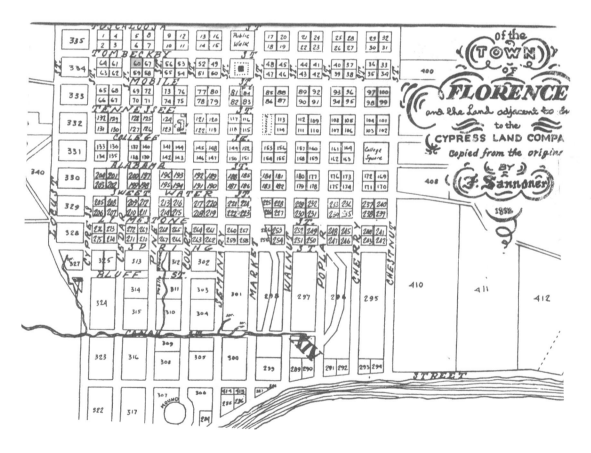

I was fascinated to learn from an article in our local paper that Andrew Jackson, long associated with the Cypress Land Company and Lauderdale County's history, owned lots in the city of Florence as late as 1840; and according to this map, one of those lots was the lot where Aunt Linnie's house once stood. Note that the street was then called Tombeckby, not Tombigbee. But that, of course, was an earlier time in an earlier century.

One unforgettable day, Aunt Linnie (undoubtedly calling upon an indisputable nursing education) whispered some secret words, rubbed smooth stones over the warts that were on my knee, and promised me that they would in time disappear. She squeezed her eyes shut, threw the stones away over her left shoulder, and warned me that if I ever found them, my warts would absolutely and for a certainty grow back. You can rest assured I never played in that part of her backyard again. My Mother gently tried to discourage my belief in such folklore, without also diminishing my faith in Aunt Linnie. But within weeks, just like Aunt Linnie promised, by whatever means or magic, my warts did indeed disappear forever.

My aunt often told me that someday her most prized possessions— her fainting couch, platform rocker, and corner chair—would be mine. They along with a framed picture of her as a lovely smiling young woman, auburn-haired as ever, were bequeathed to me in her will.

Aunt Linnie always kept her promises like I always knew she would.

Aunt Linnie's Sugar Biscuits

Aunt Linnie was never known as the world's best cook, so there is little reason to include much of anything from her kitchen in this book, except that I wanted an excuse to share with you my memories of this loving and delightful great-aunt of mine. She was the closest thing to a grandmother I had on my Daddy's side of the family. I do remember that she did use recipes because, like many of her generation, she called them "receipts."

And, of course, there is really no recipe as such for the sugared biscuits Aunt Linnie used to fix for me. She simply buttered the halves of left-over biscuits, sprinkled them with sugar, and pressed them back together sandwich-style. Or she served them toasted with thick homemade preserves made from figs we'd picked the summer before from the fruit-laden tree by her back door. I do wish I had Aunt Linnie's Fig Preserves recipe, but if I did I'm not sure where I'd find the figs to make them.

What is important to understand is that even such simple foods as sugared biscuits become delicacies when served with hands as loving and a heart as warm as my Aunt Linnie's.

Clouds In a Milk Bottle

THOUGH I WAS ONLY ABOUT SIX OR SEVEN YEARS OLD, I vividly remember the breathtaking panoramic views, the dizzying hairpin curves, and the deep green forests of the Smoky Mountains on the way to visit Mother's sister Lenice (whom we called Auntie), Uncle Weymond, and my favorite cousin Serrill in North Carolina.

When I became excited over the knowledge that in the mountains we could drive through and even above the clouds, I innocently set myself up to become the butt of a family joke. I was told that if I would carry a milk bottle with me on our drive through the mountains, I could catch a cloud to take back home to Alabama with me. For those of you too young to remember, a milk bottle looked sort of like a wine carafe and was back then what the milkman picked up empty and delivered full to your doorstep early in the morning.

How disillusioned I was to discover that clouds up close do not look like clouds far away and certainly do not lend themselves to being captured in milk bottles by gullible little girls. Oh, how early and easily one's innocence is lost, and what an uproariously good laugh

everybody had at my expense! Janna wryly reminds me that when she and Laura were little and making their first trip to the Smokies, we pulled this age-old trick on them.

Throughout our childhood summers, Serrill and I loved the time we visited together and were more like sisters than cousins. I always looked forward to when Serrill and later her sister Martha Elizabeth (called "Bud") came to Alabama to visit us, or when Grandmother and I traveled together by train to visit them in North Carolina. These are some of my most special childhood memories.

Auntie's Bran Muffins

This muffin mix can be stored up to 6 weeks in the refrigerator.

1. Mix and set aside:

   1 c boiling water

   1 c 100 percent Bran

2. In a large mixing bowl, cream:

   ½ heaping c shortening

   1 ½ c sugar

3. Add **2 eggs**.

4. Sift together:

   2 ½ c plain flour

   2 ½ t soda

   ½ t salt

5. Mix sifted dry ingredients with **1 pt buttermilk**. Alternate liquid and dry ingredients.

6. Fold in **2 c All-Bran**, and mix only until moistened.

7. Store and cover in refrigerator.

8. Fill greased muffin tins ¾ full.

9. Bake at 350 degrees for 15-20 minutes.

From Scratch To Sin

BACK IN THE OLD DAYS, I would never have considered making biscuits any way except "from scratch." To have made them any other way, I was led to believe, was daringly close to mortal sin. But somewhere in my quest to become a liberated woman, I discovered that the biscuit mix that comes in boxes made better biscuits than I did. Then through my newfound confidence, I discovered I could make biscuit mix just as good or maybe even better than they did.

Biscuit Mix

1. Sift together all ingredients in a large bowl:

   8 c all purpose flour

   4 T baking powder

   2 T soda

   1 T sugar

2. Cut in **1 ⅓ c shortening**, using 2 knives (or better yet, use a food processor).

3. Mix well, and store in plastic bag.

Buttermilk Biscuits

1. Mix together **2 ½ c mix with 1 c buttermilk,** and stir lightly.

2. Sprinkle flour on a piece of waxed paper.

3. Roll out dough about ¼ inch thick.

4. Cut with a biscuit cutter. (Or the rim of a glass the size you like. I prefer a wine glass.)

5. Place fairly close together on cookie sheet.

6. Bake at 450 degrees for 10-12 minutes or until brown.

Bread By Committee

THE GIFT OF HOMEMADE BREAD from the Hamlin kitchen was special. Of course, so were our neighbors Jack and Corinne Hamlin and their now grown children: Mary Ellen, Nancy, and Reuben who was our Dee's age. We shared a lot through the years, beginning soon after we moved to the neighborhood when Reuben shared a case of the Measles with Dee, and later when Pop Hamlin moved in with the Hamlins and became the neighborhood Grandfather.

I always wished the Hamlins could witness what happened to their warm loaf of bread when seven hungry Musslemans attacked it. For the peace-loving family that we are, it was a violent scene. Bread was torn apart, spread with butter and jam, and then hungrily devoured. Only crumbs, sticky fingers, and smiles remained.

Before he left for college, Reuben dedicated an entire Sunday afternoon to teach our family the art of bread making. But, as usual, our schedules were such that no one was home long enough to stay for the complete lesson, and bread simply cannot be made by committee! So we savor our fond memories of warm, fragrant loaves of homemade Hamlin bread, regularly delivered to our door.

Hamlin Bread

1. To **¼ c lukewarm water,** add:

   6 T sugar   **1 pkg yeast**

2. When yeast looks spongy, pour into large bowl and add:

   2 T salt   **4 T shortening**

   1 c molasses

3. Stir in **3 ½ to 4 lb of 100 percent whole wheat flour.**

4. Stir until mixture becomes stiff and does not stick to your hands, place on floured dough board, and knead several minutes.

5. Place dough in oiled bowl, cover with a towel, and let rise in warm 80-85 degree location (out of drafts).

6. Let rise, punch down 2 times, knead again, and place in greased loaf pans.

7. When dough has risen, bake at 350 degrees for 30-35 minutes.

8. Remove from pans when slightly warm.

Simple Southern Cornbread

1. Place 3 T cooking oil in 12-inch skillet (preferably cast iron) in oven preheated to 450 degrees.

2. Mix together in bowl:

   2 c self-rising corn meal

   2 T self-rising flour

   1 ½ c buttermilk

   1 slightly beaten egg

3. Stir hot oil into cornbread batter, and sprinkle corn meal in skillet.

4. Pour batter into skillet, and sprinkle corn meal on top of batter.

5. Bake at 450 degrees until edges are brown, about 20 minutes.

Cracklin' Bread

I include this recipe for a time when one of you dear children may be far away, homesick, and overcome with the "hongries" for good ole Southern soul food. I want to be sure you know how to soak and soften the cracklin's in boiling water BEFORE you put them in the batter. Otherwise, you may think you have mistakenly added rocks instead of cracklin's, and you and your teeth may be too far away for an emergency visit to Uncle Rivers, DDS.

1. Cover ½ to ¾ c **cracklin's** with water.

2. Heat to boiling in microwave, and soak for a few minutes.

3. Place **2 T oil** in 12-inch iron skillet in oven preheated to 450 degrees.

4. Mix:

   2 c self-rising corn meal

   1 egg

   1 ¼ c buttermilk

   2 T hot oil from skillet

5. Add **cracklin's**, water and all.

6. Pour into hot greased cast-iron skillet.

7. Bake at 450 degrees until edges are brown, about 20 minutes.

Here's To Friends and Neighbors

PEGGY AND GERALD WADE HAD BEEN OUR FRIENDS since school days, and neighbors since we both built our homes here on Cypress Creek and lived next door to each other for more than forty years. Believe me, things happen that would never happen unless you lived next door to the Wades. Let me cite some examples.

In the summer of 1978, Dee was kicked by a horse at our barn. He lost his spleen, one kidney, and very nearly lost his life. He spent one month in the local hospital and another month in Birmingham's University Hospital. I believe that Dee is living proof of the exceptional surgery skills of famed Dr. "Midnight" McDowell, as well as the living proof of the power of prayer.

When Dee returned home from Birmingham, looking like an emaciated war prisoner (but Thank God, alive), the Wades organized a surprise Get Well Parade for him. Marching down our driveway came the entire collected neighborhood, all wearing bright yellow T-shirts emblazoned with "The Dee Mussleman Get-Well-Club-and-Marching-Band." Shirts were compliments of the Wades who had the first screen print shop in town. Nancy McIntyre, strutting with her daughter Donna's baton, led the band; octogenarian Pop Hamlin played a pan with a spoon; Gerald, triumphantly beating a big bass drum, brought up the rear. Everybody in the neighborhood, musical or not, played something, and I've never heard before or since sweeter music. The neighbors gave their love, support, visits, cards, and prayers all summer long. They truly were Dee's "Get Well Club" and even his marching band!

The Wades founded the Great Cypress Creek Raft Race, and for several years running, Janna and Laura with friends Cindy and Lori Davis won the Best Decorated Float Award. Lindsey, Dee, and Matt, sporting their Raft Race Staff T-shirts, always worked the waterfront. One year, Dee and Laura placed second in the Mixed Doubles Watermelon Seed Spitting Contest at the race-end festivities, and the next year I and Stacy, our special Boy's Ranch son who visited us each summer, continued the family tradition by competing in and winning the same Seed Spitting Contest, thus repeating their achievement.

The Raft Race spawned lots of parties at homes along the creek, and the Hendrix' family next door annually hosted a University of Tennessee Alumni Picnic. One year, Maggie (our bloodhound) crashed the UT picnic wearing her Auburn T-shirt: Her own idea, of course. The first time I ran for public office, Maggie went to the Raft Race dressed on my behalf in her "Mussleman For Mayor" T-shirt.

Through the years, among the many things we shared with the Wades was an occasional neighborly glass of wine. One such evening, we were laughing about Gerald's *Time Magazine* interview. A reporter had heard tales of our county's archaic "dry" status and came down South to do a story titled, "In Alabama: Voting Dry and Practicing Wet." Hearing of Gerald's well known way with words and wit, the reporter sought him out for an interview. Gerald waxed eloquent. Gerald waxed candid. Gerald waxed himself right into Peggy's doghouse by making her private life public to millions of *Time* readers when he commented that his own wife voted dry the last time around but that they had a little glass of wine nearly every night.

One Christmas, our gift to Gerald, himself a master wood crafter, was a cedar log from our woods. We delivered it (bedecked with a huge red bow) by jeep and trailer to his front door. The Christmas following, the Wades' gift to us, adorned with a fat red candle, was a beautifully turned cedar candlestick.

Gerald was a Civil War buff, and when sons Scoot and Robin were little, he led a band of boys (including our sons Dee and Matt when he was old enough) called the Rangers, in all sorts of activities: hikes, camp-outs, train rides, and excursions to such historic sites as Shiloh Battlefield. They paraded down our road carrying Gerald's own Confederate flag, and their ingenious leader eventually built with his own hands his own cannon.

David hand-built our downstairs Pub, and when we dedicated it, the Wades presented us with a hand-hewn sign that proclaimed:

and on the other side poetized:

"Here's to friends and neighbors
To Jazz, Easter and more
And here's to our fantastic luck
To have a pub built right next door."

229

Now very few historians have ever heard of the Wade-Mussleman War, but if you lived around here on Cypress Creek, you surely would have heard the sounds of it being waged. Actually, this was a friendly war … the weapons being the Wade's cannon and the Mussleman's anvils. I'd rather not discuss the time when in the heat of battle a new neighbor's newly hung pictures came crashing down, and the frightened lady of the house ran screaming from it. The negotiated peace included the removal of the anvils to the farthermost property line.

If the Wades had guests worthy of a cannon shot, the cannon was aimed our way in the hopes we would man battle stations and shoot back with the anvils. When we had guests worthy of an anvil shot, the Wades reciprocated, and the war was on.

What a wonderful world it would be if the only wars that threatened our world were no more threatening than the friendly, noisy, neighborly Wade-Mussleman War.

Dee and His Derby Party

MANY FAMILIES ARE HELD TOGETHER by such things as love and loyalty, but never overlook the strength of the glue of tradition that bonds us together. Dee began his own unique tradition with what would become his annual Derby Party. That first year (as a single man), Dee served the food (mainly M&Ms, potato chips, and cookies) in little bowls on the coffee table. How times changed! With Amy's touch, it is a gala affair and a firmly established family tradition. These days, a Derby Flag bids us welcome at the door, and tables are laden with a variety of delicious homemade food appointed with a centerpiece of traditional Derby red roses.

Excitement mounts as we each drop our $1 bet in and draw a horse's name out of the hat. With such high stakes, we gather around the TV way before post time to check out our horse's odds, our horse's number, and our jockey's colors. The spirited, high strung thoroughbreds prance and parade to the starting gates … AND THEY'RE OFF!! All twenty three of us cheer enthusiastically for our horse and jockey by name, screaming the entire two minutes that it takes to run the race. I'm not sure which is more fun: for our horse to win the Kentucky Derby or for the winner to win the dollars in the hat!

Mexican Cornbread

I first tasted Mexican cornbread when the young Wade boys, Scoot and Robin, appeared around suppertime at my kitchen door with a neighborly plate of it. I'm sure it was not what they were supposed to say, but what I remember one of them saying was: "Mama said to give this to you. We don't want any more of it."

1. Mix together:

3 c self-rising corn meal	**3 T sugar**
½ t salt	**1 ½ c milk**
3 eggs	**1 chopped onion**
2 chopped hot peppers	**1 can cream style or niblet corn**
1 ½ c grated cheese	

2. Pour into large well-oiled cast-iron skillet, preheated in oven.

3. Bake at 400 degrees for 20 or 25 minutes.

Broccoli Cornbread

Another great variation on Southern cornbread and a variation of 2 recipes from the latest First United Methodist Church Cook.

1. Mix together in large bowl:

   2 boxes (6 ½ oz) corn muffin mix

   1 pkg (10 oz) chopped broccoli, thawed

4 eggs	**1 c sour cream**

   1 small onion, chopped

2. Melt stick of oleo in 9x13 baking pan.

3. Pour over mix and stir together, leaving pan coated with oleo.

4. Pour mix into baking dish.

5. Bake at 375 degrees for 35-40 minutes or until golden brown.

PICKLES & POSSUM

Old Dogs and New Pickles

IN EARLIER DAYS, MUCH STOCK was put in one's own special pickles: in their flavor, crispness, and artistic arrangement in sparkling jars. They were exhibited with no less pride at the church dinner-on-the-ground or the family reunion than they were at the North Alabama State Fair. My daddy never competed for blue ribbons, but his Squash Pickles certainly won him a blue ribbon reputation. Daddy had little patience with "old dogs" who claimed they could not learn new tricks. He, after all, learned how to pickle squash well past his eightieth birthday.

With a Master's degree in Vocational Agricultural Education from Peabody College, Daddy was at one time both principal of our five room country school and farmer to our 500 or so acres of cotton, corn, soybeans, and cattle, all reigned over by a massive but gentle Registered Hereford bull named Big Boy. He was so gentle, in fact, that I could ride around the barn lot on his broad back, holding onto him by his long ferocious looking horns that, like my short little legs, stuck straight out on both sides.

During these Depression years and before, many country folks in the South (themselves poorly educated) didn't put much stock in book learnin' and didn't send their children to school on much on a regular basis if there was farm work to do, and, of course, there always was. Many rural families struggled simply to survive those hard times. Black families, not that many years removed from slavery, struggled to overcome the past and their less than equal opportunities. Back then, too, many children, both black and white, had grown up without ever learning enough readin,' writin,' and 'rithmetic to make a notable difference in their future.

During these times, we maintained in our basement a commissary of supplies and staples for our farm hands and sharecroppers. Orders were sometimes filled from lists whose phonetic spellings were a wonderment and a puzzle to my school-teacher parents, especially to my city-bred mother. One day, a child from the farm handed mother an empty jug and a crumpled scrap of paper which read:

> 1 jug Kolol
> 1 bx sat
> 10 # shug
> Lonydog

After examining the list, Mother filled the jug with 1 gallon of coal oil (kerosene), sealed it with the corn cob it came with, set out a box of salt, and weighed out 10 lb of sugar in a paper sack. The two of us together puzzled over the list, but neither of us could figure out the final item. Ultimately, we had to call on the colloquial common sense and handwriting-reading skills of my country-bred daddy who correctly translated Lonydog as … a stick of bologna.

Dada's Squash Pickles

I proudly pass this recipe on to you as Daddy so loved making it and gifting others with it. I cherish my copy of the recipe, written in his hand. However, I am translating it for you since (as you children know) his handwriting bordered on the illegible.

1. Place **8 c sliced squash** in large pan.
2. Sprinkle with **2 T salt**, let stand for one hour, and drain.
3. Chop and set aside:

   2 c onions   **2 bell peppers**

   2 hot peppers

4. Add to squash:

   1 c vinegar   **2 T celery seed**

   2 T mustard seed   **3 c sugar**

   1 T salt   *continued* ☞

233

5. Bring to boil.

6. Add pepper and onions.

7. Bring to boil again.

8. Remove from heat.

9. While hot, pour into jars and seal.

Cute and Lula

FARM ACCOUNTS TO BE SETTLED at the end of the crop year were entered in Daddy's old canvas-bound ledger. The following entries appeared in ledgers from the 1930s, showing the accounts of Cute Ellis Jackson, his wife Lula, and of their son-in-law Jerry Martin, and Ruthie Mae ("Sister" as we all called her). It looks like Jerry was getting ready to put his spring crops in with a new pair of $125.00 mules. Note the five cents for horseshoe nails, apparently charged to Daddy's account at Mr. Arthur Smith's Store, then transferred over to the debit column of his ledger.

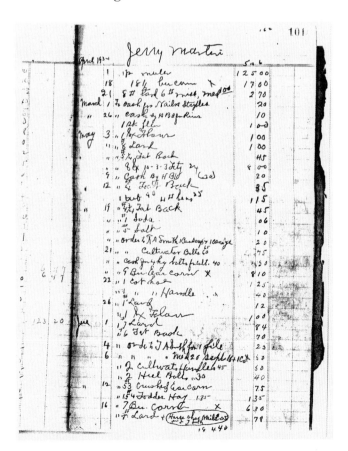

Lula planted her vegetables and flowers by the moon, and she observed an assortment of superstitions that I never fully believed, but I didn't "not" believe either. After all, Lula, whom I so adored, was known for miles around for her beautiful, bountiful gardens as well as her beautiful, bountiful spirit. A gracious lady if there ever was one, Lula's face fairly shined with goodness, and she was always doing a kindness for someone.

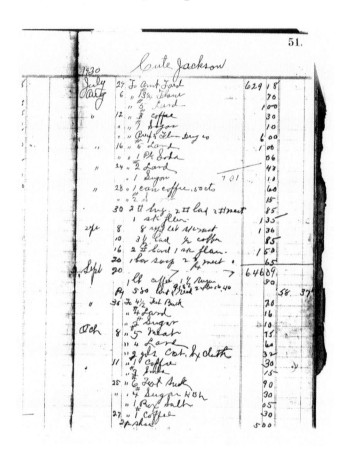

Lula knew my Daddy well enough to know how much he loved to eat possum, and she also knew my mother well enough to know she was not about to cook possum. So the kindness Lula did for Daddy, about once a winter when she was fixing it for their supper, was to send him over a plate of possum and sweet potatoes. Daddy consumed every bite of this delicacy, for I assure you that nobody else in the family would touch it, much less taste it.

If this recipe I once saw in an old cookbook doesn't whet your appetite for possum, perhaps it will at least pique your curiosity about foods that used to be common to the South, when from the Civil War forward Southerners learned to survive on whatever it was that was available.

As I recall, the recipe, in dialect, read something like this:

Possum 'n Sweet Taters

Catch a possum, skin it and wash it good with water.

Boil it in a pot of salt water until tender.

In another pot boil a few sweet taters 'til done.

Place possum in baking pan.

Salt and pepper it real good.

Put sweet taters around it.

Cook in oven 'til brown.

They say that possum tastes a lot like pork and is just as good, but I am quite willing to take their word for it!

Lula always promised me that she would make me one of her beautiful quilts when I got married. Sadly, with advancing age came failing eyesight, and the tiny, delicate stitches of earlier years were gone forever. But this quilted love gift, my wedding gift from Lula, is no less a cherished treasure.

Through the years, I have known several generations of Cute and Lula's descendants. I have tried to repay a debt of love by sharing with them my memories of these two dear, hard-working, God-loving souls at whose knees I (unlike them) was privileged to sit.

A Nickel's Worth of Alum

THIS RECIPE, DATING BACK TO THE 1800S, came from Charlotte King, a longtime Leighton friend. I might explain that Leighton is a wealthy farm community south of the Tennessee River, where acres of fertile bottom land are interrupted only by distant tenant houses or by the impressively big houses of the landed gentry. There, if time has not exactly stood still, it at least has paused a bit along the way.

I remember Charlotte's chuckle as she read to me over the phone this original recipe that called for a nickel's worth of alum. Thank goodness she revised the recipe to an inflation-proof form!

Leighton 8-Day Pickles

1. Make **salt water mixture strong enough to float an egg.**

2. Add **whole washed cucumbers,** and push under liquid.

3. Leave in brine 3 days.   Day 1-2-3

4. Change to clear water on 3rd day.   Day 3

5. Change to clear water for 3 days.   Day 4-5-6

6. Slice up on 6th day.   Day 6

7. Measure to make ½ **gal sliced cucumbers.**

8. Mix:

   1 pt vinegar   **2 pts water**

   2 t (a nickel's worth) of powdered alum

9. Place sliced cucumbers in mixture, leave 2 days.   Day 7-8

10. Rinse cucumbers.   Final Day

11. Mix in large pot, and boil slowly for 15 minutes:

    4 c sugar   **1 pt vinegar**

    1 T pickling spices

12. Dump in sliced cucumbers.

13. Bring to a boil and remove from heat. Repeat 3 times.

14. Pour hot cucumbers and juice into jars and seal.

Friends Forever

OUR FATHERS WERE BOTH SCHOOL PRINCIPALS in Lauderdale County: my daddy, Rivers Lindsey, at Oakland Elementary School, and Peggy's daddy, Linden Reeder, at Central High School. My mother Pauline and her mother Marvinee were both Elementary teachers and both active Methodist women. Peggy and I played together as children but never dreamed how intertwined our lives would become and what a deep and lasting friendship ours would be. Meanwhile, on the other side of the county, David and his cousin and neighbor, James Edward (known widely as Chicken), were growing up best friends. They played together, went through high school, and worked together. They were activated in the National Guard during the Korean Conflict, and were sent (together, of course) to Fort Jackson, South Carolina. Peggy was dating Chicken, and I was dating David, so it didn't take long for us to renew our friendship. David was a groomsman, and I was a bridesmaid in their wedding. Chicken was a groomsman in our wedding.

The years have passed too quickly, but family ties are strong, and the four of us have remained close friends. After Chicken retired from the City Electricity Department and Peggy retired from teaching at Weeden School, they traveled extensively, rarely missed a University of Alabama football game (wherever it was played), and enjoyed retirement as much as any couple I've ever known. And what a blessing they did, because all too soon their life took a turn in a tragic direction.

Chicken suffered a massive stroke. He who was a people person (knew more people by name and more about the people than most politicians). He who loved to talk and make people laugh now had an impaired ability to speak as well as a limited capacity to move independently. Chicken now lives in a nursing home, where Peggy spends much of her day with him in loyalty and love. He has many friends who visit, even a group of retired buddies who play dominoes with him every first Monday.

There is always beauty in a love story, and in spite of the sadness of this one, when David visits Chicken it is an act of love that has become an important part of both of their lives. Several times every week, David visits his beloved friend, whether it means carrying both sides of the conversation, lifting up familiar memories and old stories from their common past, or simply waiting for him to wake up from his nap. With words or without them, I hope David's presence reassures Chicken that he is there for him and that the two of them are, come what may, friends forever.

Watermelon Rind Pickles

This recipe came years ago from Peggy Price's mother, Marvinee Reeder. And at the bottom of the recipe, in her hand, was the reminder: "Invite friends over to share." No Southern cook should be without this distinctively Southern recipe, a delicious accompaniment to any meal and a good conversation piece.

1. Cut into small pieces **7 lbs watermelon rind (white part only).**
2. Soak overnight in **1 c lime,** dissolved in **2 gal water.**(Lime is usually found with canning supplies at grocers.)
3. Wash 3 times in water.
4. Cook 2 hours in water until rind looks clear.
5. Boil together:

    1 qt vinegar

    3 ¾ lb sugar

    1 T whole cloves

    2 sticks cinnamon
6. Drop rinds in liquid.
7. Cook until rinds are clear and liquid is syrupy.
8. Fill jars and seal.

DRINKS

Mayor Bill

Aɴʏ ᴍᴇɴᴛɪᴏɴ ᴏꜰ ᴋᴇɴᴛᴜᴄᴋʏ ᴛʀᴀᴅɪᴛɪᴏɴ, Mint Juleps, or the Kentucky Derby brings fond memories to that place in our hearts reserved especially for Mayor Bill Stansbury. His zest for life and the way he included us (his in-laws) as family in all that he, Mary Ellen, and Louisville had to offer will be part of us forever.

We never left his city without some memento—a poster, a mug, or their trademark Fleur-de-lis pinned to our lapels—to prove his hospitality. Always the gracious host, he opened doors that only he could for us to visit exclusive thoroughbred farms or inside Churchill Downs.

The year we went to the Derby as Bill and Mary Ellen's guests, we ourselves experienced the infamous "Blue Light Rides" through the city we had theretofore only heard tales about. There were three lengthy limousines to get the Mayor's party to and from all the parties and places we had to be, with too little time to get there. The breath-taking, siren-screaming, blue-lights-flashing rides were almost more excitement than my faint heart was equipped to handle. I was terrified when the police escort led us through a tunnel (going the wrong way), but Bill (who thrived on this kind of excitement) only chuckled at me. If any man ever lived his life to its fullest, it was surely Bill Stansbury.

That sad day at Saint Francis Catholic Church in the Louisville he so loved, Bill's most fitting eulogy was taken from one of Bill's own speeches and best reflected who the man really was. With tears in his eyes and in his voice, Bill's dearest friend quoted as eloquently as his grief allowed:

> *"Allow me to share with you one of my most earnest wishes. I believe the time is now for people to direct the way as we reach beyond our remarkable scientific achievements and begin to translate mere technological progress into meaningful human achievements.*
>
> *If we all work together, we can, and one day will, eliminate prejudice and injustice and spread human rights throughout the world. then, opportunity will be even brighter for future generations, and life for everyone will be rich, secure and filled with the dignity that is, and ought to be the birthright of every citizen."*

Mayor Bill Stansbury's Mint Juleps

1. Prepare Simple Syrup:

   Mix **1 part sugar, two parts water**

   Boil to dissolve

   Cool to room temperature

2. Fill 1 Julep Cup with **crushed ice.**

3. Pour **1 oz Simple Syrup** over ice.

4. Add **3 oz Kentucky Bourbon.**

5. Garnish with **fresh mint.**

6. Enjoy, but designate a driver.

Bloody Marys

Served peppery hot and spicy with celery sticks, Bloody Marys have always been a traditional favorite of horse folk, be they Polo, Hunt, or Derby. Remember that you can always get Tabasco refills here at home. The generous gallon Lindsey brings her dad from New Orleans may provide a life-time supply for us all!

1. Mix together:

1 can (46 oz) tomato juice	**3 T Worcestershire sauce**
3 T Tabasco	**3 T horseradish**
1 t salt	**Juice of 2 lemons**

2. Pour **1 jigger of vodka** over **ice** in a glass, and add juice mix.

3. Serve with a **celery stick** in each glass.

Mom's 3-B Punch

Both the thirstiest kids and the most sophisticated ladies appreciate a cool refreshing glass of punch. And believe it or not, the same punch can meet the needs of both. It just must be served a little differently; that's all. This recipe is scarcely a recipe, but it does suggest how simple punch is to create.

There are three kinds of ingredients. The measurements are approximate.

If it tastes too sweet, add lemon juice … too tart, a little sugar … too strong, more bubbly.

1. Base:

   2 qt of lemonade, tea, KOOLAID (or if you need a bright color or flavor, add liquid JELLO).

2. Basic:

   1 can (46 oz) of pineapple juice (a great mixer and equalizer of flavors) is essential to any good punch. **Orange juice** is optional but adds both flavor and nutrition.

3. Bubbly:

   Add just before serving: **1 large bottle of gingerale,** seven-up, lemon-lime soda, or anything clear and carbonated.

   Note: For the ladies, add a **cartwheel of citrus**, a sprig of mint, or frost the glass by dipping the rim first in liquid and then in salt.

4. If you wish to call forth a fourth B, (Booze) for grown-ups, add **champagne** or **white wine.**

KD Punch

This punch recipe, from our local Kennedy Douglas Art Center, beats all others for simplicity and tastiness.

1. Chill:

   1 can (46 oz) of pineapple juice

   2 bottles (2 liters each) of lemon-lime soda

2. Mix chilled ingredients in punch bowl. Add **frozen fruit ring**.

Manure Wine

WHEN DAVID'S VETERINARY CLIENT, MR. BROWN, used our prized (at least he thought so) thoroughbred horse manure* to fertilize the grapes of his backyard vineyard, he brought back in gratitude almost more homemade wine (in bottles, fruit jars, and jugs) gallon for gallon than he carried off truck load for truck load of manure.

One time, Mr. Brown delivered a big jug to David's Veterinary Hospital. David accepted the gift (well-wrapped in a plain brown paper sack, of course), placed it on a shelf in his closet, and promptly forgot about it. Months later, a small explosion brought everyone running to David's private office, where they discovered a warm purple liquid oozing out from under the closet door. That was when David remembered Mr. Brown's wine.

When in the presence of guests we would jokingly refer to this as Manure Wine, there was always a momentary pause in wine sipping until we gave (at least what we considered to be) our entertaining explanation of why we called this rich, sweet, homemade wine … Manure Wine.

*This is not thoroughbred ie. elite manure, but only manure from thoroughbred horses.

243

Coffee-In-Bed-In-The-Morning

THIS RITUAL HAS BEEN PART of our morning so long I cannot remember exactly when it began; I can only tell you why it began. Given our busy, hectic schedules in separate directions, this is the one time of day that belongs solely to David and me. This is our time to catch up on each other's news, to discuss, debate, or to arrive at family decisions. It is our special time to share a laugh or a tender moment. We take turns padding back and forth to the kitchen for the first, second, and, if we wake up early enough, third cup of coffee.

You know, the communication between husband and wife, especially after more than fifty years of being so, can be an intriguing and sometimes unspoken phenomenon. Our private signal that says, "Now it's your turn to get the coffee," is a gentle rattle of empty cup against saucer. If he/she is not quite ready for his/her next cup, the impatient spouse is permitted to rattle a little more insistently until the other one is coaxed into refills. Marital equilibrium is thus restored as we savor a few more sips of coffee and a few more moments of togetherness.

Overlooking the creek, our floor to ceiling bedroom windows capture the reason we built our home on wonderfully wild and natural Cypress Creek. Cypress knees edge the water and all kinds of trees lean protectively over both deep water and rushing rapids. And, as they, too, come awake to the world, our woods and water friends join us in greeting the new day.

We delight in the tree-to-tree antics and aerobatics of the frisky squirrels, listen for the hammering of the bigger-than-life Piliated Woodpeckers, and watch for the water's wake made by beaver, muskrat, or fish. Our Mallard Ducks, charming us with their grace and beauty, placidly paddle into view. We catch the majestic morning flight of our resident Blue Herons and marvel if perchance we glimpse a rare hawk. In the spring, amorous owls whoo-whoo by night, then settle by day in nearby trees to court their mates, blinking boldly at us with their huge hooded eyes.

We greet the early morning beauty of God's world and observe the subtle seasonal changes in the private panorama framed by our windows. My day has not truly begun until I have said to Him who created all of this … and all of us … a profoundly felt and simply stated, "Thank you."

It is very special when our grown-up children and grandchildren drop by to share a cup of coffee and a few moments with us, which to our great pleasure, on many Saturday mornings, they do.

Some weekend mornings get busy. Once, while they were our house guests, niece Courtney impishly invited husband Danny and young daughter Elisabeth to join us as she unceremoniously hopped into bed between David, me, and our coffee cups. With a twinkle in her eye and this explanation to her family, she teased, "See, didn't I tell you? They ALWAYS have Coffee-in-bed-in-the-mornings!"

Perked-Up-Coffee

A simple pot of coffee can be perked up, jazzed up, or transformed into a gourmet's delight with a dash of imagination.

- Break a few pieces of **cinnamon stick**, or snip a few bits of **orange peel** into the **ground coffee**.
- Garnish a steaming cup of **coffee** with **1 T of whipped cream** sprinkled with **cinnamon**.
- Add **1 T of hot cocoa mix** and **1 t creamer to cup of coffee**.
- For Cafe' au lait, make **coffee** double strength, and mix coffee and **half-and-half** with **hot milk**. Top with **whipped cream**.

Good Morning!

ARE YOU READY TO BE PERKED UP? Whether perked, pressed or dripped, adding a little cinnamon or orange peel to your beverage helps start the day right!

CHILDREN'S RECIPES

Let Me Tell You About My Grandchildren

I SMILED AND LOOKED AROUND ME, and I counted again just to be sure that all were present and accounted for, and sure enough all twenty three were. That's five grown children, five spouses, eleven grandchildren, and two grandparents (G-Doc/David/Dad and Memaw/I/Mom). We were on our way to Atlanta in a customized everybody-can-ride-together-in-one-big-happy-party-vehicle that G-Doc had located in Birmingham, complete with a driver and enough seating and walking around room for everybody. It had taken us from Christmas to July to find a weekend the children were ball game free, when the adults could arrange to be work free, and for G-Doc to take care of all the rest. "All the rest" involved a lot: arranging for this incredible transportation and hotel accommodations; reserving tickets and a sky box with all the amenities for the Braves game at Turner Field; and, of course, planning the day at the Atlanta Aquarium. We even overcame the fact that I was still recovering from a recent hospital stay. We simply rented a wheelchair, and away we went!

Everybody was settling in for the trip, and the noise level was high but happy. Laura's children had brought a huge bag of craft loops, and in no time all eleven kids were busily creating multi-colored "jewelry." We probably looked like we had toured a potholder factory, but by the time we got to Atlanta, we were all proudly adorned with bracelets and necklaces. Soon, food and drink appeared, and everybody began to move around, visit, and enjoy being together. These were good times, special times, and no one was enjoying the moment more than was I. I asked myself, "What more could a grandmother possibly want?" I looked around me, taking a whole roll of mental snapshots, remembering a jumble of special stories about each and every one of them. By the way, have I ever told you about my grandchildren?

Rebecca (Lindsey and Butch's first child, our first grandchild) held Mary (Laura and Jim's last child, our last grandchild) in her lap. The oldest patiently helped the youngest with the loops, and their loving bond shined through. With a gift of working with children, Rebecca has a beautiful smile and is the only grandchild with naturally curly hair (and the one who hates curly hair). She is dedicated to her church and its ministries and also is involved in school activities. I see in Rebecca the same qualities of faith, strength, and leadership that her mother Lindsey possesses. Like her mom, she is a great tennis player.

Rebecca's younger brother Forrest was the only child I knew who wore out his Halloween costumes. One year, Buzz Lightyear flitted around the neighborhood in costume for the rest of the year. Because he (like his dad, Butch) loves to cook, his chef's hat and apron are also wardrobe essentials. Forrest hangs out in the kitchen a lot, where he is an excellent chef-in-training. Hanging out in my kitchen, he has apprenticed with me in Chicken Stew making. He plays center for the football team and has earned the honor of singing in the Alabama All-State Boy's Choir.

Matt and Deanna's first child Alex was our second grandchild, and the best part of the week was when he and Rebecca came to Saturday morning breakfast at our house. In time, we had so many grandchildren, they preferred to run and romp and play together, but our favorite time with the first two was reading stories. Alex loved the "Three Little Pigs," a big board book with three stuffed pigs dressed in red, blue, and green overalls; VELCRO on their backsides attached to different scenes. Alex never tired of hearing this age old story and rearranging the pigs on the pages. By the time he outgrew this pastime, our bedraggled little pigs were ready for retirement. Today, Alex plays football on his Tennessee high school team, has his own car, is quite a hunter, and bags a deer every now and then.

Alex's younger sister Macie is a petite fireball of energy, but what she lacks in size she makes up for with spunk, a dimpled smile, and twinkling blue eyes thrown in for good measure. I believe she inherited my love for cats because she is always ready to take in another one. She enjoys her own four-wheeler. She is rightfully excited, and we are rightfully proud of her for being chosen for the second year as a cheerleader for her school.

Sydney, Janna and Blaine's only child (unlike some only children), is loving and well mannered; she is generous with her hugs and ready with her beautiful smiles complete with dimples. She is creative, artistic, and thoughtful, just like her mom. Sydney adores her two dachshunds, also like her mom. As a seventh grader, her exceptional tennis skills have earned her a position on the Varsity Tennis Team.

James, the oldest and biggest brother in his family, has set the pace for the affection that Laura and Jim's children show for each other, especially in the care the two brothers show their two little sisters. All four have their mother's warm, loving nature. James was early on fascinated with balls, and could bounce a ball almost as soon as he could hold one. Then came little brother Liles, who before long was big enough to throw it back to James, and the brothers have been playing ball ever since. James' love affair with balls is as strong as ever. A gifted athlete, he plays on his school's varsity basketball and baseball teams.

At Liles sixth grade graduation, each teacher was to stand and receive a flower. The program continued, the perceptive Liles walked across the gym and retrieved the one flower left. With a broad smile and a big hug, he delivered the flower to the one tearful teacher who had failed to get one, then returned to his seat. It was one of the most beautiful acts of kindness I have ever witnessed. Liles, also talented in baseball and basketball, has a laid back sense of humor and a unique voice that carries across a room or a ball field. Once, while at bat, a baseball hit him on the hip, hard. Without flinching or hesitating, he trotted off toward first base. With a smile on his face, in a voice heard by all present, he reported: "Well, I took one for the team!"

Nobody can agree on which child looks like Jim and which looks like Laura, but to me Laura Alice is the spittin' image of her mother. With her blonde hair, brown eyes, and quick smile, she is a classic All American girl. Laura Alice can ask very thoughtful, challenging questions. I am so pleased she inherited my love of reading, but she also excels in math, and she sure didn't inherit that from me. This was Laura Alice's first year to play softball, and she not only played, she made All Stars! And we all cheered.

Mary Pauline, the "baby of the family," is special because she is our only grandchild named for my mother Pauline. And sometimes, I see in Mary a smile or an expression that reminds me of my mother. Her pixie size and winsome ways work wonders for her. Her September birthday gave her an additional year of preschool, and Mary entered kindergarten well prepared. In sports terms, I call her a fifth year senior. Guess who is following in her big sister's footsteps and has signed up to play softball?

We welcomed Lauren and Anna Beth into our family as new grandchildren when their mother Amy married our son Dee. Both girls are beauties. Lauren is blonde, trim, and fit; she is a talented, dedicated athlete, and is passionate about volleyball. She has graduated from high school and now attends the University of North Alabama where she has earned a volleyball scholarship.

Anna Beth, the younger, is dark haired with flashing eyes and a warm, loving smile. She is full of spirit and follows her own path. She has been taking cheerleading lessons, and we were all excited when Anna Beth was chosen as a seventh grade cheerleader. Of course, neither one remembers it, but Anna Beth and Sydney were both born the same day, month, and year and in the same hospital. It's no wonder they are such soul mates!

Dear grandchildren,

The following children's recipes are dedicated to you, my beloved grandchildren, with the hope that Family will always be as meaningful and as precious to you, growing up together as cousins, as it was to your parents, growing up together as siblings, and to your grandparents who so dearly love each and every one of you.

The chronology … the who-begat-whoms of families … is the framework on which we build the heritage that is unique to each of us. It is important to realize that each distinctive one-of-a-kind one of us is the present link between our past and our future. By sharing the stories of our family's past, and even the recipes that were theirs, we can better learn about ourselves.

It has been said that life must be lived by looking forward, but life may best be understood by looking backward.

Few of us are destined to be noted or even footnoted in any annals of history, yet all of us, by virtue of the families to which we belong, may illuminate, if only briefly, the way for our heirs. It is through Family then that each of us may secure for ourselves our special place in history.

In biblical times, worship and teaching began early … at the family table. There, values were taught and values were learned. Given the nature of modern day living, we need renewed commitment to the preservation of these traditions, and there

at table

together

celebrate Family.

I love every one of you SOOOOOOOOOOOOOOOOOOOOOOOOOO Much!!

Memaw

Children's Fun, Food, and Philosophy

IN ADDITION TO LEARNING THEIR WAY AROUND the kitchen, it is here that children can develop confidence and competence; here children can learn about good nutrition and discover the satisfaction of sharing with others a homemade gift from the kitchen.

It seems to me, litters of pups and large families have something in common in that both not only require sharing but also engender enthusiastic eating habits.

Our growing-up family consumed such quantities of milk that at one time Dad suggested we pasture a milk cow in with the horses. However, the children's zeal waned when I explained that somebody would have to milk this new moo-pet every morning and every evening. Furthermore, I categorically stated and established that said somebody would not be me.

David contends (not true, of course) that Mother Superior's single dissenting vote somehow constitutes a majority. Anyway, the milk cow proposal was defeated by a 6-1 vote. Or was it 1-6?

Since I hold that we are what we eat, during the children's growing up years, there was a minimum of junk food and a maximum of nutritional treats around our house. I am convinced that if junk food is available, children will learn to eat junk food; if fruit, cereal, milk, and juice are available, children will as readily learn to eat nutritional food. By early establishing healthy eating habits, we can give children a gift that not only may last a lifetime but may even extend a lifetime.

Children should early on be involved in such activities as meal planning, cooking, and grocery shopping. Let a child sift the flour, break an egg, grate the cheese, cut out the cookies, and of course lick the bowl and beaters. For holiday dinners, encourage each child to prepare (and clean up after) one simple dish.

Let children clip coupons, help with the grocery list, pick out the cereal, and learn to properly put away everything from ice cream to dog food. A grocery store can be both a learning place and a fun place. We all held a contest at check-out time, and as the children grew older, wiser, and more aware of food prices, one of them usually won. Contestants each submitted their best guess of what the total grocery bill would be, including tax. We were absurdly specific—$96.98 or $103.17—because the one whose guess came closest (without exceeding the total) won. As we waited in the checkout line, it was not uncommon for fellow shoppers to get caught up in the excitement. When the checker finally rang up the total, the losers groaned, and the triumphant winner was awarded the ultimate positive reinforcement: the left-over change from my grocery check, rounded up to the next dollar or two.

Children need some free and creative time in the kitchen, too. However else would Dee and Matt have discovered that ketchup on vanilla wafers (so they say) tastes just like hush puppies? Or that they loved (their own invention) Ketchup-Mayo-Mustard Sandwiches? Of course, these are the same two boys who claimed that dog food tasted pretty good, too. You just never know what creative children turned loose in the kitchen might learn. However else would Lindsey learn how not to burn the brownies (family joke), as well as how to become such an eminently good cook (not a joke)? However else would Laura learn to like pepper on banana sandwiches? And Janna learn to like Tabasco on almost everything except ice cream?

Wherever else would they all have learned (some better than others) that if you mess up the kitchen … you clean up the kitchen?

Basic Blender Shakes

Milk Shakes not only taste good but are excellent sources of nutrition. It doesn't take kids long to figure out a blender shake tastes fun, too. The "head" on this frothy shake makes marvelous milky mustaches.

Children also enjoy foods with fun names. A grape milk shake is bound to taste better when it's called a Purple Cow.

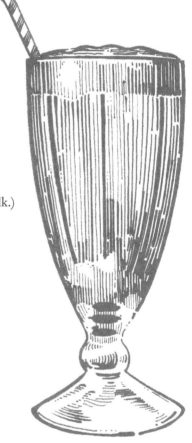

1. Beat in blender until fluffy:

    1 egg white

    2 or 3 t sugar

2. Add and blend until smooth and creamy:

    1 c milk

    1 t vanilla

    1 scoop ice cream

    (Add extra nutrition with 1 or 2 spoons of non-fat dry milk.)

3. For variety, blend in 2 T of any one of the following:

    Frozen orange or grape juice concentrate

    Chocolate milk mix

    Crushed pineapple

    Strawberries

    Or yum - **1 banana** (of course, you peel it!)

4. Don't forget to let the kids name the shakes.

Old Fashioned Drugstore Sodas

1. Put **2 scoops ice cream** (your favorite flavor) in a tall glass.

2. Fill glass with a **cold foamy coke**.

3. Top with splash of **whipped topping and a cherry**.

4. Serve with a straw and an ice teaspoon.

Monkey Dog

This sandwich is more fun than a barrel of monkeys!

1. Spread a **hot dog bun** with **peanut butter.**
2. Wrap the bun around a **whole peeled banana.**
3. Eat! Are you having fun yet?!

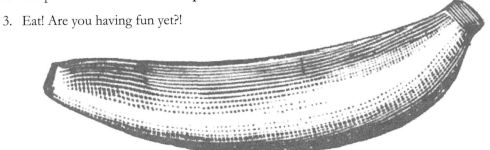

Rice Krispie Treats

Treats made from enriched cereal are nutritional and, like this one, simple to make. When Laura, the family's red hot cereal lover was little, she staunchly and periodically proclaimed that when she got married she was going to fix her husband cereal for supper every … single … night.

1. In a large sauce pan over medium heat, melt **¼ c margarine.**
2. Add **1 pkg marshmallows.**
3. Stir until melted.
4. Remove from heat and stir in **6 c Rice Krispies.**
5. (If adding any **candies, nuts or raisins**, do it now)
6. Cool slightly.
7. Spread in greased 9x13 pan with your hands (also greased).
8. Cut into squares when cool.

Oatmeal Cookies

1. Cream together:

   1 c margarine

   1 c brown sugar

   1 c white (granulated) sugar

   2 eggs

   1 t vanilla

2. Sift together and add to first mixture:

   2 c flour

   ½ t baking powder

   1 t soda

   1 t salt

   1 t cinnamon

3. Fold in:

   2 c oatmeal

   1 c chopped nuts

   ½ c coconut (optional)

4. Drop by spoonfuls on greased cookie sheet.

5. Bake at 350 degrees until lightly browned.

6. Remove with spatula to plate or rack to cool.

Almost Home-Made Cookies
(Note: this "recipe" is addressed to parents)

Always keep refrigerated ready-to-bake sugar cookies on hand for the day you have been non-stop on the go, finished your grocery shopping, rounded up the kids, and you are pulling into the driveway, home at last. Then it happens. A still small voice from the back seat remembers that he/she needs dozens of home-made (of course) cookies-for-school-the-next-morning.

Save the day (and your sanity) with sugar cookies to the rescue.

Children can have fun decorating these cookies with chocolate chips, raisins, nuts, or painting them with a Q-tip dipped in a mixture of egg yolk and food coloring. Be creative. Make designs by pressing a fork or anything around the kitchen (including thumbs) that makes a good impression or a design. Keep on hand an assortment of cookie cutters and a large portion of patience.

Bake cookies according to package directions. Package them ready for school delivery in zip-lock bags.

Cinnamon Snips

1. Open **1 can of refrigerated biscuits.**
2. Cut each biscuit into 4 pieces with kitchen shears.
3. Dip pieces in ¼ **stick melted margarine.**
4. Roll pieces in ⅓ **c brown sugar.**
5. Place in a greased pie pan.
6. Top with remaining sugar and margarine.
7. Sprinkle with ½ **t cinnamon.**
8. Bake at 375 degrees, 12-15 minutes or until brown.
9. Serve warm.

Biscuit Animals

After Mom has rolled out biscuits and has scraps leftover, create some fun animals. Cut out a round body and head for a dog. Roll up a piece of dough for a tail, add four legs, and don't forget two big eyes and two goofy ears. Use a drop of water to help "glue" pieces together. Now then: what animals do you want to try next?

Bake along with the biscuits. When cooked, they look even funnier!

Fruit Kabobs

1. Assemble:

    Cubes of Velveeta cheese

    Thick-sliced bananas

    Maraschino cherries

    Strawberries

    Pineapple chunks

    Or any other canned or fresh fruits that can be skewered

2. Dip a plastic drinking straw in water, and carefully thread your choice of fruit and cheese on the straw, beginning and ending with a cube of cheese.

3. Drain on a paper towel a minute or two before serving.

Frogs (or Bugs) On A Log

1. Wash **4-5 stalks of celery**, and dry with paper towel.
2. Cut each stalk into 3-4 pieces (logs).
3. Using a knife, spread cream cheese into logs from **1 tub (8 oz) soft cream cheese spread.**
4. Count out **24 raisins** (bugs), and press 4-5 bugs into each log.

Caramel Corn

1. Boil rapidly for 5 minutes:

   ½ c white corn syrup

   1 box light brown sugar

   2 sticks oleo

2. Stir constantly and add **1 t soda.**

3. Pour mixture over **5 qt of popped popcorn** in a flat pan.

4. Bake for one hour at 200 degrees.

5. Store in a closed container.

Popcorn Catch

WHEN OUR NOW GROWN-UP CHILDREN were little, got grumpy, and everybody needed a break, we used to spread a bed sheet on the floor.

Next, we would set up an electric corn popper (without its top) in the middle of the bed sheet.

Then we would settle the children around the edge of the sheet. Before you knew it, we would have squealing un-grumpy children chasing and catching the wildly bouncing popping corn.

If you have one of the kind of corn poppers that works this way, I'd like to suggest: "Try it, it's fun!"

But if you don't, try this! One day when you are feeling a little grumpy or bored, use your imagination! Close your eyes tight, and imagine your mom or dad leaping around on a bed sheet, chasing popping corn, or trying to catch the corn in his or her mouth. Imagine the laughter and the squeals. Such visions may chase away the grumpies or the boredom, and you'll have had a good laugh!

Aunt Janna's Turtle Dessert

1. Place **8 ice cream sandwiches** in a 9x13 dish.
2. Pour **1 jar (12 ½ oz) caramel topping over sandwiches.**
3. Sprinkle **1 c chopped, toasted pecans** over topping.
4. Spread **2 c of topping** from **1 carton (12 oz) whipped topping**
5. Layer **8 ice cream sandwiches** on topping.
6. Spread rest of whipped topping over sandwiches.
7. Sprinkle **¼ c of chopped, toasted pecans** over topping.
8. Cover and freeze for at least 2 hours
9. Before serving, pour **¾ c of hot fudge topping** over dessert.

Home-Made Play Dough
(Not For Eating!)

1. Bring to a boil **1 ½ c water and ½ c salt.**
2. Add:

   2 T cooking oil

   2 T alum

   2 or 3 drops of food coloring
3. Quickly stir in **2 c plain flour.**
4. Knead on a flat surface until smooth.
5. Store in air tight container.

Hot Drinks For Children

All dressed up in a be-ribboned container, these hot drinks are tasty on cold wintry days and they make great gifts for special friends. Remember to put a label with directions on each and every container.

Hot Chocolate Mix

1. Put all ingredients in a large plastic bag and mix.
2. Secure with a twist tie or zip lock and shake:

   1 lb box of instant cocoa mix (the kind you add to milk)

   1 jar (6 oz) coffee creamer

   4 qt size powdered dry milk
3. Optional: 1 T instant coffee (if for grown-up gifts).
4. Store in a covered container.

   • Directions for making hot chocolate: Add ⅓ c mix to 1 c hot water.

Spiced Tea Mix

1. Put all ingredients in a large plastic bag and mix.
2. Secure with a twist tie and shake:

   2 c Tang

   ¾ c instant tea (with lemon and sugar)

   2 t ground cinnamon

   1 ½ t ground cloves

   ½ t ground all spice

   • Directions for tea: Add **2 t of mix to 1 c hot water**

Recipes For Bird Friends

THINK OF YOUR FELLOW CREATURES, as did Victor Hugo when he wrote:

> *Be like a bird*
> *That, pausing in her flight*
> *Awhile on boughs too slight,*
> *Feels them give way*
> *Beneath her and yet sings,*
> *Knowing that she has wings.*

Peanut Butter Cones

1. Tie a **string or ribbon** securely to the top of a **large pine cone**.

2. Spread lots of **peanut butter** on tips of pine cones.

3. Sprinkle with **bird seed**.

4. Tie with the ribbon onto a low limb or shrub.

Garlands

1. String **Cheerios** on a piece of **brightly colored yarn**.

   (Birds are attracted to bright colors.)

2. Thread **cranberries or popcorn** on **heavy thread**.

   (Be sure to use a **needle** and **thimble**.)

3. Hang garland from a tree branch or decorate a bushy shrub.

   For all creatures great and small, pray this blessing:

> *Dear Father,*
> *Hear and bless*
> *Thy beasts and singing birds,*
> *And guard with tenderness*
> *Small things that have no words.*
> *Amen*

Timothy Tadpole Tales

DEAR CHILDREN,

I HOPE YOU WILL TAKE THE TIME to do something very important … to add to mine your favorite recipes, fondest memories, or any bits of family fact or fiction you care or dare to record.

Perhaps you'll do for your children what I never found time to do for you … and write down your favorite one of Mom's created-just-for-you Timothy Tadpole tales.

Remember? They always began, "Once upon a time, a long time ago, there was a little tadpole named Timothy … "

Remember how he, like you, loved to play in his sand box, explore the woods and, as tadpoles do, loved to splash and swim in the creek … Remember how he cried when he had to take a nap, a bath, or come from the outside in?

Remember when Mother Frog called Timothy the first time, her voice was sweet and melodic, "Timothy … Timothy Tadpole … "

When she called the second time, she was more business-like.
" TIMothy. Timothy TADpole."

But if she called the third time, it was in her big frog voice,
"TIM-O-THY! TIM-O-THY MATTHEW TADPOLE!!!"

And believe you me, that little tadpole answered … fast.

Remember that no matter how much mischief he had been into, no matter what he had said or done, nor how much he had cried and tried to get his own way, the adventure-some Timothy, like you, was always welcomed back into a family circle of

forgiveness,

acceptance,

and love.

Mom

My dearest children,

The time has come for me to share these few final thoughts with you. Acknowledging all the blessings that God has granted us, I pray that you will be true to the faith of your church and family.

May you be guided by Christ's teaching to love God and to love your neighbor as yourself. Pray often. Forgive. Offer hospitality. Use your God-given gifts to serve others. Learn grace. Live love.

You may find yourself incorporating some of our old family traditions into your new family with its very special character, lifestyle and its own traditions. Never mind whose or which family traditions get preserved. What is important is that families do have traditions.

Understand that research can never fully explain nor comprehend

the learning … the living … and loving … of families.

Research may never confirm one of my pet traditions, and one we followed … that especially in large families such as ours, with so much sharing and so many hand-me-downs, each child needs his/her very own personal cat … an oft overlooked furry, purring source of unqualified acceptance and unconditional love.

Recent research has confirmed what I have instinctively known and as a parent practiced, that family rituals and traditions provide to children, a valuable sense of

security … stability … and continuity.

So Dear Ones, in addition to the valued gifts of roots, wings and the heritage of a deep faith there is one other gift that I entrust to you and lovingly place in your hands and hearts … the priceless heritage of family traditions.

I love each of you so dearly,

Mom

POTPOURRI I

ANY GOOD COOKBOOK WORTH ITS SALT provides complete tables of measurements, equivalents, and substitutions. I am including abbreviated lists of the ones I most frequently use and least frequently remember.

— ⧜ —

From Pinches to Pounds
(You can figure out most other measurements from these)

Pinch	=	less than ⅛ t
Dash	=	2 or 3 drops
1 c	=	8 fluid oz
4 c	=	1 qt or 2 pts
1 T	=	3 t
2 T	=	1 fluid oz
8 T	=	½ c
1 lb granulated sugar	=	2 c
1 lb brown sugar	=	2 ½ c
1 lb confectioner's sugar	=	3 ½ c
1 med lemon	=	3 T lemon juice
¼ lb nuts	=	1 c
¼ lb cheese	=	1 c
1 med onion	=	1 c chopped
1 apple	=	1 c sliced
2 bananas	=	1 c mashed
1 big marshmallow	=	10 little ones
23 soda crackers	=	1 c crumbs
15 graham crackers	=	1 c crumbs
2-3 slices of dry bread	=	1 c crumbs
1 stick of margarine	=	½ c or 8 T

(I prefer brands that mark it on the wrapper)

This For That

2 egg yolks	=	1 whole egg
3-4 T cocoa + ½ T margarine	=	1 (1 oz) square chocolate
1 c milk + 1 T vinegar	=	1 c buttermilk
or + 1 T lemon juice	=	1 c sour cream
1 c yogurt	=	1 c buttermilk
1 lb fresh mushrooms	=	6 oz canned mushrooms
1 t dry mustard	=	1 T prepared mustard
1 t dried herbs	=	1 T fresh herbs
2 T flour (to thicken cooked sauces)	=	1 T cornstarch

POTPOURRI II

I REALIZE IT SOUNDS ELEMENTARY, but it is important to know:

How To Follow a Recipe

- Read the entire recipe before you begin.
- Assemble all necessary ingredients and utensils.
- Do ahead any chopping, cutting, grating, melting.
- Clean up as you go, or at least place all the dirty stuff in the sink to soak.
- Measure accurately and mix carefully.
- Bake or cook as directed, but understand that there are individual differences in ovens … utensils … and cooks.

Cookbooks and Recipe Cards

COLLECT COOKBOOKS, ALL KINDS—old ones passed down from friend or family, ones discovered at yard sales or church bazaars. Look for unusual cookbooks as you travel— airport gift shops often carry good regional cookbooks. Wherever they come from, these books provide us adventures in reading, in cooking, and in eating.

Only those recipes I have tried, enjoyed, and plan to use again are honored with a recipe card in my file.

For old time's sake, I like to note who gave me the recipe. For time's sake, I sometimes make a locator card for a favorite recipe found in one of my recipe books, noting simply the book and page number. I maintain several special sections in my recipe file:

- One is for Quantity Cookery, with the recipe on one side of the card and the shopping list on the other.
- There's a special one for Children's Recipes, fun and easy even for the little ones.
- And then there are the Non-Food Recipes.

Chubby's Fine Furniture Food
(Good for spring cleaning or for furniture that has been stored and/or neglected)

I appreciate the caring approach that Chubby, our hometown furniture mover, took toward his work and, on occasion, our furniture. Chubby gave me this recipe, all the while muttering darkly about folks who can't seem to understand that in addition to being cleaned, fine furniture—like fine folks (editorial comment)—must also be nourished.

1. Mix well, equal parts of:

   Mineral spirits

   Linseed oil

   Turpentine

2. Using **finest grade (#00) steel wool**, rub furniture lightly with the grain. Work on a small area at a time.

3. Polish with a soft cloth after 3-5 minutes.

   Congratulations! You have just fed your hungry furniture.

Spice Potpourri

The warm and welcoming aroma of this mix simmering before guests arrive provides the final fragrant finishing touch of hospitality.

1. Mix together:

   12 T whole cloves

   12 broken cinnamon sticks

   6 T whole allspice

2. Store in a jar.

3. Add **1 T mix to small pan of water.**

4. Simmer for 30 minutes or more.

5. Optional: add a last minute slice of **fresh lemon, lime, or orange.**

POTPOURRI III

How To Season a New Iron Skillet

NO SELF-RESPECTING SOUTHERN COOK could possibly survive without a collection of iron skillets, griddles, and corn stick bakers. Prized most are ones that have been handed down through the family from one's mother, grandmother, mother-in-law, or maiden aunt. Believe me, these cherished old blackened utensils have character. Proper care is essential. Wash with warm water and little or no soap. Rub lightly with oil if you see rust. Sometimes the old may need to be re-seasoned, just as new cast iron must be seasoned before use.

New cast iron is gray but cooks best when it turns black with use. Any protective coating will be burned off during the seasoning.

---

10 Steps to Seasoning

1. Wash skillet in hot soapy water, rinse and dry thoroughly.

2. Rub thin coating of vegetable oil to inside of skillet with a paper towel.

3. Place foil covered cookie sheet on bottom oven rack.

4. Preheat oven to 350 degrees.

5. Place skillet UPSIDE DOWN on top oven rack.

6. Bake in oven for 1 hour.

7. Turn oven off. DO NOT OPEN OVEN.

8. Cool down for several hours.

9. Remove, rub lightly with oil, then wipe with dry paper towel.

10. Repeat seasoning, as needed from time to time.

Anybody who knows how to season a skillet is well on the way to becoming a true Southern Cook! Congratulations y'all!

Potpourri IV

Sometimes the most gracious way to treat guests is to treat them not as guests at all but as family, which in turn suggests that family should be accorded the same courtesy as guests.

My Recipe for Enjoyable Entertaining

- 3 parts planning and preparation,

  So there's time to enjoy your guests and yourself.

- 2 parts attitude:

  A warm and gracious one makes everyone feel welcome.

- 1 part having the right tools for the job:

  The right size cooking utensils,

  The right kind of serving dishes,

  The right number of settings (in-house) of china, silver, and glassware to serve as many guests as you choose to cook for.

Preparation for Entertaining

When planning for guests, I write my menu on one half of an index card and my shopping list on the other half. On the flip side, I remind myself to press the table cloth, polish the silver, or other such pre-party chores that the inimitable Peggy Clay describes as, "Spraying the cobwebs with glitter."

In order to arrive at the appointed dinner hour with everything in readiness, I note the time to brown the casserole, un-mold the salad, or warm the rolls.

My checklist stays posted on the refrigerator door until the party is over (the 'fat lady has sung' and is ready to go to bed). Just as surely as spices enhance the flavor of foods, a considered mix and blend of guests can enhance the flavor of a party. And don't hesitate to include family. Children can be taught company manners, and those who have been need not be excluded from all the festivities. And isn't it nice how willing these included children also include themselves in the chores of preparation and even, believe or not, clean-up?

Be a Kitchen Gadget Collector

EXPERIENCE THE VISCERAL PLEASURE of reaching into the kitchen drawer and finding the old reliable potato peeler, egg slicer, melon baller, strawberry capper, pizza cutter, pasta scoop or grapefruit spoon. What great satisfaction for such a small price!

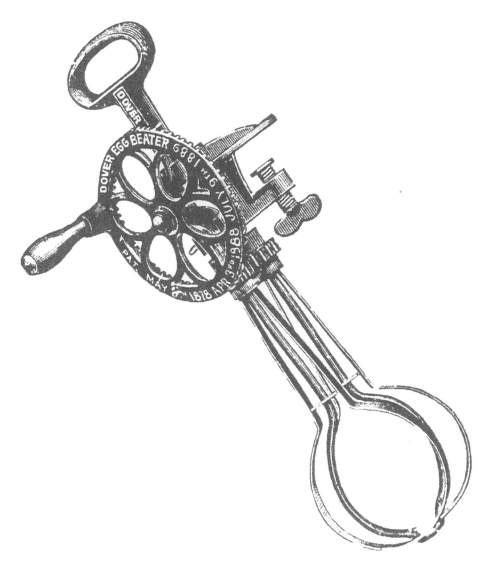

POTPOURRI V

My-Tricks-of-the-Cooking-Trade

- Rub the mold lightly with mayonnaise, and make un-molding a congealed salad easy in and easy out.

- Remove the lettuce core by smashing it smartly with the heel of the hand or against the counter top. Remove core and discard.

- Roll out dough between two sheets of wax paper. Use a few drops of water to anchor the bottom sheet to the counter top.

- Dip spoon in hot water before measuring butter or serving ice cream.

- Meat slices better after it cools for 15-20 minutes.

- Add a few drops of olive oil or lemon juice to the water to keep pasta from sticking together.

- Then there is the rather messy off-the-wall tip of throwing a string of spaghetti up against the refrigerator door to check for doneness. (If it sticks, it's done; if it slides, it's not.)

- Be as wise as Aesop's thirsty bird who raised the level in the water jug with pebbles. For example, when measuring ⅓ c of shortening, fill cup ⅔ full of cold water, and add shortening until cup is full. Pour off water. Shortening slips easily from cup with minimal mess.

- Add salt early to soup, late to meats, and to the water when cooking vegetables.

- Even the trivial may be valuable: A casserole is done when it bubbles in the middle.

- A cake is done when it shrinks from the sides of the pan or springs back when lightly touched in the center.

- If you like coffee, soup or supper served hot, warm mugs, bowls or plates in the microwave for 20-30 seconds per unit.

- Of course, use only microwave safe dishes.

But Enough!

IN TIME YOU WILL FIGURE OUT YOUR OWN BEST TRICKS, so I shan't bother you with more of mine! Enjoy!

LIST OF PHOTOGRAPHS

INDEX